24 HOURS IN CHARLOTTESVILLE

24 HOURS IN CHARLOTTESVILLE

AN
ORAL HISTORY
OF
THE STAND AGAINST
WHITE
SUPREMACY

NORA NEUS

BEACON PRESS, BOSTON

BEACON PRESS
Boston, Massachusetts
www.beacon.org

Beacon Press books
are published under the auspices of
the Unitarian Universalist Association of Congregations.

Printed in the United States of America
26 25 24 23   8 7 6 5 4 3 2 1

This book is printed on acid-free paper that meets the uncoated paper
ANSI/NISO specifications for permanence as revised in 1992.
Text design by BookMatters

All maps © Nat Case, INCase, LLC.
Detailed maps are derived from those in Spencer, Hawes, *Summer of Hate:
Charlottesville, USA* © 2018 by the Rector and Visitors of the University
of Virginia. Reprinted by permission of the University of Virginia Press.

Library of Congress Cataloguing-in-Publication Data is available for
this title.

Hardcover ISBN: 978-0-8070-1192-8
E-book ISBN: 978-0-8070-1194-2
Audiobook ISBN: 978-0-8070-1289-5

For Heather Heyer

"If you're not outraged, you're not paying attention."
  —*Heather Heyer's Facebook post*

"If you are neutral in situations of injustice,
you have chosen the side of the oppressor."
  —*Desmond Tutu*

CONTENT WARNING

This book includes graphic descriptions of white supremacist violence, including blood, injury, and death. It also includes incidents of racism, antisemitism, homophobia, transphobia, and Nazi imagery and language.

CONTENTS

MAPS OF CHARLOTTESVILLE

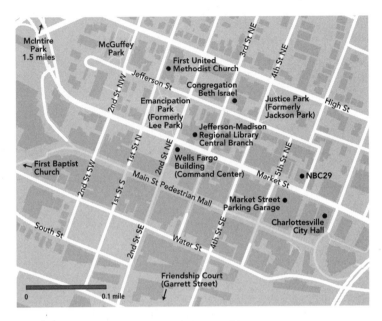

Downtown Charlottesville, Virginia, as of Summer 2017
© 2022 Nat Case. Based on maps in *Summer of Hate* by Hawes Spencer
(University of Virginia Press, 2018).

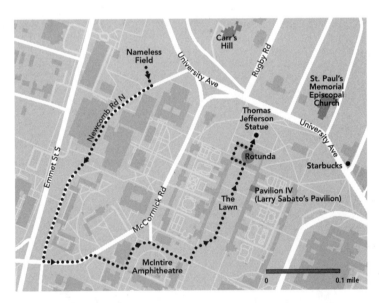

**Torch march path at the University of Virginia and surrounding
areas, August 11, 2017**
© 2022 Nat Case. Based on maps in *Summer of Hate* by Hawes Spencer
(University of Virginia Press, 2018).

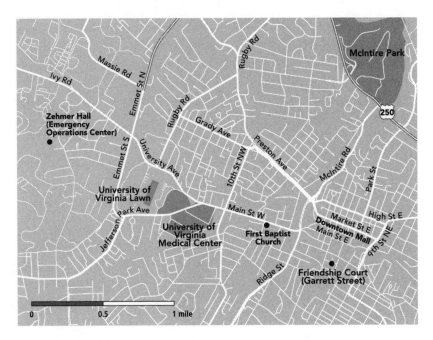

Charlottesville, Virginia, as of Summer 2017

© 2022 Nat Case.

AUTHOR'S NOTE

It was standard hotel fare: lukewarm eggs made from powder, tiny boxes of sugary cereal, and a dirty waffle maker dripping batter onto a Styrofoam plate underneath.

I wasn't hungry but I knew I had to eat. That was the first piece of advice I'd been given when starting as a producer at CNN: During breaking news, eat when you can because you don't know when you'll next have access to food. So before 8 a.m. on August 13, 2017, I swung by the breakfast nook at the Hampton Inn in Charlottesville, Virginia, before embarking on what I knew would be a 15-hour-plus day producing breaking news for Anderson Cooper.

It was the morning after the Unite the Right rally that had taken place in downtown Charlottesville. Hundreds of white supremacists and neo-Nazis had rioted, killing one woman and gravely injuring scores more. Many of the demonstrators were members of avowed white nationalist groups, including Vanguard America (an antecedent of Patriot Front), the Traditionalist Worker Party, the League of the South, and the Ku Klux Klan. They had come in from 35 states and from Canada. That morning, the local community woke up in what felt like a stunned silence, the reality of what had happened crashing back into our collective consciousness. I'd been a part of this community for years and had just moved to New York one month earlier, leaving my job as a local news reporter and fill-in anchor for a new gig at CNN. I had happened to return to Charlottesville that weekend, coincidentally, to pick up the last of my boxes from my old apartment. Now, I was in a war zone.

It was the waffle maker that caught my eye: Standing there were two white men, politely discussing who would pour their batter first. Probably in their thirties, both clean-shaven with close-cropped haircuts, they each respectfully deferred to the other.

One was a uniformed Virginia State Police officer; the other appeared to be a white nationalist, down to the khaki pants and white polo shirt, even balancing a homemade plastic shield on top of his rolling suitcase—the exact type of shield the nation had watched demonstrators use to pummel counterprotesters the day before.

And they were polite. Gracious, even. To each other, that is.

They made their waffles, I grabbed a yogurt cup, and then about 10 minutes later the three of us each made our way to the parking lot just as the sun was coming up. The state trooper got into his squad car and drove away. The other man heaved his bag and shield over the open back of his red Jeep and then hopped inside. By the time I'd started my rental car and looked back, he was gone too.

I thought a lot about those men in the weeks, and then months, and then years that followed. Their blasé interaction belied the deep trauma that a horrified community was just beginning to come to terms with. I watched, shell-shocked and nauseous, while they acted as if the previous day had never happened.

I have since wondered if this was one of the white nationalists later arrested by police. Could his arrest have even been at the hands of that officer at the waffle maker? Or, more likely, did he just melt seamlessly back into his life with few to no consequences?

Then, last year, I had a new question: Could that man have stormed the Capitol on January 6, 2021?

By the time we found ourselves together in that Hampton Inn breakfast nook, a woman had already been killed by a white nationalist. Two Virginia State Police officers were dead. Scores of people had already been injured; some were waking up in the hospital. The damage was all around us. But that police officer and that white nationalist peacefully shared the waffle maker and then went their separate ways. And the stage was set for the continued trauma to come.

History often has a sense of inevitability. We tell stories of the past with the benefit of hindsight; we already know what is going to happen. However, history-in-the-making takes us by surprise. In the cloud of adrenaline and in-the-moment myopia, it can be hard to tell what is about to happen next.

That was not the case in Charlottesville. Many knew what was coming—people of color, especially.

Activists, progressive clergy, and private citizens repeatedly warned local lawmakers, police, and University of Virginia leadership that extreme violence would break out when the neo-Nazis and white nationalists came to town that August. They were largely ignored.

The cost of this refusal to listen, and the resulting lack of police response, was human life. And yet we have seen this same stonewalling, whether willful or unwitting, play out over and over again in the years since, as the white supremacist threat only increased in America.

The story of August 11 and 12, 2017, in Charlottesville is the story of activists explicitly sounding the alarm on a specific, credible threat and the failure of city leadership and law enforcement to protect their citizens.

Much ink has been spilled in trying to make sense of what happened in Charlottesville during those 24 hours, from about 7 p.m. on Friday, August 11, until about 7 p.m. on Saturday, August 12. But the harrowing, traumatic events of that day have also been largely overshadowed by what came next: President Donald Trump declaring that there were "very fine people on both sides," and a rise—or at least an increase in visibility—of white supremacy in the United States.

The voices leading our national conversation about what happened on August 11 and 12 have largely been outsiders: people who were not in Charlottesville that day, who were not the ones "staring Satan in the eyes," in the words of Don Gathers, a cofounder of Charlottesville Black Lives Matter.

This book is different.

This book tells the story of those 24 hours in Charlottesville in the voices of the survivors, activists, politicians, and journalists who were actually there. The bulk of the words you're about to read were collected in dozens of individual, original interviews conducted specifically for this project and totaling over 150 hours of audio recordings. I granted anonymity for those who feared violent retaliation for speaking out, identifying them by initials only. Best practice in oral history work is to compensate the "narrators," or folks being interviewed, both for their time and for the emotional labor of telling their stories. Too often, projects like these rely on unpaid labor from local activists—especially Black women—for their success. For this project, every survivor and activist was offered compensation for their time; some chose to donate that money to charities. Politicians were not compensated. (I should note that while compensation is best practice in oral history interviews, it is *not* standard in journalism and I have never offered compensation for an interview or information in my role as a CNN producer.) Not everyone I approached for this project agreed to be interviewed; some declined to comment or did not respond to repeated interview requests. However, I did request an interview with any public figure mentioned by name in this book. Other sources quoted in this book include court testimony, government reports, and contemporaneous news coverage and social media posts.

One category of voices is very intentionally missing: those of white nationalists and neo-Nazis. I have actively chosen not to interview any Unite the Right participants or sympathizers. They, unfortunately, already have a platform. In some places, I have included words spoken by the rioters that day as recorded in audio or video, or as remembered by witnesses, in order to provide deeper clarity about what happened. In those cases, I contextualize the comments and provide rebuttals on the page.

A further note on language: Many descriptors exist for the participants of Unite the Right. They include, but are not limited to, *white nationalist, white supremacist, neo-Nazi, alt-right supporter,* and *white rights activist.* Many scholars and activists have dedicated extensive time to studying the importance of accurate language to describe these abhorrent individuals—a critical discussion but one beyond the scope of this work. In most cases, I have kept the language that each individual used themselves.

The quotes you'll find in this book have been condensed and edited for clarity and flow. I've taken out many *ums, likes,* and *you knows,* and in some cases corrected location names for accuracy. (For example, there are many parks involved in this story. More than one person mixed up the names of parks, but after I queried, they clarified which park they meant.) One additional note on park names: As part of the reconciliation efforts in spring 2017, Lee Park was renamed Emancipation Park and Jackson Park was renamed Justice Park. I have used the official reconciliation names that were current on August 11 and 12, 2017. Those names were later changed again in 2018 to Market Street Park and Court Square Park, which stand currently. For ease of reading and historical accuracy, I have at times edited quotations to correct verb tenses or make clearer to what the subject is referring. Finally, the names, titles, and occupations of the interviewees are recorded as they were on August 12, 2017.

This project also benefited from the labor of an incredibly talented oral historian, Noor Alzamami, who conducted nine interviews. Research assistant Arya Royal also contributed heavily to the project. Any mistakes that remain, of course, are my own responsibility.

These are the voices of Charlottesville, telling their own story.

CAST OF CHARACTERS

Note: Names and titles reflect those as of August 12, 2017.

Activists

Chelsea Alvarado, counterprotester
Wednesday Bowie, counterprotester
Bill Burke, counterprotester
Kristin Clarens, lawyer and activist
Lisa Draine, local activist
I.B.F., local activist
Jeff Fogel, lawyer and activist
Don Gathers, cofounder, Charlottesville Black Lives Matter
Brennan Gilmore, counterprotester and former US Foreign Service
    Officer
Emily Gorcenski, local activist
DeAndre Harris, counterprotester
S.L., counterprotester
Corey Long, counterprotester
Sabr Lyon, counterprotester
Marcus Martin, counterprotester
Rosia Parker, local activist
Tom Perriello, counterprotester and former US congressman
Star Peterson, local activist and street medic
L.Q., counterprotester and car attack survivor
Elizabeth Shillue, Quaker activist

David Straughn, local activist and car attack survivor
Katrina Turner, local activist and car attack survivor
Melissa Wender, street medic
Constance Paige Young, counterprotester

People of Faith

Rev. Brenda Brown-Grooms, pastor, New Beginnings Christian
    Community
Brittany "Smash" Caine-Conley, cofounder, Congregate C'ville
Michael Cheuk, secretary, Charlottesville Clergy Collective
David Garth, retired pastor
Rabbi Tom Gutherz, Congregation Beth Israel
Rev. Dr. Cornel West, civil rights leader, pastor, and writer
Rev. Seth Wispelwey, pastor and cofounder, Congregate C'ville
Rev. Phil Woodson, associate pastor, First United Methodist Church
Alan Zimmerman, president, Congregation Beth Israel

Journalists

David Foky, news director, NBC29
Henry Graff, anchor and reporter, NBC29
Nicole Hemmer, journalist
Kasey Hott, anchor, NBC29
Ryan Kelly, photojournalist
Chuck Modiano, reporter
Zach Roberts, photojournalist
Chris Suarez, reporter, Charlottesville *Daily Progress*
A. C. Thompson, journalist
Zack Wajsgras, freelance photographer
Allison Wrabel, reporter, Charlottesville *Daily Progress*

University of Virginia Faculty

Emily Blout, UVa professor and Mayor Mike Signer's wife
Aniko Bodroghkozy, UVa professor and Congregation Beth Israel member
Allen Groves, UVa dean of students
Walt Heinecke, UVa professor and activist

Willis Jenkins, UVa professor

Larry Sabato, UVa professor, political pundit, and pavilion resident on
   the Lawn

Jalane Schmidt, UVa professor and cofounder, Charlottesville Black
   Lives Matter

Teresa Sullivan, UVa president

Lisa Woolfork, UVa professor and member of Charlottesville Black
   Lives Matter

Students

Diane D'Costa, fourth-year UVa student and Lawn resident

Tim Dodson, managing editor, *Cavalier Daily* (student newspaper)

Alexis Gravely, senior associate news editor, *Cavalier Daily*

Kendall King, third-year UVa student

Natalie Romero, second-year UVa student

Elizabeth Sines, UVa law student

Malcolm Stewart, fourth-year UVa student and senior resident on
   the Lawn

Devin Willis, second-year UVa student

Government Leaders

Andrew Baxter, Charlottesville fire chief

Wes Bellamy, Charlottesville vice mayor

Terry McAuliffe, Virginia governor

Brian Moran, secretary, Virginia Public Safety and Homeland Security

Mike Signer, Charlottesville mayor

Kristin Szakos, Charlottesville city councilor

Government Documents

Independent Review of the 2017 Protest Events in Charlottesville,
   Virginia, compiled by attorney Timothy J. Heaphy, known colloquially
   as the "Heaphy report"

"Virginia's Response to the Unite the Right Rally: After-Action Review,"
   by International Association of Chiefs of Police

Healthcare Workers

Tom Berry, director of emergency management, UVa Medical Center
Beth Mehring, emergency services nurse manager, UVa Medical Center
Alex McGee, chaplain, Sentara Martha Jefferson Hospital
Jane Muir, emergency room nurse, UVa Medical Center
Jody Reyes, incident commander, UVa Medical Center

Community Members

Susan Bro, Heather Heyer's mother
Dr. Andrea Douglas, executive director, Jefferson School African
    American Heritage Center
Yolunda Harrell, CEO, New Hill Development Corp.
Micah Washington, car attack survivor
Tadrint Washington, car attack survivor

PART 1

WARNING FLARES

CHAPTER 1

"This isn't just a bunch of weird LARPers on some dark corner of the internet."

FRIDAY, AUGUST 11, 2017

CHARLOTTESVILLE, VIRGINIA

CHRIS SUAREZ, REPORTER, CHARLOTTESVILLE *DAILY PROGRESS*: It was like waiting for a natural disaster, like a storm, something you had seen the forecast for days ahead.

ELIZABETH SHILLUE, QUAKER ACTIVIST: We knew this thing was coming, like a tsunami headed our way, and it was hard to think about anything else.

REV. BRENDA BROWN-GROOMS, PASTOR, NEW BEGINNINGS CHRISTIAN COMMUNITY: The air just crackled.

MIKE SIGNER, CHARLOTTESVILLE MAYOR: There were some flyers from the alt-right that were being put on people's windshields, and maybe even people's doors, in the North Downtown neighborhood. And I remember getting a message that said, "They're here."

FLYER: Diversity is a code word for white genocide.

#whitegenocide[1]

CHRIS SUAREZ: It'd been a weird few months before that, going on in May and June.

ALAN ZIMMERMAN, PRESIDENT, CONGREGATION BETH ISRAEL: Through the spring of 2017, there was definitely something happening here in Charlottesville. And as Jews, we knew it involved us, but it wasn't completely clear yet.

INDEPENDENT REVIEW OF THE 2017 PROTEST EVENTS IN CHARLOTTESVILLE, VIRGINIA, compiled by attorney Timothy J. Heaphy, known colloquially as the "Heaphy report": The racially charged events that roiled Charlottesville in the summer of 2017 did not occur in a vacuum. These demonstrations have deep roots in our community and stem from events that occurred much earlier . . . [and are] rather particularly sad chapters in a lengthy record of social and racial discord in Charlottesville.

Charlottesville is famously the home of America's third president, Thomas Jefferson, his house, Monticello, and the university he designed, the University of Virginia.

TIM DODSON, MANAGING EDITOR, *CAVALIER DAILY*: We see a very white-washed version of American history living here in Virginia and of Thomas Jefferson in particular. We live in the shadow of Monticello. We grow up in the Charlottesville-Albemarle area, learning about Thomas Jefferson as this amazing founder: He is an inventor and he's a president, he's an author and a writer and a scientist. You learn all this stuff about him, but in elementary school we don't talk about Sally Hemings. We don't talk about the horrors of slavery or the repercussions of that, like with the University of Virginia. Yes. It was built by Jefferson, like it was designed by him, but was he the person who actually laid the bricks? No.

Enslaved laborers were the ones who laid those bricks.

STAR PETERSON, LOCAL ACTIVIST AND STREET MEDIC: It is a very small, little university town, obsessed with Thomas Jefferson and not really seeing, *Oh, but remember he was a slave owner?*

WALT HEINECKE, UVA PROFESSOR AND ACTIVIST: Thomas Jefferson was the popularizer of the ideology of white supremacy in the United States as the country formulated.

THOMAS JEFFERSON, in *Notes on the State of Virginia*: ...the blacks, whether originally a distinct race, or made distinct by time and circumstances, are inferior to the whites in the endowments both of body and mind.2

DR. ANDREA DOUGLAS, EXECUTIVE DIRECTOR, JEFFERSON SCHOOL AFRICAN AMERICAN HERITAGE CENTER: Charlottesville is a hugely racist city. It's a Confederate city. When the Articles of Secession occurred, the university raised a Confederate flag—the students did. The Lost Cause Narrative is essentially written in this area, in this community. So as a city, this is as South as you can get. It may not be the deep, Deep South, and so maybe some of the *violent* acts that occur in the Deep South don't occur. The ways in which white supremacy is maintained here, it's not through violence, physical violence. It is maintained through a kind of legal violence. Anytime that you can have an educational system, for instance, where Black children remain in the lower 30 percent of scores over time—that's racism. So anybody who wants to say that Charlottesville is not a racist space doesn't understand what racism actually looks like in its broadest sense. They just believe that if you are racist, you must be violent.

STAR PETERSON: Lots of liberals, great place to eat, lots of really fun, locally owned restaurants. Beautiful, just drop-dead gorgeous, easily the most beautiful place I've ever lived. But then also, yeah, a lot of division, right? A lot of people who are very wealthy, and then people who are getting paid next to nothing to work at the University of Virginia in the cafeterias or cleaning the floors. A lot of the hourly staff refer to the University of Virginia as "the plantation."

REV. BRENDA BROWN-GROOMS: Charlottesville is a very beautiful, ugly city. It's a very beautiful place, physically, with a very ugly underside, of poverty, inequality. And the policies don't line up with who we say we are.

DR. ANDREA DOUGLAS: Charlottesville is a place that is largely based on having a good time: going out into the mountains and enjoying yourself there, or learning a little history and having a little wine. We live in a city where most of the people who *maintain* the city don't even live here. The police don't live here. The fire people don't live here. Schoolteachers don't live here. So it's a very lopsided place in that way, especially when you have so much concentration on someone else's good time.

Marcus Martin, who is Black, lived in nearby Nelson County, but worked and socialized in Charlottesville.

MARCUS MARTIN, COUNTERPROTESTOR: I am the image when they think of a thug. I have that image. I have a beard, I have tattoos. I have a deep raspy voice. I might wear the latest Jordans. I might wear a jersey or white T-shirt. That's what you consider a thug. But I have a gigantic heart—I wouldn't say it's a gold heart, but I have a good heart.

And when you come down there, even if you show a lot of people respect—like as you walk past, *How you doing today, ma'am?* or *How you doing today, sir?*—a lot of people don't even give you a response. Or if it's me holding the door for somebody, don't look at me like I'm *supposed* to hold it for you.

YOLUNDA HARRELL, CEO, NEW HILL DEVELOPMENT CORP.: We can't say that we're this great, award-winning city when it doesn't work for everyone and people that live here are living in two different cities.

For almost 100 years, downtown Charlottesville had centrally featured two statues of Confederate leaders: General Robert E. Lee and General Thomas "Stonewall" Jackson. Discussions about removing the statues had been ongoing for many years, led by city councilors Holly Edwards and Kristin Szakos, but gained new traction in 2016 when high school student Zyahna Bryant started a petition to have the statues removed. The cause was then taken up by Vice Mayor Wes Bellamy, who is Black.

HEAPHY REPORT: This conflict played out in a public discussion facilitated by a Blue Ribbon Commission on Race, Memorials, and Public Spaces, a group convened by City leaders to evaluate the future of the iconic statues.

UVA'S CARTER G. WOODSON CENTER: Like other localities across the nation, Charlottesville erected its Confederate monuments during a period of peak activity from the Ku Klux Klan. In May 1924, Charlottesville unveiled its statue of Robert E. Lee. Leading up to and in the months following the fanfare, the Klan burned crosses and set off explosions in Charlottesville and the surrounding areas. Months later, Charlottesville would unveil its statue to Thomas "Stonewall" Jackson to ever more throngs of expectant guests.[3]

I.B.F., LOCAL ACTIVIST: They were built in the 1920s when there was a growing Black middle class in this area. They are Confederate statues because the subject matter is Confederate, but they weren't from the time. They were really using history to intimidate and subjugate.

JALANE SCHMIDT, UVA PROFESSOR AND COFOUNDER, CHARLOTTESVILLE BLACK LIVES MATTER: During those Blue Ribbon Commission meetings, whenever I would go up to speak, I would just hammer on: *Over half the population was enslaved at the time of the Civil War. Fifty-two percent. Therefore, these statues have been lying to us from the moment they were put in, because we know that Union support was strong here in Charlottesville.* Think about it. Rather than statues telling us that there was some sort of a consensus that these Confederates were heroes, like, no—actually *most* people were glad about Union victory. Most people who lived here were relieved.

HEAPHY REPORT: After receiving recommendations from the Commission, the City Council voted to remove one of them from the park where it stood for years.

Many members of our community embraced the effort to remove the statues, believing them symbols of white supremacy. They began talking not just about the statues, but more systemic issues like race, immigration, and economic opportunity.

The election of President Trump further motivated progressives in Charlottesville. City leaders encouraged this liberal activism. Newly elected Mayor Mike Signer declared Charlottesville the "capital of the resistance" to oppressive policies and systemic inequality.

KRISTIN CLARENS, LAWYER AND ACTIVIST: As soon as we declared our-selves the center of the resistance or whatever, there were some people who wanted to fight against that. When we were talking about becoming a sanctuary city or really signaling to the world that we were this progressive bastion, I think it just invited attention.

TERRY MCAULIFFE, VIRGINIA GOVERNOR: You know, I'd worked hard to rebuild the Virginia economy. And I don't want our cities to be the center of resistance. I'd rather have our cities [be] the center of innovation.

KRISTIN SZAKOS, CHARLOTTESVILLE CITY COUNCILOR: We had declared ourselves a welcoming city. We were committed to our refugees. We were talking a lot about racial justice. We had Vice Mayor Wes Bellamy, who had joined us on council not too long before, who was certainly outspoken and was pulling no punches and talking about the need for racial justice in this town, for a reckoning for the centuries of a lack of racial justice here.

WES BELLAMY, CHARLOTTESVILLE VICE MAYOR: Challenging the status quo or even demanding that Black people be treated as equals was seen as an im-mediate threat. Yes, our community may vote blue and we believed that we were progressive, but our values were deeply rooted in traditional Southern beliefs. Beliefs that meant people of color, specifically Black people, were seen as inferior. I knew that I couldn't stand idle.[4]

KRISTIN SZAKOS: And I think those things, these folks found very threaten-ing and they wanted to stamp it out—or at least frighten it, make it go away.

One of those people was a local man named Jason Kessler.

CHRIS SUAREZ, REPORTER, CHARLOTTESVILLE *DAILY PROGRESS*: Jason, I mean, I talked to him a lot through that year. He was just some local townie, just this random guy, unassuming person. We figured out pretty fast that this guy was a UVa graduate, someone who was in his mid-thirties. It seemed like he didn't have a lot going on for himself. We came to find out that he had self-published some books, like poetry, on Amazon. He just seemed like this local weirdo. He had this sort of political agenda, very strong feelings about what was going on with the Lee statue and upsetting the status quo. A lot of what he was doing was sort of inspired and informed by that very nascent alt-right movement online.

And it was still kind of all under this pretext of *Oh, this is just about the Confederate statues.* But I had picked up on very, very quickly that these are actual neo-Nazi groups and actual white supremacists. And this is actually kind of terrifying.

Kessler began attracting followers.

REV. SETH WISPELWEY, PASTOR AND COFOUNDER, CONGREGATE C'VILLE: The statue was just an excuse. At the same time, the statue represents a lot, and it's very telling that the threat of removing a Jim Crow–era white supremacist participation trophy from a college town that prides itself on being blue was all it took to generate the largest neo-Nazi rally in God knows how many years.

MAY 13, 2017
FESTIVAL OF CULTURES
CHARLOTTESVILLE, VIRGINIA

KRISTIN CLARENS, LAWYER AND ACTIVIST: They came for Mother's Day, that year.

KRISTIN SZAKOS, CHARLOTTESVILLE CITY COUNCILOR: The first thing that made us realize that we were on this national agenda for these white supremacist folks was in May at the multicultural festival, which is this incredible festival that Charlottesville's had for years. All of the immigrants and people of all races and nationalities and languages and colors and sizes—all come together and there's Sufi dancing and African drumming and all the different things that make this community rich and so complex being celebrated in a beautiful way.

EMAIL FROM CITIZEN TO CITY OFFICIALS, 12:49 P.M.: Reports from Festival of the Culture that White Nationalists are converging...Reports are that there are currently over 50. They are holding signs and protesting the imposition of minority stress on whites.

KRISTIN SZAKOS: We were part way through it and we realized that these khaki guys were in the park and they started marching toward us.

The group included white nationalist leader Richard Spencer.

KRISTIN SZAKOS: I hadn't known that they were coming, but folks with the multicultural festival had known. They were ready and they had done some training and they just created this human cordon as those guys were coming down the street. And they just blocked the entrance to the park and said, *You're not coming in.* And they were very nonconfrontational. They were very calm and just held their ground.

Next, the white nationalists marched on then-named Jackson Park. There, a small group of antiracist activists confronted them, attempting to disrupt their speeches and force the demonstration to end. The activists say they asked the general community for help shutting down the demonstration but were left largely unsupported. The activists point to this as an early example of feeling left on their own to confront the white nationalist threat against their city that summer.

Then, night fell.

ALLISON WRABEL, REPORTER, CHARLOTTESVILLE *DAILY PROGRESS*: I was at my boyfriend's house in North Downtown. He worked at the *Daily Progress* with me and lived with other news people. We were going to get some beers and some dinner. We started walking. I distinctly remember not really noticing anything at first, but somebody on the road passes on a bike, and he looked up and he said, *Oh my God.* We looked up, and there was a long line of people with the tiki torches and they were starting to light them.

I remember this feeling, almost like when your stomach drops on a roller coaster. *What is this? Are they going to come attack me for standing here? Are they going to run with these torches and try to light something on fire?*

I remember someone saying, *Is this like a UVa graduation ritual thing or what?*

I was like, *I don't think so.*

HEAPHY REPORT: [They] marched in two single-file lines...carrying lit tiki torches. The group formed into ranks five lines deep in front of the statue of Robert E. Lee, and chanted "blood and soil," "you will not replace us," and "Russia is our friend."

ALLISON WRABEL: I had tweeted something like, *Oh, I've heard it might be Richard Spencer, but we're still working to confirm that,* and he replied with a picture of himself holding a torch.

It really all kind of ended pretty quickly, but everyone was like, *What the heck was this? What the heck just happened?*

WES BELLAMY, CHARLOTTESVILLE VICE MAYOR: Jason Kessler and his minions were not there to defend the statue; they were there to defend their whiteness.[5]

YOLUNDA HARRELL, CEO, NEW HILL DEVELOPMENT CORP.: It was definitely something that spread through the community pretty quickly. When I was a little girl, I was with my stepmother in Montgomery, Alabama, and we accidentally found ourselves in the middle of a KKK march. She turned down the wrong street and I remember her telling us to get down on the floor of the car and we was suddenly surrounded by people in white sheets. I will never ever forget that as a kid and just the fear in her voice. And so for me, it was a flashback to that moment as a kid and thinking how scared we was in that moment. And then thinking, *Wow, like this is what our community is about.* And wondering how much more was going to show itself before it was all said and done.

KRISTIN CLARENS, LAWYER AND ACTIVIST: This isn't just a bunch of weird LARPers on some dark corner of the internet. They have such firmly held convictions and they want violence. And they will show up and they want to scare us. And we've got an environment that's making them feel comfortable doing that here.

TWEET FROM AN ALT-RIGHT MARCHER: This is just the beginning. #saveJacksonAndLee #Charlottesville[6]

FACEBOOK POST FROM A CITIZEN: Where is the loving and nonviolent counter protest?[7]

EMAIL FROM LOCAL LAWYER TO FRIENDS: What do you do when White Supremacists/White Nationalists come to town?

My answer starts with I have no idea. For those in Charlottes-ville, yes, it did happen.[8]

KRISTIN CLARENS: People had a lot of different reactions. *Did we invite this or are we the victims? Whose fault is this and why? And what do we need to do? And how significant are those changes we need to make?* And people were starting to argue. And it was starting to get tense.

One of those voices was activist Emily Gorcenski. She had been living in Charlottesville with her wife for the past 10 years, but it had never really felt like home.

EMILY GORCENSKI, LOCAL ACTIVIST: I was in Berlin when Richard Spencer came the first time with the torches. And I think that's the moment that Charlottesville became home. It became home when it became a place that I was willing to fight for. It became something I was willing to stand up for and I felt bad that I wasn't there.

ALAN ZIMMERMAN, PRESIDENT, CONGREGATION BETH ISRAEL: Right after that, the Ku Klux Klan announced that they were coming and having a march at the Stonewall Jackson statue.

The Ku Klux Klan march would occur July 8.

EMILY GORCENSKI: And so with that, I was like, *Well, what's my place?* I'm not going to go up and fist-fight a Nazi, because I'll get my ass kicked. I'm not as good a fighter in real life as I am in my head. And so, I realized that the weapons that I had were my words, and my platform, and my ability to shape relationships with media and to have connections with media. I know how this is going to go down in today's media ecosystem. And so that's when I decided that's what I wanted to put my energy into.

When I transitioned, I made a conscious choice to do things under my real name, under my real identity, because I wanted to show...I really be-lieved in being that kind of trans person that I didn't have as a role model. And so I think that it definitely informs every bit of my activism. Because in everything that I fight for, I can see very clearly how queer people are oppressed and get the short end of the stick in all of these conversations. The white supremacist movement is about whiteness, but whiteness is not just about skin color. It's about patriarchy. It's about heteronormativity, cisnormativity. Trans people are one of the most targeted groups by the current white supremacist movement. So I think that being trans informs what I do and that having lived a life of not speaking under my real voice, I know what the power of speaking under my real voice is.

It made me a target, but I also made myself a target. I became a lightning rod on purpose. And the purpose of this was to divert the attention away from the people who were on the ground, doing that organizing, to give them free space and just make it look like Emily Gorcenski is this huge Antifa bigwig or whatever, when really all I'm doing is just shit-posting on Twitter.

Her plan worked. While the white nationalists largely focused on her, groups of activists in Charlottesville organized secretly.

Activists including Rev. Seth Wispelwey and Brittany "Smash" Caine-Conley started a progressive faith group later called Congregate C'ville. They organized counterprotesting trainings with civil rights activist Rev. Osagyefo Sekou.

REV. SETH WISPELWEY, PASTOR AND COFOUNDER, CONGREGATE C'VILLE: I put out the call to friends and clergy we knew and everything: We're bringing in a well-regarded, well-known organizer who's been arrested in Ferguson. Sekou is going to come down and do one of his little workshops. This was top secret because Kessler was trying to dox people. We're like, *This is on the DL. No one's to know that Sekou's in town.*

We had this big open floor plan and piano and he played some music and he did a little theological spiel. We ended up doing our first "ass in the grass" simulations in our backyard. It was like a trial run.

Other activists in Charlottesville were also training within their own organizations. That included Katrina Turner and Rosia Parker, both citizen leaders in Charlottesville's Black community.

KATRINA TURNER, LOCAL ACTIVIST: When we found out the Ku Klux Klan, the KKK, was coming to Charlottesville? We started training immediately. Yes.

ROSIA PARKER, LOCAL ACTIVIST: We don't do nothing without each other.

DAVID STRAUGHN, LOCAL ACTIVIST: Katrina and Rosia are town matriarchs.

ROSIA PARKER: We met at a rally and we've just been connected ever since, and we're both grandmothers and 'splain about our babies. When we got together, it was unstoppable.

You know, a lot of people call us Double Trouble.

So that summer we would go to church, we wouldn't even come home. We would be even training in our church clothes, high heels, shoes, dresses, purse. Myself, Katrina, and her son, Timmy. We trained and we trained and we trained.

Two or three months, we have already trained through to the KKK rally.

JALANE SCHMIDT, UVA PROFESSOR AND COFOUNDER, CHARLOTTESVILLE BLACK LIVES MATTER: There was immense social pressure to not counterprotest. *It's the leftists that are gonna be the problem.* That was the mood all summer. So you really, as an activist, felt like you had to defend your position to counterprotest.

HEAPHY REPORT: The City made a concerted and unified effort to discourage attendance at the Klan event and to schedule alternative events. Chief [of Police Al] Thomas's approach to public communications was "don't take the bait," which he repeated to multiple audiences as a means of encouraging people to stay away from the Klan event....

YOLUNDA HARRELL, CEO, NEW HILL DEVELOPMENT CORP.: I remember [Police] Chief Thomas coming to our church to talk about the KKK coming and asking us to please stay at home. *Don't give them an audience. The best thing we can do is for you all to let us do our job and to not put us in a position where we gotta try to figure out how to protect you while also—unfortunately they have the right to hold this rally.*

So my husband and I talked about it and we're like, *Yeah, we're not gonna go. We're not gonna give them an audience.*

HEAPHY REPORT: The City's attempts to discourage counter-protests at the Klan rally alienated some members of this community.

JALANE SCHMIDT: There just wasn't institutional support for the resistance to this stuff. And in fact, in the lead-up to the Klan rally and stuff, I call it the Phalanx of the Four P's—by which I mean, the politicians, the police, the preachers, and the professors—they're all in lockstep saying, *Don't protest, don't counterprotest, you'll just encourage them, you'll just add fuel to the fire, better to just ignore them.* It's like, *Oh yeah, that worked so well for the good people of Weimar, Germany, didn't it?* You don't ignore fascists when they're coalescing and mobilizing and organizing and coming in public, you don't just let that go.

We were like the hand-waving alarmists and we kept saying, *This is dangerous and it's leading places that are dangerous and it's not just something you can ignore.*

LISA WOOLFORK, UVA PROFESSOR AND MEMBER OF CHARLOTTESVILLE BLACK LIVES MATTER: What you often find when someone is advising you to respond to something that is harmful to you with civility, is that person is not equally harmed or even harmed at all.

I think that one of the reasons that civility gets used is because it's a way to control people's behavior, but in a way that doesn't seem as autocratic as it really is. Civility itself is a kind of a smoke screen.

REV. SETH WISPELWEY: In terms of my own worldview, that I think is also objectively verifiable, white supremacy is a governing and violent ethos for this entire country that informs policies, politics, procedures, the privileges, the power, and wealth of white people, not just in general but over and against people of color.

If white supremacy is the governing and prevailing order, and white supremacists threaten violence and do violence and are looking for violence, you can't ignore it because it is the oxygen we breathe.

When the KKK finally came to town on July 8, the counterprotesters were ready.

HEAPHY REPORT: Eyewitnesses estimated that the Klan had 40 to 60 members while the crowd contained 1,500 to 2,000 counterprotesters.

KASEY HOTT, ANCHOR, NBC29: They ended up being drowned out by so many people, so many counterprotesters, which was wonderful.

JEFF FOGEL, LAWYER AND ACTIVIST: It was like a joke. They were more pathetic than dangerous.

LISA DRAINE, LOCAL ACTIVIST: It was kind of clownish really. It was a small crowd, but they were in their full regalia, the hoods and the insignia and all. It was really very bizarre, but there was nothing frightening about it.

ALAN ZIMMERMAN, PRESIDENT, CONGREGATION BETH ISRAEL: There was nothing scary about it, really. I thought the feeling in the air was triumphant, almost: *Oh, the big, bad Ku Klux Klan came to Charlottesville and we shouted them down, a thousand to one.*

Despite the relative triumph, many people were still extremely disturbed.

DEVIN WILLIS, SECOND-YEAR UVA STUDENT: I was really optimistic and outgoing at 18, and I think the KKK rally burst my bubble for sure. It grossed me out. If a Black counterprotester or whatever got too close, they would do monkey noise or monkey motions in their direction.

ALAN ZIMMERMAN: What surprised us in our congregation and in our temple leadership was the signs that the Klan brought with them were steeped in antisemitism. And we were not ready for that. Like a lot of Americans, we thought of the Klan as being against people of color. We didn't think of them as an antisemitic organization. I mean, we knew it, but we didn't think that was their focus.

HEAPHY REPORT: At approximately 4:25 p.m., the Klan left Justice Park.

That's when the tenor of the day changed.

HEAPHY REPORT: Police lined up the Klan and told them to move quickly. Police formed a wall to separate the Klan from counterprotesters.

KRISTIN CLARENS, LAWYER AND ACTIVIST: When the Klan guys were leaving, [the Klan members'] cars were at the very end in the underground parking lot by one of the police stations downtown. And that felt really infuriating. When the people in the crowd were like, *Wait, what do you mean? You've got their cars there. You're giving them a police escort?*

HEAPHY REPORT: Photographer Patrick Morrissey said that police made repeated demands over bullhorns to disperse and threatened to use tear gas if counterprotesters did not leave the area. Reverend Seth Wispelwey recalled seeing troopers put on gas masks but did not hear any warning regarding the impending tear gas deployment. Alan Zimmerman, president of Congregation Beth Israel, similarly observed law enforcement donning gas masks but did not recall any warnings from police before the release of tear gas.

Then, Virginia State Police officers released tear gas directly into the crowd.

HEAPHY REPORT: Emily Gorcenski told us that at the time the gas was deployed, a line of counterprotesters stood about 15 feet in front of the VSP Field Force, though they were not obstructing or blocking the street. Gorcenski heard screams of pain in the crowd when VSP deployed the first tear gas canister. She was also affected by the tear gas and was forced to flush her eyes. Less than a minute later, Gorcenski heard a second tear gas canister fired by police. Reverend Seth Wispelwey remembered seeing people in the crowd washing their eyes out due to tear gas exposure while police escorted arrestees away for processing. Ann Marie Smith saw people struggling after exposure—crowd members laid down on the ground and received treatment from street medics using milk and water.

TERRY MCAULIFFE, VIRGINIA GOVERNOR: The state police...were able to get the KKK safely out of the garage. Nobody injured or anything, but tear gas. And I guess down in Charlottesville...they didn't like the idea of any police doing anything or tear gas or anything like that. But I mean, they got 'em out and nobody injured.

ZACK WAJSGRAS, FREELANCE PHOTOGRAPHER: It felt very much like just, they were...without *directly* supporting the Klan, they were reacting with violence to one group of people and completely protecting another, so.

COUNTERPROTESTER CHANTS: Cops and Klan go hand in hand! Cops and Klan go hand in hand!

KRISTIN CLARENS: Why is one side getting a police escort and one side getting tear gassed in the street? I understand that the nuances are complicated in terms of providing police protection or security to people and their right to protest. I get that; I'm an attorney. I understand that tension between First Amendment and violence. But I think we had opportunities to provide security and not also provide a welcome mat. And I don't think we got it right. I think history shows we did not get it right.

CHAPTER 2

"Take away the permit, bad people are coming."

HEAPHY REPORT: Jason Kessler obtained a permit to convene a rally at the Lee statue [on August 12] at which he planned to bring together a wide array of right-wing and white nationalist groups. This event was called "Unite the Right" and was expected to be a much larger event and more significant public safety challenge than the July 8 Klan rally.

Kessler had filed the permit request on June 13, but it was after the KKK rally on July 8 that fears heightened.

ALLEN GROVES, UVA DEAN OF STUDENTS: By then, the flyers for the Unite the Right rally had started showing up and they had very neo-Nazi imagery, a fascist eagle.

I remember saying to some colleagues at the university, *This is the one I'm worried about. Not these clowns that came up from North Carolina. I'm worried about this one. I think this could attract a lot more people.*

Not all university administrators agreed.

TERESA SULLIVAN, UVA PRESIDENT: In the beginning, it didn't look like it was going to be much. The notion that you needed to *unite* the right suggested they were somehow not united.

That view changed over time. I think it began to look more threatening, though we still had a pretty imperfect idea of who was engaged and how many groups there were, and so on. I was expecting something more or less along the lines of the KKK rally, focused downtown on the park by the statue of Robert Lee.

Some city officials were concerned, however, especially after witnessing what they described as an unorganized and unprepared emergency response to the July 8 KKK rally.

ANDREW BAXTER, CHARLOTTESVILLE FIRE CHIEF: The KKK rally was a dress rehearsal. There were huge red flags.

The city had established a command post to monitor the rally—a central location at which first responders and city leaders would observe events and plan their response. But Chief Baxter remembers it as unorganized and ineffective.

ANDREW BAXTER: You could've walked into the command post on July the 8th and if you'd asked seven people, you would've got at least three different answers about who was in charge. There was a complete lack of clarity based on a complete lack of understanding about what being the incident commander means.

According to US federal government guidance and procedure under the National Incident Management System (NIMS), a single incident commander should head the chain of command and give orders.

ANDREW BAXTER: I hate to be critical of Al, of [Police] Chief Thomas, but he didn't have that understanding.

What should have happened in my view on July the 9th, if not before, was a weekly meeting, if not more frequently, of the president of the university, the city manager, the county executive, and their respective public safety teams.

All right, what do we know, what don't we know, how do we find out what we don't know, who's done this before, who's going to be... You see what I'm saying? Just at a high level, that never happened. . . . They were doing it like somebody would call Chief Mike Gibson at the university police, and then he would call so-and-so, like there was going to be a football game or something. It was terrifying.

Law enforcement and senior executives and others should have been actively seeking out communications from other communities that had been through this: Portland, Berkeley, there's some of the communities in Kentucky. *Hey, we just had this event and we dodged a bullet, and we had some problems, but this other group has applied for a permit and we're getting intelligence, consistent intelligence that this is going to be a major event. Here's what we've got planned. What are we missing?*

It takes an incredibly mature, confident professional when put under pressure to say, *What am I missing? Does anybody else in this room know anything?* And we did none of that, not a bit.

BRIAN MORAN, SECRETARY, VIRGINIA PUBLIC SAFETY AND HOMELAND SECURITY: We got intel here that this thing could be substantial in size and in nature, of potential violence. And as the date approached, we became very concerned to the point that I started to ask for briefings with Governor [Terry McAuliffe] and the chief of staff, and I would bring in the superintendent of state police. The superintendent shared with me that he was concerned that the city wasn't taking adequate preparations. He specifically expresses, *You know, I'm not sure they're taking this to the level that it should be taken.* And so that's when my involvement became more intense.

At one point I actually went to the governor, I said, *Governor, we continue to be very concerned that this thing could get out of hand.*

TERRY MCAULIFFE: They were very concerned at this point that the city just was not listening to any of the recommendations coming in from the state.

BRIAN MORAN: At that point, we talked about what state resources are available, what state resources we should apply to the situation. And the governor was very receptive, said, *You do whatever you think you need.*

The state government later ended up activating the Virginia National Guard.

TERRY MCAULIFFE: Now we tried to do this secretly. I wanted to make sure we had all the assets down there, but the last thing I wanted was CNN to say, *Terry McAuliffe, the governor of Virginia, has called a state of emergency, is sending the national guard.* Because all that's gonna do is be like Woodstock, everybody [would say], *Ooh, I gotta get to Charlottesville.*

We almost got caught. We didn't *lie* to the press, but we skated it a little bit and said, *Well, we have training exercises going,* which happened to be true. But the truth is we were moving everybody to Charlottesville.

DAILY PROGRESS: While police prepare for protests, local hospitals also are gearing up. Both Sentara Martha Jefferson and the University of Virginia Medical Center are making preparations for the rally by increasing some medical and security staff during the event.[1]

MIKE SIGNER, CHARLOTTESVILLE MAYOR: It was the worst-case scenario that UVa hospital had in mind. I always thought that was interesting, that the public health experts, like just looking at the variables, like in a clear-eyed way, they were like, *There's gonna be mass casualties.*

TOM BERRY, DIRECTOR OF EMERGENCY MANAGEMENT, UVA MEDICAL CENTER: I wasn't getting a lot of intel through law enforcement. They kept it very close and that wasn't surprising to me. And so because of that, I went out and looked for stuff on my own.

Tom Berry had 21 years of experience in the US Army and had participated in the emergency response at the Pentagon on September 11, 2001.

TOM BERRY: It wasn't hard to do through the unclassified network. It was pretty easy to see that people were interested in violence. It wasn't just *likely;* to me, it was more *imminent* based on a lot of the websites that I was looking at. And so from that, I felt it was pretty easy to determine that *something's* going to happen.

BETH MEHRING, EMERGENCY SERVICES NURSE MANAGER, UVA MEDICAL CENTER: I'm very thankful that Tom was as diligent as he was getting intel about what to expect in August because I don't think people would've taken it as seriously had he not done that. I can honestly say if we had had other people in place, we would not have been prepared to the level that we were.

Tom Berry chose Jody Reyes, the medical center's cancer services administrator, to serve as the weekend's incident commander. She too came from an armed services background.

JODY REYES, INCIDENT COMMANDER, UVA MEDICAL CENTER: You have to be able to sit and look forward and say, these are all the different paths that this could take. And one of those would be, you're down on the Downtown Mall, somebody sets off a bomb, you've got a hundred patients. What are you gonna do? Well, you're gonna need to have nurses and doctors available and you need to have beds available. So, how do you do that?

TOM BERRY: I can remember working with UVa health systems executive Dr. Rick Shannon. He was asking me, *Tom, what do you want me to tell the physicians?* Because, I mean, they'll listen to him, a physician, a clinician.

JODY REYES: Some people can see it and they understand, but you're a surgeon and you have had a patient waiting to get their hip replaced for the last six months, and you're supposed to do surgery on them, and a day before, all of a sudden, some leader manager comes to you and says, *You've gotta cancel that surgery 'cause we can't have elective things scheduled because of what might happen?*

There's going to be a handful of people who understand and recognize that it's not convenient and the timing stinks, but it's the right thing to do for everybody. And then you're gonna have people who don't understand it at all.

TERESA SULLIVAN, UVA PRESIDENT: We began having meetings every morning, you know, just as a precaution to think about what could happen.

TOM BERRY: Dr. Shannon was taking me to President Sullivan's meetings. He asked me to give an overview to President Sullivan about what we were doing. And I could see shock in her eyes. I think they always thought, it's just Charlottesville, it's never going to happen here. And so that was the approach they took.

And to be honest with you, I felt bad for her because I honestly felt like her staff should be doing more for her. She gave some explanations of some dreams she was having.

TERESA SULLIVAN: There was no question. I was very anxious. The closer we got to the event, the more concerned I became and the more of my daily space it occupied, you know, trying to think about it and plan for it and not really knowing what was coming.

TOM BERRY: After that time where I really explained how we were taking those actionable steps to prepare ourselves, decompressing the hospital in terms of ICU beds, I could tell she really didn't want that to be communicated out. And I think in her mind, she thought that it would make people very fearful. She didn't say those words specifically, but the look I saw in her eyes was that, *Tom, what you just briefed to me, I really don't want that to be our message out because I think it's going to scare people.*

President Sullivan recalls those conversations—and her reaction —differently.

TERESA SULLIVAN: Well, Rick had told me that they were prepared for it, but he also said to me, *We do regular drills for this* and so on. And he seemed quite confident that they were ready to take care of it. But also when he spoke of "mass casualty," I was thinking, you know, more along the lines of things that we would see at football games where you'd have people who had heat exhaustion and stuff like that, the occasional heart attack or stroke. I didn't actually think of it in terms of orchestrated violence.

Five miles down the road at the only other hospital in Charlottesville, Sentara Martha Jefferson Hospital, leaders were having similar conversations.

ALEX MCGEE, CHAPLAIN, SENTARA MARTHA JEFFERSON HOSPITAL: Mass casualties. They were preparing for mass casualties.

I was three months into this new job. I had been asked as a chaplain to attend the senior leadership meetings of the hospital. I was hearing them talk about, if they had to get the stable patients out of the hospital to nursing homes, what routes would be accessible and how were those routing instructions going to be given to ambulance drivers. What surgical materials were likely to be needed ahead of time and how were those gonna be obtained? There were conversations about if people had tear gas on them and they needed to be hosed down how would that occur? Where outside the emergency room were those curtains and hoses or water going to be set up? There was very, very thorough thinking ahead.

I think I was standing there stunned like, *Oh my gosh, these people are so on the ball and these people are here to save lives and to heal people. They're not joking around.*

Charlottesville Fire Department Chief Andrew Baxter was also coordinating his firefighters, paramedics, and staff for the weekend.

ANDREW BAXTER: Our big concern was a Las Vegas shooting style event and, quite frankly, open combat on the streets of the city with high powered weapons, with rifles. So we were trying to prepare for multiple, what we would call red patients, priority one traumas. We had plans in place with the National Guard to land Blackhawks on the football field at Charlottesville High School. That's the level of contingency planning we had done. Because if we needed to evacuate, if we had that many people with gunshot wounds, some of them were going to Richmond, some of them were going to Fairfax, some of them were going to Roanoke. We can't take care of all them.

What really made me nervous was the physical safety of our firefighters and EMTs and paramedics. They're hearing from a lot of the CPD [Charlottesville Police Department] folks—excuse my language—really scary shit. Really, like officers telling their wives, *Honey, this may be it.*

A number of us had been trying to get City Manager Maurice Jones to declare a state of emergency.

HEAPHY REPORT: The executive power for the City Government is vested in a City Manager. Selected by City Council, the City Manager is the "chief executive and administrative officer" for the City Government and thus responsible for enforcing

the laws of the City and ensuring that City employees faith-
fully perform their administrative responsibilities. The City
Manager is also explicitly named as the "director of public
safety" and given general powers of supervision over the
Charlottesville Fire Department (CFD) and the Charlottesville
Police Department (CPD).

ANDREW BAXTER: He wouldn't do it. He didn't want to. Even if it was just
declare a state of emergency because we're going to be shutting down traffic
on so many streets, likely increased response times...

We didn't want to alarm people. Well, sorry. The only person who's not
alarmed is you.

KRISTIN CLARENS, LAWYER AND ACTIVIST: We get more information about
a snowstorm or something than we did about this.

JALANE SCHMIDT, UVA PROFESSOR AND COFOUNDER, CHARLOTTESVILLE BLACK
LIVES MATTER: The week before, there was a little baby bear that was loose
near the children's hospital. You know, wandering wildlife. And the university sent out a campuswide alert: *Stay away from the hospital! There's wildlife!
The fish and game people are handling it. You stay!* And then by comparison, the
next week, 300 Nazis with torches? Nothing, no warning.

CONGREGATION BETH ISRAEL
DOWNTOWN CHARLOTTESVILLE
EARLY AUGUST 2017

ALAN ZIMMERMAN, PRESIDENT, CONGREGATION BETH ISRAEL: As the Unite
the Right rally drew closer, we started to look at some of the online postings,
just on websites, Twitter, stuff like that, and we became really concerned:
95 percent of that stuff was about Jews and was sophomoric humor about
the Holocaust, jokes about ovens and exterminating Jews. And we started to
see this and just become more and more concerned. We really didn't know
what to expect that day.

EMILY BLOUT, UVA PROFESSOR AND MAYOR MIKE SIGNER'S WIFE: The Jewish community in Charlottesville is about 400 families, and the synagogue is the only synagogue in all central Virginia.

Congregation Beth Israel is one block from Emancipation Park, where Kessler had applied to hold his rally.

ALAN ZIMMERMAN: We have services on Saturday morning and we thought about canceling services, but we ultimately decided not to.

MICHAEL CHEUK, SECRETARY, CHARLOTTESVILLE CLERGY COLLECTIVE: They decided to have their regular Shabbat service almost as an act of resistance.

ALAN ZIMMERMAN: We started an hour earlier, so if people wanted to get out of downtown before the march officially started at 12 o'clock, they could do so.

We'd hired a security guard the weekend of the Ku Klux Klan march, but we asked him not to come armed. But for the Unite the Right march, we had the security guard come back. He said, *Can I come armed?* And we told him it was OK to do that.

HEAPHY REPORT: Rabbis also removed the synagogue's sacred scrolls for safekeeping outside of the downtown area.

RABBI TOM GUTHERZ, CONGREGATION BETH ISRAEL: We said to ourselves, *Is there anything in this building that just can't be replaced?*

And when we thought that through, we realized this Holocaust Torah, which is a special scroll that our synagogue has…I mean, it couldn't be replaced. So a couple days before August 12, we just sort of quietly removed that Torah. A member took it to their home for safekeeping.

We left one Torah there because we wanted to read from it on Saturday morning.

WES BELLAMY, CHARLOTTESVILLE VICE MAYOR: The activist community had been scouring the internet and dark net for a while now, and they were adamant that the people coming here on August 11th and 12th were serious people who wanted to invoke pain, terror, and real violence.[2]

DAVID STRAUGHN, LOCAL ACTIVIST: We had people inside that were also looking at 4chan and 8chan and Discord and all of these websites that white nationalists run through.

DON GATHERS, COFOUNDER, CHARLOTTESVILLE BLACK LIVES MATTER: It was very much clear to us that we could expect for people to die.

REV. SETH WISPELWEY, PASTOR AND COFOUNDER, CONGREGATE C'VILLE: Our trainings became less and less about, *Here's how to not get your shoulder dislocated if the police drag you away,* and more like, *Here's how to go serpentine and crouch through the ground and cover the body of someone in a live-fire situation.*

LISA DRAINE, LOCAL ACTIVIST: The leaders were saying, *If you decide you wanna be on the street and nobody's pressured to do so, you should make sure that you have some training. You don't wanna go into that situation, not knowing what to expect or how to act.*

DAVID STRAUGHN: We trained for bullet fire: Get down in serpentine in case you hear fire. We trained for chemical warfare, we trained for audio warfare 'cause we heard that they might bring sonar guns that would pierce the ears.

REV. SETH WISPELWEY: Our house became kind of a safe zone. Sekou lived with us for six weeks in our basement during the time in training. We had like 60 to 80 people at any given training. We're doing this in a field behind Sojourners United Church of Christ on these hot-ass muggy days. It was just community members, though, doing this on their free time. That was what was so striking about it. We were building an airplane while flying. I was running out buying cases of LaCroix and snacks for the trainings.

What I'm trying to say is we were taking it really fucking seriously.

Congregate C'ville decided to organize an interfaith prayer service the night before Unite the Right. In a planned demonstration of unity, they invited hundreds of clergy from around the country in what they named the #ClergyCall.

REV. SETH WISPELWEY: That idea originated on my back deck one night where Sekou and I got high after a training. And he goes, *This is going to be big, this is going to be so fucked up, holy shit.* We were saying, *There's going to be so many Nazis.* We didn't know how many.

He's like, *You know what we're going to do? We're going to put out a call.*

And he's stoned. And I'm just looking at the moon and being like, *Uh-huh. Yeah.*

And he's like, *We're going to put out a call. We're going to ring that park.*

That is explicitly where the clergy call came from.

The trainings grew in intensity as August 12 approached.

REV. SETH WISPELWEY: By the last training, the white men in the simulation had to play the parts of the cops and the white supremacists. We were having to pretend to be white supremacists! Like, not saying anything, but beating on... It was crazy.

DAVID STRAUGHN: Everything was placed on the down low, 'cause we didn't know when individuals would strike. We didn't know if they would come early and try to take us out during an organizer's meeting or a training like this or what. I can't tell you how much weight I lost, how much I didn't sleep, how much I didn't eat.

REV. SETH WISPELWEY: In other words, just full-time organizing, around the clock. It's hard to believe it was in four and a half weeks.

REV. SETH WISPELWEY: A lot was happening at city council meetings.

I.B.F., LOCAL ACTIVIST: We'd been trying all summer for that permit to be revoked. Don't let people come.

EMILY GORCENSKI, LOCAL ACTIVIST: There was one city council meeting between the July 8th rally and the August 12th rally, because the summer break was there.

The activists thought their best bet to get the city council to listen to their concerns was to put together a physical document detailing the threats.

EMILY GORCENSKI: We had all of this evidence and all of this chatter about the violence that was going to be created. So we put together a document to try to say, *Look, they're planning. They're talking about how many Black people they're going to beat up. They're talking about how they're targeting Wes Bellamy, specifically. Jason Kessler is organizing with a motorcycle gang. We've got militias that are coming here and saying that they're going to kill people.* All of this stuff.

And we're like, *Here you go. Here's all of this evidence of the very intentional violence that these people want to bring into our community.*

EMILY GORCENSKI'S DESCRIPTION OF DOSSIER CONTENTS: One militia man posted on Facebook, "I can assure you there will be beatings at the August event." Of Black Lives Matter activists, he promised that his fellow militia members "will finish them all off." On the neo-Nazi media portal Daily Stormer, user Exterminajudios (Exterminate Jews) posted, "Antifa and [N-words] will be out in force. We need some military guys there to crack skulls."[3]

EMILY GORCENSKI: The purpose of the dossier was multipurpose, a lot of layers to it. This was not merely an effort to say, *Take away the permit, bad people are coming.* One part of it was, yes, you hope that they listen and you hope that they act and that they do something with the information that you give them. But you don't bank on it, you don't depend on it because most of the time, power is going to let you down.

And so, the secondary purpose of this dossier was to put it on record that we told them so. So that when the ship went down, we could then point back at it and say, *We told you that they would be violent. We told you that they were going to be violent and you're incompetent.*

DOSSIER, AS PRESENTED TO CITY COUNCIL ON JULY 17, 2017:

Dear Esteemed Council Members,

With respect to the issue of public safety surrounding the "Unite the Right" rally currently scheduled for 12 August 2017, we present evidence of threats of violence planned to take place during the event...

Part 3.4.5(b) of the Special Event Regulations of the City of Charlottesville states that a "permit may be denied in writing" if "it reasonably appears that the proposed activity will present a danger to public safety or health...." On these

grounds, we submit the following to support the claim that
it reasonably appears that the proposed activity will present a danger to public safety and formally request that the
Event Coordinator revoke the permit for the proposed August 12
event.[4]

MIKE SIGNER, CHARLOTTESVILLE MAYOR: Emily Gorcenski was so furious at
us when she brought that dossier, and it included a lot of that open source
stuff. And she told me actually in another meeting, she's like, *Yeah, I had
other stuff that I can't produce. But what I brought to you, you should have been able
to stop it or turn down the permit.*

But I went through everything that had happened legally and what we'd
been told. We couldn't legally have stopped the rally.

**It's not clear that is true, given the city code allowing for the city
to deny permits out of concern for public safety, but multiple city
officials say that is what the city lawyers told them at the time.**

KRISTIN SZAKOS, CHARLOTTESVILLE CITY COUNCILOR: We kept being told
by our advisers, legal kind of advisers, that there was nothing we could do
about it. It was just a free speech issue, and we were just going to have to
take it.

Soon, city councilors tried a potential middle option.

KRISTIN SZAKOS: We tried to get the rally moved outside of downtown,
because we were worried [that with] so many people in such a dense area,
it was just going to explode.

**The Unite the Right organizers sued to keep the rally at its original
location, and the federal court agreed to take the case. Now, more
uncertainty around the rally: Where would it even take place?**

REV. SETH WISPELWEY: I remember that feeling once the calendar hit August, like, *Oh God, it's here.* Like a hurtling snowball down a mountain.

I remember days feeling long, but of course they were really full. Things were in motion. And we had prepared. We were preparing.

I.B.F., LOCAL ACTIVIST: I wore a hijab at the time and my parents were really, really worried about my safety. They still lived with me. And so, the Thursday before, I moved out of our home. There was this fear that people might follow you and I didn't want to put them in any kind of danger. So I left home, I packed up my things and I stayed with a friend who was also organizing.

Vice Mayor Wes Bellamy says that white nationalists were threatening him with injury and death via email, social media, and even mailed letters, but he still wanted to go to the rally to counterprotest.

WES BELLAMY, CHARLOTTESVILLE VICE MAYOR: A few guys from the barbershop told me that they wanted to meet...and it was mandatory. I'm normally not one who likes being told what to do, but I sensed the seriousness of the tone in their voices...I walked in, sat down, and knew immediately that this was not going to go well.

These guys, most of whom were from here, who had been here for years and had a strong footprint in the city, were there that night for one reason: to tell me that I wasn't going to the rally on Saturday.

We had a long conversation, and went back and forth about why I felt I needed to be there, how I didn't want to let the community down. I refused to allow this group to come to our city and simply think that they can take over without any kind of pushback. For them, my brothers standing before me in the barber shop—it was more so about safety. They'd been there for the KKK rally and believed, had I been at that one, that things would not have turned out well for me. In their eyes, going to this rally would be even worse.

I was hell-bent on going to Unite the Right, and eventually they realized that the only way to stop me was by them physically knocking me out. We agreed on a compromise.[5]

Wes Bellamy promised that he would go to the counterprogramming events around the city, and not the rally itself. Then, he too left home for the weekend.

WES BELLAMY: I was informed by the police that it wouldn't be a good idea to stay at my house, so I made other arrangements.[6]

REV. SETH WISPELWEY: On our last training, we encouraged people to write a letter to a loved one just acknowledging with informed consent, like, *I'm going to go out. It's going to be dangerous and volatile.*

ROSIA PARKER, LOCAL ACTIVIST: We was prepared because we had intel. We already knew that they was coming here to kill. They wanted to kill us.

PART 2

THE RIOTS

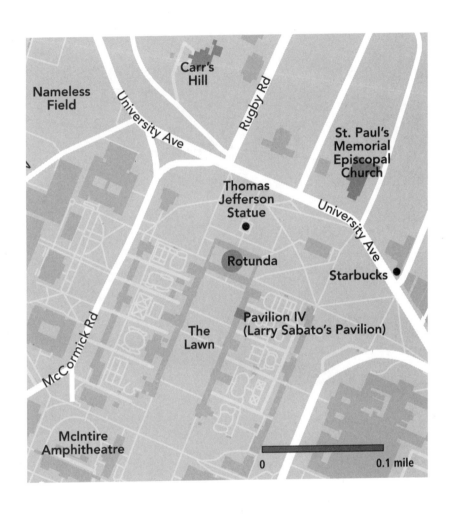

Carr's Hill

Nameless Field

University Ave

Rugby Rd

St. Paul's Memorial Episcopal Church

Thomas Jefferson Statue

University Ave

Rotunda

Starbucks

McCormick Rd

Pavilion IV (Larry Sabato's Pavilion)

The Lawn

McIntire Amphitheatre

0   0.1 mile

CHAPTER 3

"Is somebody going to respond to this? Because this sounds really bad."

FRIDAY, AUGUST 11

REV. SETH WISPELWEY, PASTOR AND COFOUNDER, CONGREGATE C'VILLE: When I woke up, it was relatively early. It was like, *OK, this is the day. Here's what we're going to do.*

I was having my early coffee and smoke with Sekou on my front porch when we got the message over Signal that the torch-lit rally, which we knew they wanted to replicate, was going to be at UVa.

EMILY GORCENSKI, LOCAL ACTIVIST: When they started organizing this thing, I'm like, *Jason Kessler is an arrogant son of a bitch. He's definitely going to try to pull something the night before, because if I were in his position, that's exactly what I would do.* And there's a handful of places in the city where that can actually be pulled off.

The activists considered several possible locations the white nationalists might hold a torch march Friday night, but soon eliminated most of them for either being too far outside of town or having no symbolism, often important to white supremacists.

EMILY GORCENSKI: We were like, UVa is the only other place that makes sense. So of course, they're going to do it at UVa. That morning we get the confirmation of where and when it would be.

That confirmation included the exact location: the statue of Thomas Jefferson at the UVa Rotunda, across the street from St. Paul's Memorial Church where Congregate C'ville would be holding an interfaith prayer service at the exact same time.

REV. SETH WISPELWEY: Our morning coffee became like, *Well, does that change anything for us?*

We thought that community members and activists would confront it, and that invariably local authorities would step in. Like, this is on UVa's campus. So we were just like, *We're going to stick to what we do, because this will be confronted in some way or another by people. And we'll do our thing and just be vigilant.*

But most people within the local activist groups actually had not decided yet whether they would confront it, and not all activists were making decisions together.

EMILY GORCENSKI: There was a big debate among activists on whether we should counterprotest it or not. Everyone's like, *Are we counterprotesting the torch march?* And I'm like, *Look, I don't care. Just decide, figure it out.*

KRISTIN SZAKOS, CHARLOTTESVILLE CITY COUNCILOR: I started getting calls about maybe noon, one or two o'clock, about the plans for a torchlight march at UVa. I was talking to folks who were monitoring some of the chat on the internet from the folks planning it.

I talked to our police department and talked to the city folks about, *Is somebody going to respond to this? Because this sounds really bad.*

TOM BERRY, DIRECTOR OF EMERGENCY MANAGEMENT, UVA MEDICAL CEN-TER: I saw it coming at probably 1 or 2 in the afternoon. Everything that I'd read and then anticipated, and we had prepared for, it was becoming real. It was obvious that the ER was probably going to become the center of gravity that evening.

I had the time to go home. I think I changed clothes into something more comfortable. I had something to eat. I got back in my car and I went straight to the ER.

EMILY GORCENSKI: So sometime around 3, [my group of activists] decide not to counterprotest the torch march. I'm like, *Fine, I'll go there. I'm still going to film it.* Everyone else is going to be dealing with the church, whatever. And then I thought about saying, *Well, if we're not going to counterprotest, should we call [the torch march] in to the police?* And I was on the fence about it. And I think it was Jalane who said like, *Oh, I've mentioned this or something like that already.* And so I was like, *All right, it's been handled, it's been gone through official channels. It's fine.*

JALANE SCHMIDT, UVA PROFESSOR AND COFOUNDER, CHARLOTTESVILLE BLACK LIVES MATTER: I really struggled with whether or not to even say anything [to warn University authorities about the torch march]. I'm like, they're not gonna listen to me. I'm like, *Oh we need a living wage, we need affordable housing, it's racist up in here, Nazis are coming.* See? You stopped listening to me three issues ago.

And I'm just like, I cannot be the messenger here. I really want this message to go through. It's not about my ego. The message needs to land.

So Jalane Schmidt found a conduit, someone she thought would be trusted: the mayor's wife.

EMILY BLOUT, UVA PROFESSOR AND MAYOR MIKE SIGNER'S WIFE: It was 2:30. I was doing grocery shopping at Barracks Road, and I get a call from a member of Antifa, which is exceptional unto itself because there's a big cynicism towards government by the far left. So I got a call from that person saying this rally was gonna happen at [UVa's] Nameless Field and that I needed to tell the chief of police and the mayor about it, 'cause it was going to happen and it was gonna happen at night. I remember calling Mike and then him promising to call not only just the chief of police, but the UVa police and the president of UVa at the time about it.

UVa Professor Louis Nelson was also warned about the march on
UVa's campus—called "Grounds"—and he in turn called the provost's office. The vice provost then notified university administrators.

3:23 p.m. email to University administrators:

Subject: Possible March tonight on-Grounds

Dear all:

You likely already know this, but if not...Louis Nelson, cop-
ied on this message, just received an informal call alerting
him to the possibility of an alt-right march on-Grounds this
evening, beginning at a Jefferson statue (not sure which one)
to St. Paul's Church, coinciding with the prayer service this
evening. Just wanted to alert you to this possibility. If you
have questions, please contact Louis directly.

Best,

Anda

Vice Provost for Administration and Chief of Staff

Why might UVa administration "likely already know this"? Private
emails obtained through a public records request filed by the *Chronicle of Higher Education* show that the university police had received
intelligence about the torch march days earlier.

CHRONICLE OF HIGHER EDUCATION: Capt. Donald H. McGee, a university police officer, appears to have heard these concerns as
early as August 8, three days before the march on the Lawn.
After a meeting that day of the Charlottesville Police Department, Captain McGee warned his superior about a possible "tiki
torch march" to be held the night before the big downtown
rally. The description proved prescient.

"It was stated that at 9PM there were plans to replicate
the tiki torch march they made last month at an undisclosed
location," Capt. McGee wrote to Michael A. Gibson, the university's chief of police, and several other officers. "There
is concern that the location could be the Rotunda or Lawn

area since Mr. Spencer, an alum, will likely be at the Friday event."

Shortly after 5 p.m., Jason Kessler called the university police department directly.

HEAPHY REPORT: Kessler called [UPD Patrol] Lieutenant [Angela] Tabler, then passed the phone to an associate, who informed Tabler that the group planned to assemble at Nameless Field on the University grounds, march to the statue of Thomas Jefferson in front of the Rotunda, and make a short speech. There was no mention of torches.

UVa President Teresa Sullivan says none of this information was escalated to her.

TERESA SULLIVAN: Somebody should have told me, and there were a lot of different people here who could have told me who knew, who didn't tell me.

ST. PAUL'S MEMORIAL EPISCOPAL CHURCH
7 P.M.

DAILY PROGRESS: After an afternoon of sunshine gave way to a brief evening rain shower and an overcast sky, clergy members and people of faith gathered in St. Paul's Memorial Church on University Avenue for a prayer service that was organized in response to the Unite the Right rally on Saturday.[1]

HEAPHY REPORT: Located on University Avenue, St. Paul's sits just across the street from the University of Virginia, a stone's throw away from the iconic Rotunda and the statue of Thomas Jefferson.

REV. SETH WISPELWEY, PASTOR AND COFOUNDER, CONGREGATE C'VILLE: We wanted to have a service that demanded in the name of God and people of conscience that white supremacy must be overcome if America is going to have a successful future.[2]

DON GATHERS, COFOUNDER, CHARLOTTESVILLE BLACK LIVES MATTER: I
picked up Dr. Cornel West from the airport and got him positioned and
situated.

BRITTANY "SMASH" CAINE-CONLEY, COFOUNDER, CONGREGATE C'VILLE:
Like, we knew what to expect, but we had no idea what to expect.

WASHINGTON POST: Doors opened at 7:30 and within minutes some
600 people filled the pews and lined its walls. Many others
were turned away.[3]

REV. SETH WISPELWEY: Boy, that church was packed. I mean, we had to turn
people away.

Rosia Parker and Katrina Turner arrived together.

ROSIA PARKER, LOCAL ACTIVIST: So we get to the church about maybe
6:30 or so.

KATRINA TURNER, LOCAL ACTIVIST: No, we were late. It was like 7:15–20.
We were late.

ROSIA PARKER: No. We first got to the church. Remember? We walked
around first before we went to the door. And so by that time it was about
7:15. So then we was told that we couldn't get in the church because the
church was packed. So, we end up sitting outside in front of the church.

**Another person in attendance: Lisa Draine. Her two daughters,
23-year-old Rebecca and 21-year-old Sophie, had just gotten home
from summers abroad only two days earlier, but they wanted to
counterprotest on Saturday. So on Friday night, Lisa brought Rebecca with her to the service.**

LISA DRAINE, LOCAL ACTIVIST: Sophie had told us that she couldn't go to
that service, that she was meeting up with her friends who were planning
what they were gonna do the next day. So Rebecca and I went to the service
and she didn't come with us.

REV. SETH WISPELWEY: We definitely came close to breaking the fire code.
There were about 675 folks packed into St. Paul's.[4]

CHRIS SUAREZ, REPORTER, CHARLOTTESVILLE *DAILY PROGRESS*: The thing that really struck me in all of that was that there was very intense security.

REV. SETH WISPELWEY: We had people within the activist security network sweeping the church for suspicious bags and stuff, making sure that only a couple of doors were open, letting in our VIPs through the back alley.

WILLIS JENKINS, UVA PROFESSOR: I [was] standing guard at the front doors. . . . A few hours earlier, for reasons that remain unclear, Charlottesville police had pulled back the officers initially promised to the church where the meeting was held, so organizers had scrambled to ask some allies for security help. I was asked to come help, not because I was experienced in security, but because I was nearby and trusted. By then organizers knew (and UVa administrators had been alerted) that there would be a torch-lit rally at the Rotunda, which was across the street from the church. About 10 of us stood on watch outside, all unarmed.[5]

WASHINGTON POST: The church service began at 8 p.m. Sitting in the pews were clergy members from all over the country who had paid their way to come to Charlottesville to support those protesting against the Unite the Right rally.[6]

There were many local residents on hand as well, including long time activists with experience in civil rights rallies and newcomers who wanted to voice their opposition to what they saw as an ugly threat to their city.[7]

REV. SETH WISPELWEY: The spirit was alive, for lack of a better word. The gospel singing, the freedom songs.

I.B.F., LOCAL ACTIVIST: It was like a pep rally, almost. It was like, *We're going to be OK, we're going to be fine there. We are here together in solidarity*, et cetera, et cetera.

REV. DR. CORNEL WEST: We have to take a stand. That's why some of us came to fight and get arrested, if necessary.[8]

MIKE SIGNER, CHARLOTTESVILLE MAYOR: Cornel West had been my professor at Princeton and when I heard that he was coming, I reached out to him.

We had this really nice conversation, but what I had seen from the clergy organizers and from the groups that were leading this was that there was enough confrontationalism in this group. I don't think—it wasn't entirely around that pole at all, but it had enough in it that I didn't think that this was gonna be the event that would somehow calm the whole city down and avoid a conflict.

So I was sitting there with a knot in my stomach during the whole service and during everything that was happening that night, 'cause I was worried about this clash that I feared was gonna come.

SINGING: We shall not, we shall not be moved
Just like a tree that's planted by the water, we shall not
   be moved
We are fighting for our freedom...
Black and white together...
Gay and straight together...
Jewish, Christian, Muslim...
We are fighting for our children...[9]

DON GATHERS: It was like Sunday morning at a Baptist church! It didn't matter about belief or sect or religiosity, it was just a commonality of people coming together to worship and to denounce evil.

RABBI TOM GUTHERZ, CONGREGATION BETH ISRAEL: There was a moment during the service when people came up to us to receive blessings from the clergy and a sense that we were entering into kind of a sacred moment, really. That this was going to be sort of a moment of...I don't want to use strong terms but...of good and evil.

We're going to go into the fray against this terrible ideology and this terrible hatred that had come to our town, and there was something sacred about that.

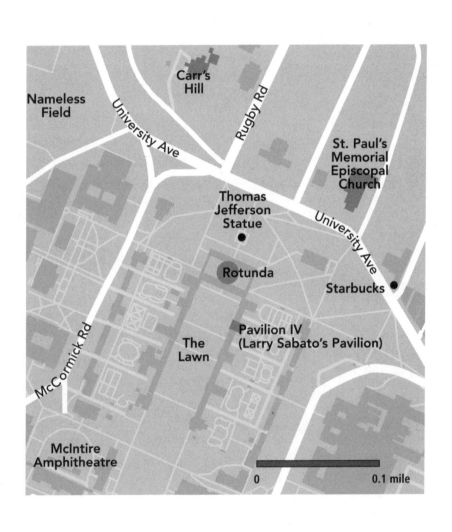

CHAPTER 4

"We have a tip that something is going to happen on Grounds."

THE LAWN, UNIVERSITY OF VIRGINIA

AUGUST 11, JUST BEFORE 8 P.M.

The Lawn is essentially UVa's central quad, designed by Thomas Jefferson himself. It's ringed by small, single dorm rooms that open directly onto the grass. Today, it is an honor for a student to be selected to live in a Lawn room, even though the rooms lack many modern comforts, including bathrooms.

MALCOLM STEWART, FOURTH-YEAR UVA STUDENT AND SENIOR RESIDENT ON THE LAWN: Around 8 that night, there was still a little bit of sunlight out. One of the Lawn residents was like, *Guys, President Sullivan's on the Lawn saying hi to people.* I was like, *Oh, you know what, T-Sully is here, let me go say hello, I haven't seen her since I moved in.*

TERESA SULLIVAN, UVA PRESIDENT: I had walked over to the Lawn after dinner because it was the day the Lawnies could move in and I just went to say hello.

MALCOLM STEWART: So we start chatting and she's like, *I just knew Lawn residents were moving in, and I want to come by and meet people and say hello.* And

I was like, *Cool.* At 7:57 p.m., a GroupMe message came from one of the other senior residents.

TEXT FROM A SENIOR RESIDENT ADVISER, 7:57 P.M.: From one of my staffers: Heads up that there might be a secret alt right rally at the rotunda tonight. Stay safe everyone.

MALCOLM STEWART: Immediately following that message, another senior resident sent a link to a website.

IT'S GOING DOWN TWEET, 7:43 P.M.: Multiple sources confirming neo-Nazis will converge at 9 PM at Jefferson Statue at UVa campus. #Charlottesville #defendcville #NoNewKKK[1]

IT'S GOING DOWN ARTICLE, TWEETED OUT AT 7:43 P.M.: Local organizers in Charlottesville have now received word from an anonymous source that Unite the Right can't wait for Saturday—they are planning a repeat surprise torchlit rally on University of Virginia (UVa) campus tonight. Sounds like Richard Spencer wants back on his old stomping grounds, right where he and his white supremacist followers can feel at home.

...As IGD reported today, the right's leaders are documented calling for armed violence against anyone who crosses them.[2]

MALCOLM STEWART: Immediately following me getting this message at 7:57, I read it, saw it, and I pulled President Sullivan aside. I said, *Hey, President Sullivan, can I borrow you for a second?* I pull her out onto the Lawn and I turn my phone around and I say, *Have you seen this?* As she took my phone, looked at it and saw the time and the location plans, she said, *Well, this is news to me.* Those are her exact words.

And I looked at her, I was like, *OK, so what would you like us to do?*

And she's like, *I need to get in touch with the police chief.*

TERESA SULLIVAN: I went back up to Carr's Hill [the president's residence] and started making some phone calls. And I talked to Marge Sidebottom, who was the emergency operations director. And she came over, and it was Marge who told me there had been a phone call that afternoon to the police department.

And she said that they had said there was gonna be a small number of people who would walk on the sidewalks up University Avenue to the Thomas Jefferson statue, read a speech, and then go home. Both the street and the sidewalks are considered public, so we actually can't control that. And that by itself didn't sound very threatening, but that also turned out not to be true. I mean, first of all, lying to a police officer is a pretty serious matter. You don't do that.

I also understand the call came from Jason Kessler, who was over and over identified as a UVa alumnus. And, you know, I think at UVa, we tend to accord to both our alumni and our students a kind of a generous belief that they're subscribing to the honor code.

At home 20 minutes south of town, Dean of Students Allen Groves was having dinner with his husband, Adam.

ALLEN GROVES, UVA DEAN OF STUDENTS: I'm thinking I need to get a lot of sleep tonight, because it's going to be a really challenging day tomorrow. And the phone rang around 8:20 and it was President Sullivan. And she said, *Allen, I just heard from a student that they're coming to Grounds tonight. They're coming to Grounds.* And I said, *I'll be right there.* So I told Adam, *I got to go back in. They may be coming to UVa.* And he said, *Well, you're not going alone. I'm going with you.*

So our dog Gracie, we piled her in the car and he got in the car and we drove and I got to UVa around nine. There's two guys helping a friend move into a Lawn room and otherwise it looks like a very quiet Friday night before students start to come. So we go to the other side of the Rotunda, the Jefferson statue side. There were those wooden benches and Adam and I sat down with Gracie at a bench and I said to him, *It seems very quiet.*

Meanwhile, the church service continued across the street.

REV. SETH WISPELWEY, PASTOR AND COFOUNDER, CONGREGATE C'VILLE: The first couple of hours flew by.[3]

At about 8:30 p.m., the US District Court issued its order preventing the city from moving the Unite the Right rally out of Emancipation Park. The park would therefore be the location of the rally on August 12.

MIKE SIGNER, CHARLOTTESVILLE MAYOR: We got the news about the court decision and I had to go draft a statement, we had to go work on it. I was sitting there not doing anything. So we left.

At 8:43 p.m., the first 911 call came in.

HEAPHY REPORT: An anonymous male caller claimed to have an AR-15 rifle and threatened to open fire inside the church in five minutes.

One block away, *Daily Progress* reporter Chris Suarez was writing his article in a Starbucks, trying to make his print deadline.

CHRIS SUAREZ, REPORTER, CHARLOTTESVILLE *DAILY PROGRESS*: Someone in our newsroom heard over the police scanner that there had been threats called in to the church. I have a distinct memory of seeing text messages from friends in the newsroom about the threats, telling me this is going on. All kinds of wild stuff, that someone was going to shoot up the church.

Unbeknownst to the organizers of the service or the worshippers inside, four responding police officers searched outside the church for a potential shooter and found none. The service continued. At 8:56, another call came in.

Heaphy report: An unidentified male called the [Emergency Communications Center] and threatened to walk inside St. Paul's and kill a large number of parishioners.

Again, police responded, but found no threat. The service continued.

At the same Starbucks down the street where Chris Suarez was working, a small group of activist street medics was holding an emergency meeting to discuss their plans for that night's torch march. They had only just found out it would take place at UVa.

STAR PETERSON, LOCAL ACTIVIST AND STREET MEDIC: There weren't that many of us, maybe eight, maybe five?

MELISSA WENDER, STREET MEDIC: I had taken on some degree of making sure things were in place and the supplies were in place. *Did we have aspirin? Did we have Gatorade? Did we have bandages? Did we have saline solution?*

STAR PETERSON: I remember us warning the Starbucks employees. We just went and told the people working there, *A bunch of Nazis are coming. I highly recommend you close and you go home now. Don't stay open late.* So, they called their manager and they're like, *We're getting out of here.* I'm glad that we did that.

MELISSA WENDER: My regular medic partner wasn't available, so I was actually partnered that night with Star. And I didn't really know Star in advance of that, but we talked enough and, you know, we go through a series of questions about whether you're willing to be arrested and your degree of medical training and this and that. And we thought we could work well together for that night.

STAR PETERSON: That was my first time running as a marked medic. Basically, if you're a marked medic, you don't protest. You wear the big cross or whatever. You don't participate in any of the actions. You're just there to provide first aid. Medics generally agree not to protest if we're marked, because then the cops will start aiming for us more than they already do.

MELISSA WENDER: Being a medic is a super interesting role because you're both involved and you're staying detached at the same time. So things were gearing up and then we decided to go over by the Rotunda.

In the student newspaper office in the basement of nearby Newcomb Hall, rising junior Tim Dodson was just biting into a takeout order of tacos. As the managing editor of the *Cavalier Daily*, Dodson was waiting for the court decision as to whether the white nationalists would be permitted to rally in the location they'd originally requested, Emancipation Park.

TIM DODSON, MANAGING EDITOR, *CAVALIER DAILY*: I'm just eating dinner and we're waiting for the injunction. Then we got word that there was going to be some sort of gathering of, at the time what we called the alt-right.

It was a really skeleton crew who was in town for *Cav Daily* at that point. The school year hadn't started yet. So I was texting different news writers trying to figure out, *Hey, is anyone able to come to UVa at this moment because this will probably be some sort of news story and we should try to report on it.*

ALEXIS GRAVELY, SENIOR ASSOCIATE NEWS EDITOR, *CAVALIER DAILY*: I was at home and going to start writing a story about the ruling. I was just tip-tapping on my laptop, writing my little story and then Tim texted me and he's like, *We have a tip that something is going to happen on Grounds. I'm not sure what it is. Can you come down?* Because we're short staffed and we're all doing everything, I was like the resident photographer for the weekend. So I just grabbed my camera and I was like, *OK, well, I'll come meet you at the Rotunda and we'll see what's happening.* I was going in kind of naively.

They got to the Rotunda, where more journalists were waiting.

DAVID FOKY, NEWS DIRECTOR, NBC29: We had been hearing this rumor that there was gonna be some sort of march or demonstration or torch thing at the Rotunda. But because we were so unsure if this was gonna happen, I didn't mind going out and hanging out on Grounds, waiting to see if these rumors were true.

There were a couple of journalists just down there sitting on the benches, just keeping an eye out, being real low key sitting around. We were just chatting.

ALEXIS GRAVELY: Tim was already there and he was talking to some other reporters there that I didn't know. Someone was from South America. And I think that was my first indication where I was like, *Whoa, this is kind of a big . . . Someone flew all the way from South America to cover this?*

We were standing there, but it was still very unclear what was happening. And so, we sort of realized that we were in the wrong place because the Rotunda was quiet, comparatively.

DAVID FOKY: We weren't seeing anything. We weren't hearing anything. Like, we were getting ready to leave.

Meanwhile, a group of student activists was gathered at Professor Walt Heinecke's house nearby, eating spaghetti he cooked for them and making protest signs for the next day.

KENDALL KING, THIRD-YEAR U.VA STUDENT: Walt Heinecke was a teacher, a friend, a mentor of mine and a couple other of the people who were organizing that summer.

WALT HEINECKE, UVA PROFESSOR AND ACTIVIST: I just really wanted to support the cause and support them personally in the work that they were doing. It's really difficult to be an activist at UVa. The culture is anti-activist, and the small group of activists that come and go in UVa's history get punished a lot and they don't have a lot of resources and they don't get a lot of support. The faculty don't really support them very much.

I considered these students my colleagues. They asked me if they could use my house to organize for August 11th, 12th. I think they felt it was a safe space to organize and it was off the grid and nobody knew about it, like nobody knew where to find them.

So they came on the afternoon of the 11th and I think there was 20, 25 of them at the house and they were getting organized and figuring out where they were gonna sleep. I mean my house isn't that big; it's three bedrooms and a living room and it's not that big. So I told them, if you guys wanna stay...and they did, they wanted to stay over. So people brought sleeping bags. I think they trusted me to create that kind of a space for them.

KENDALL KING: That night we were going through the day's agenda for August 12th and we were saying, *OK, does everybody have a buddy? Does everybody have water? Here's our starting point.*

Professor Heinecke left the students in his house to finish eating while he headed to the church service at St. Paul's.

DEVIN WILLIS, SECOND-YEAR UVA STUDENT: At some point during the dinner, somebody came in—I don't remember who it is anymore—and informed us like, *Hey, we heard that Jason Kessler and some of his people are going to have something and it might be at UVa.*

KENDALL KING: So we were just like, *All right, drop everything. Let's go. Get your buddy.*

DEVIN WILLIS: One of the signs was already finished that we had intended to use for Unite the Right. So they were like, we're going to take this sign and go over there. And it will be like July 8th. They say their part, we say our part, and then everyone goes home.

Devin, Kendall, and other friends drove over to Grounds, parked, and then met up with a few more friends at the Jefferson statue outside the Rotunda. There was only a handful of students there. They didn't see any white supremacists, only the few journalists waiting.

DEVIN WILLIS: We're like, *OK, so we got here first.*[4] Someone decided the plan was that we're going to link arms and we're going to form a circle at the base of the statue.[5]

KENDALL KING: We had no intention of it being any sort of message about protecting the institution or defending Jefferson. A common civil rights tactic is to hold hands and form a blockade.

At the statue, Devin met up with his friend Natalie Romero, also a UVa student.

NATALIE ROMERO, SECOND-YEAR UVA STUDENT: I was wearing flip-flops, a little tank top, some knitted shorts.[6] Like, in no way was I trying to meet protesters. I was just, you know, it's your school. I'm walking distance, really. I just wanted to witness it for my own eyes.[7]

DAVID FOKY, NEWS DIRECTOR, NBC29, AT THE ROTUNDA: All of a sudden, somebody said that there were people gathering at Nameless Field. I'm a townie, I know UVa a little bit, but like I had no idea where Nameless Field was.

CHRIS SUAREZ, REPORTER, CHARLOTTESVILLE *DAILY PROGRESS*: Someone texted, *They're at Nameless Field.* Like that's where they're meeting. And I was like, *What the—is that a made-up name?* Like, what?

Nameless Field is the actual name of a large field at UVa.

DAVID FOKY: So once we figured that out, we went down there.

While the students continued to wait at the Rotunda, the journalists walked to Nameless Field to find the white supremacists.

TIM DODSON, MANAGING EDITOR, *CAVALIER DAILY*: I remember walking down to Nameless Field, and I recognized Jason Kessler, I think because he had been on TV and I was seeing photos of him in the *Daily Progress*.

Emily Gorcenski had also arrived at Nameless Field. She was alone because on Friday afternoon she'd received a call from the FBI asking her about her plans for the weekend.

EMILY GORCENSKI, LOCAL ACTIVIST: The FBI calls me and they're like, *So Emily, we hear you're planning a terror attack at the [Saturday] rally.* And I'm like, *Well, you heard wrong.*

They're like, *Yeah, we got an anonymous tip. These are usually false, but we have to investigate.* Da, da, da, da, da, da.

And so, I know that they're following my Twitter. I know that they're seeing that I'm an antifascist or whatever. And so I don't want to talk to them, but at the same time, I'm just like, *There's no plans for violence. It's been really clear what I've been doing, what I've been organizing. I can document everything if I need to. No, I'm not planning a terror attack, but have you considered the Nazis might be planning a terror attack?*

But because the FBI called me, I was like, *Well, I can't network anymore with the rest of the activists because the Feds are on me.* So then, I had pulled myself out of the network. So I went basically alone that night.

I livestreamed it. I wanted to show how pathetic they were. And they were very pathetic until somehow the 40 people turned into 400 like that. I mean, it was freaky. And then, things got real and then things got serious.

DAVID FOKY: Then we realized in the dark, there were hundreds of people down on that field and it became apparent that something was happening.

CHRIS SUAREZ: I came upon them, like, *Oh my God. This is a ton of people. And that's a lot of torches.*

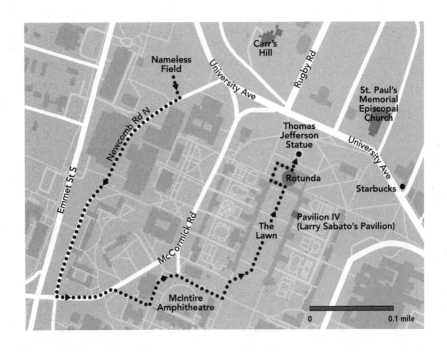

CHAPTER 5

"These are racist people carrying torches."

DAVID FOKY, NEWS DIRECTOR, NBC29: There were just scores and scores of people down there and they started handing out the tiki torches.

CHRIS SUAREZ, REPORTER, CHARLOTTESVILLE *DAILY PROGRESS*: I could tell immediately—this might be hyperbole, but this was four to six times, maybe up to ten times, as big as May. That was the first sign of like, *This is gonna be nuts.*

TERESA SULLIVAN, UVA PRESIDENT: I could barely make them out from where I was on Carr's Hill [across the street and up a hill]. And it was really too late to stop it at that point, particularly since at that point, I still thought it was going to be on the public sidewalks and therefore First Amendment protected.

ALEXIS GRAVELY, SENIOR ASSOCIATE NEWS EDITOR, *CAVALIER DAILY*: When we got there, the torches weren't lit yet, so it still wasn't very clear what was happening. And then I turned because Jason Kessler was behind me and there were a lot of people talking to him. So I looked to see what he was talking about. And then I turned back, and then Nameless Field was completely lit up. It just happened so quickly. It was just all very coordinated.

TERESA SULLIVAN: Then I saw the flames light up and I said to Marge [Side-bottom, emergency operations director], *What is going on here?* And Marge said, *I don't know. I don't know about this.* And she got on her cell phone too. So I don't think anybody was prepared for the torches.

I was pretty alarmed about this. First, there were so many more people and I knew we had very few police on Grounds that night because we had every-body on duty the next day. And we had everybody on 12-hour shifts the next day. And so we didn't have very many police. I didn't know if [the marchers] were armed or not. I could tell they were chanting, but I couldn't understand what they were saying. And so the lack of knowledge was scary, I think.

After that, it went really quite quickly. They obviously were quite organized.

TIM DODSON, MANAGING EDITOR, *CAVALIER DAILY*: There were people shouting, *If you're over 190 pounds, you need to get on the side.* I think it's 'cause they wanted larger men to protect the marchers.

EMILY GORCENSKI, LOCAL ACTIVIST: You could really tell that a lot of them were edging for violence. There's some pushing, shoving. I figured as long as I'm around the media, I'm not going to get picked up, because they're not going to beat somebody up on camera. And if they do, then great, we've made our point. Hopefully, the Saturday rally gets shut down.

REV. SETH WISPELWEY, PASTOR AND COFOUNDER, CONGREGATE C'VILLE, AT ST. PAUL'S: The service was running a little long, but we were nearing the end with some of our last singing.

SMASH CAINE-CONLEY, COFOUNDER, CONGREGATE C'VILLE: Seth and I were sitting next to each other and he leaned over and said to me that there was something going on over on UVa Grounds.

REV. SETH WISPELWEY: We were getting texts that there was a lot of white supremacists out, through a group message chain with my fellow clergy colleagues and a couple of people who were out in front of the church.[1]

The first time I heard that the march was approaching the church, we didn't know where it was headed. We actually thought it was approaching the church. We didn't know what we couldn't see, so I went outside on the front steps of St. Paul's.

**He couldn't see anything, but checked in with the volunteer secu-
rity team.**

REV. SETH WISPELWEY: And they were like, *Well, we're going to keep eyes, but
yeah, keep it going a little bit longer.*

At this point we're closing out with freedom songs, but we're meant to
be at the end. And so Sekou is stretching it out more with "This Little Light
of Mine" and this and that. And so at that point, the crowd doesn't know.

I.B.F., LOCAL ACTIVIST: Reverend Sekou was looking out and he was singing
"This Little Light of Mine," and everybody was singing along as a powerful song.

And I don't know how he knew. I don't know who told him, but he
turned around and his face changed. He turned towards the back where
most people couldn't see him and his face changed. And I remember in that
moment just being like, *Something is wrong.* It's not even like I'd known him
so long or so much, but something about that. I felt my whole body buckle
and I was like, *Something is very wrong and I don't know what it is.*

ROSIA PARKER, LOCAL ACTIVIST, OUTSIDE ST. PAUL'S: We sat outside maybe
45 minutes, I guess, maybe an hour almost. And then somebody came outside to get us and told us that we needed to go inside because something was
getting ready to happen.

KATRINA TURNER, LOCAL ACTIVIST: We started seeing lights coming towards
us. And so that's why they hurried us up in the church because they didn't
know what was going on.

ROSIA PARKER: We couldn't get into church at first because it was full. And
now that the danger is approaching now y'all made space to allow us in
church? Y'all knew we were out there. You all knew the intel that they were
coming. So even if the church was full, how did y'all make space?

So that kind of makes us feel some type of way, a little bit.

ALLEN GROVES, UVA DEAN OF STUDENTS, ON THE LAWN: I was communi-
cating with President Sullivan and all of a sudden, there's this huge roar in
the distance, kind of like a football game in the distance. I texted her. And
I said, *Did you hear that?* Because she's at Carr's Hill across the street. And

she said, *I did.* And I said, *Do you know where it's coming from?* And she said, *I don't, maybe Nameless Field?* Because it was that direction. And so at this point, I'm like, *Something is happening.* What, I didn't know. Candidly, there was a lack—the president and I didn't know what the university police knew at that moment.

Brian Moran was already in Charlottesville doing a preparatory walk-through of Emancipation Park downtown with Virginia State Police Superintendent Steve Flaherty. He also says he didn't know the torch march was coming.

BRIAN MORAN, SECRETARY, VIRGINIA PUBLIC SAFETY AND HOMELAND SE-CURITY: While I'm walking with Steve, he says, *We just got word that there's a protest on the Grounds.* And it turns out the state police had never been told about the protest, which goes to some of the communication breakdowns. So I said, *Well, where is it?* And he said, *Well, I think that they're going to the Rotunda.* And so I drive over to the Rotunda, try to find it.

And my first thought: *Where are the police?* That's what I was saying: *Where the heck are the police?* There's nobody there.

I said well, if there's a large demonstration, I don't see any police presence. So I was skeptical of the intel, but then I saw the lights.

DAVID FOKY, NEWS DIRECTOR, NBC29, IN NAMELESS FIELD: They all took off marching. And they climbed the hill out of Nameless.

TIM DODSON, MANAGING EDITOR, *CAVALIER DAILY*: It's kind of a steep hill between the parking lot and Nameless Field. I start to follow them.

DAVID FOKY: We ran along with them, our photojournalist Jeremy and I.

ALEXIS GRAVELY, SENIOR ASSOCIATE NEWS EDITOR, *CAVALIER DAILY*: They were chanting, *You will not replace us.* It was just so loud. And we were just following them. And I remember being struck by how coordinated it was. Like, this was not some impromptu thing.

I remember that's when I started getting a little emotional, which I almost felt ashamed by because I feel like journalists are always... Like, it's sort of shunned if you get emotional covering things because you're supposed to be neutral.

ALLEN GROVES, AT THE ROTUNDA: I'm trying to figure out what's happening. And now it's getting dark. And I do remember at one point President Sullivan texted me, I think it was one word, *amphitheater*, that she had heard from someone. And so I went around, I told Adam, *Keep Gracie, be safe.* I ran around to the Lawn [to find the white nationalists].

TIM DODSON: The march winds its way onto McCormick Road and they march past the amphitheater.

ALEXIS GRAVELY: The sidewalk is very narrow there. And so we were feeling a little cramped in. And I was like, *I'm a Black woman and these are racist people carrying torches, so maybe we should go elsewhere.* And so we went around and walked up past the Lawn rooms, sort of ahead of them.

TIM DODSON: Then they ended up on the southern part of the Lawn, and that's when it became clear they were going to the Rotunda.

BRIAN MORAN: Sure enough, I see these lights, near the Lawn coming toward the Rotunda. And so I pull over, I walk up to the Rotunda.

LARRY SABATO, UVA PROFESSOR, POLITICAL PUNDIT, AND PAVILION RESIDENT ON THE LAWN: All of a sudden, we heard this chanting and this noise, even before we saw anybody.

WASHINGTON POST: . . .the marchers continued their rapid trek across the university campus, their torches a line of fire as they hurried in formation past the school's iconic buildings. At times running to keep in formation they passed. The campus was almost entirely empty and silent except for the marchers and their threatening chants.[2]

ALLEN GROVES: Larry Sabato was out on the Lawn at this point. And so I see Larry and I go over and I said, *They're coming, apparently.* And he said, *Yeah, I've got some students in my Pavilion basement.*

It's now dark. It's about 10 o'clock and you could see them now coming and turning from where the amphitheater was, up the Lawn.

We were just blown away by both the numbers and all the flaming torches. And there were probably two- to three-hundred of them. And as they're coming up, they're probably four to six abreast in a column coming up, and they're chanting, "You will not replace us."

BRIAN MORAN: They walked in unison, like you did when you were in elementary school, walked to the cafeteria.

ALLEN GROVES: And at one point when they come up to that last higher level of the Lawn where the rooms are, they change it to, "Jews will not replace us." And they start laughing.

LARRY SABATO: My jaw hit the floor. It was right out of the 1930s, really. And it *looked* like it was out of the thirties. I'm sure they were modeling it after the old newsreel films of the Nazis in Germany.[3]

WHITE NATIONALISTS: You will not replace us!
Jews will not replace us!
You will not replace us!
Jews will not replace us!

MALCOLM STEWART, FOURTH-YEAR UVA STUDENT AND SENIOR RESIDENT ON THE LAWN: They were escorted by police officers. Anytime someone kind of stepped out of it, some of the officers basically seemed to coax them back in with the crowd to just walk up the Lawn.

In the dark and chaos, it was unclear which department the officers were from.

MALCOLM STEWART: I went and found Larry Sabato and Dean Groves.

ALLEN GROVES: The bigger guys were on the outside. The not-as-big guys were on the inside and some women, not a lot of women, but some women. And I saw a couple of sheathed knives, I did see a couple of handguns as they're coming up.

TIM DODSON, MANAGING EDITOR, *CAVALIER DAILY*: This felt like some really absurd nightmare. It didn't feel like I was at UVa. It felt like I was in some other dimension.

LARRY SABATO: They had the meanest look on their faces, just full of hate. Contorted, really. And they were spoiling for a fight, no question about it, they were spoiling for a fight.

Lawn resident Diane D'Costa had just moved in that day.

DIANE D'COSTA, FOURTH-YEAR UVA STUDENT AND LAWN RESIDENT: I was in my room. As I'm putting sheets on my bed and trying to get my stuff together, 'cause I have like boxes and things all around, that's when I heard them outside of my door.

It was the guttural belly chant of, *Jews will not replace us.* It just sounded like an angry guttural chant of like an angry mob.

I just looked out my peephole. All I could see was just the flames.

At that point I was just kind of in shock. I was just trying to understand what was happening. My body is physically reacting, like in fear. It looked like a river of flames. It was flowing from the south end of the Lawn coming from the amphitheater, up towards the Rotunda. And you could just see this river of flames moving.

My door opened straight onto the Lawn. They were no more than four yards in front of me. Just the sidewalk and then the grass, and they were right on the grass. I was terrified. As a Jewish person, hearing "Jews"...[4] I was scared for my life. My chest started tightening up, and there was ringing in my ears. I was kind of in shock of what was happening and trying to process what was going on, but I was terrified.

WHITE NATIONALISTS: You will not replace us!
Jews will not replace us!
One people, one nation, end immigration.
You will not replace us!
Jews will not replace us!

DIANE D'COSTA: I took off my Hamsa necklace, an upside-down hand with an evil eye for protection, and my Shema ring, with Hebrew letters in a circle just on the ring, and threw it away and grabbed a sweater to leave.[5]

I just tried to hide any part of my Jewish identity. And looking back on it, I was really upset with myself that I did that. But I just didn't want any markers of who I was to cause me to be harmed. So I just did those things instinctually.

When I opened my door to walk out, the person closest to me had a swastika on his arm. I could see the mass of people carrying flames, walking, marching towards the Rotunda. They were still chanting *Jews will not replace us.*

It was the most traumatized I ever felt as a Jewish person. I was scared for my life. I thought that I was going to die if people knew who I was.

UPD TIMELINE: 10:07 p.m. Group begins to go up Rotunda stairs.

ALLEN GROVES, UVA DEAN OF STUDENTS: They're clearly moving around to the Jefferson statue side.

NATALIE ROMERO, SECOND-YEAR UVA STUDENT, AT THE STATUE: We weren't there for long before they arrived. [The students] kind of embraced each other.[6]

DEVIN WILLIS, SECOND-YEAR UVA STUDENT: We didn't have enough people to form the ring around the base of the statue. I could hear them talking about it on the other side: *We don't have enough, we don't have enough, we don't have enough.*[7]

I'm holding hands with Nat. It was just a lot of really loud and deep shouting coming from the other side of the Rotunda.[8]

NATALIE ROMERO: I just heard loudness, almost like thunder, like the earth was growling, essentially.[9] When we heard the roaring, we were like, *What should we do?* We just linked arms and held hands and started to sing.

I looked down, closed my eyes, prayed a little bit. I was terrified.[10] To my right was Devin. And we were just holding hands. We just looked at each other like, *It's OK, we're going to be OK.*[11]

DEVIN WILLIS: You start to see the glow, this mysterious glow on the other side of the Rotunda. And the shouting and growling gets louder, and these people, these lights, start rushing over the steps. I can see the steps from where I'm standing, and this ocean of light and flames just starts spilling over both sides of the steps and washing down.[12]

I was really scared because it looked like a lynch mob. Fire is a very intentional thing and it's a very scary thing.[13]

NATALIE ROMERO: The swarms of people coming down at us, just...the sky was dark with flame, dark and angry. It just felt like war. It literally was like a scene straight out of a movie swarming down towards us.

You wouldn't even understand the magnitude. They were coming from either side, it felt like hundreds of people. Angry, upset, screaming, yelling.[14]

We were singing at first. Then it was like complete silence. Like, what do we—what am I going to sing right now? I'm terrified.

EMILY GORCENSKI, LOCAL ACTIVIST: That's when I realized it was real. That's when I realized that this was no longer...that this was something much more serious than even I had imagined it to be. And when I got to the square around the statue and saw the students, my heart sank.

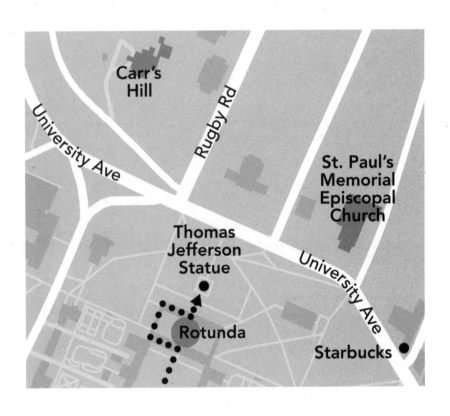

CHAPTER 6

"If they could have killed us all right then, they would have."

DEVIN WILLIS, SECOND-YEAR UVA STUDENT: You start to hear what they're saying.

WHITE NATIONALISTS: Blood and soil!
One people, one nation, end immigration.
You will not replace us!
Jews will not replace us!

DEVIN WILLIS: The vast majority of the men were white, adult-looking. A lot of them had the same haircuts. And almost all of them were wearing some combination of a white dress shirt or polo shirt and khaki pants. I also saw several people who had holstered weapons on the side of their hip.[1] And they basically just rushed the entire area and surrounded all of us in a matter of seconds.[2]

I realized as they were coming, and as it was too late to go anywhere, that I was really wrong about how many people would be there.[3]

The students were vastly outnumbered by the white nationalists, though they were not entirely without allies.

KENDALL KING, THIRD-YEAR UVA STUDENT: I think we felt really safe because Emily was there and there were a couple other community members who we had organized with.

EMILY GORCENSKI, LOCAL ACTIVIST: And at that point, I'm like, *OK, well, I came here to film. I'm going to film.* At that point, my only thought was, *Keep the camera going at all costs. You have a job, you have to do it.*

Because it's one of the few ways that we have as individuals to have a voice greater than what we would normally be able to achieve. It shows what's going on in real time. It uses the power of the networks that we have already built. It gives you a perspective that's nearly a first-person perspective of what's happening. It's unedited, it's uneditable. Then, they completely surrounded us and wouldn't let us out.

COUNTERPROTESTERS: Black lives matter! Black lives matter!

KENDALL KING: I was with my buddy, who was Devin. We just chanted and chanted and chanted, but then it became clear once they surrounded us, it was like, *Oh shit, what have we done?*

The street medics arrived on scene. From the Rotunda, they watched the situation at the statue as the student activists there, along with the handful of community activists and Emily Gorcenski, were surrounded by white nationalists.

STAR PETERSON, LOCAL ACTIVIST AND STREET MEDIC: I wanted so badly to jump in with my friends who were around the statue. My medic buddy was like, *Nope, you are a marked medic. You stay out until they need you to come in and fix somebody.* I was like, *Well, fuck this. I will never be a marked medic again.* Yeah, so I had to stand there and watch this hoard surround some of the people I love most in the world.

MELISSA WENDER, STREET MEDIC: They were saying, *Jews will not replace us.* And I'm Jewish myself.

ELIZABETH SINES, UVA LAW STUDENT: Through the chaos, there were students at the base holding a sign: *VA Students Act Against White Supremacy.*[4]

That was the sign completed at Professor Heinecke's spaghetti dinner.

NATALIE ROMERO, SECOND-YEAR UVA STUDENT: Once they started to sur-round us, they kind of directly came at Devin and I. And they were saying very specific things to us:

Go back to where you came from.

Stupid bitch.

Stuff like that. Monkey noises.[5]

DEVIN WILLIS: I've really tried to drive these comments out of my mind, but I know that the monkey noises were happening again.[6] And it's extremely hot because of all the flame.[7]

NATALIE ROMERO: Devin and I were the only people of color on that side. And it was very, very obvious and very apparent. They were screaming at us.[8] I tried to jump up onto the statue, but there's literally no little platform or anything. And I'm wearing sandals. So I'm like, I'm going to get tram-pled. For reference, I'm 4'10" and a half. I'm tiny. And everyone is just giant, screaming.[9]

Across the street, the prayer service was still ongoing.

WALT HEINECKE, UVA PROFESSOR AND ACTIVIST: I'm on that grassy area in front of St. Paul's chatting with SURJ [Showing up for Racial Justice] secu-rity folks and this activist from the anarchists of color group came up to me. And she looks up and sees me and says, *Hey, Walt, your students are surrounded by neo-Nazis at the Rotunda.* And for a minute, I didn't quite—it didn't quite process, but she came back and she said, *Hey, Walt, man, these, these kids are surrounded and it's not pretty.*

So I ran over there and lo and behold, I saw these 150, 200 neo-Nazis with torches. The students were in a circle, locked arms around the statue. And I looked around and I didn't see any police presence.

The unidentified police who had been walking alongside the march-ers earlier were no longer visible, according to scores of witnesses. It's not clear where they went.

ALLEN GROVES, UVA DEAN OF STUDENTS: Walt comes running up to me and says, *Allen, where are the police?* I said, *I don't know.*

And so he said, *The students are surrounded.* And I said, *What do you mean the students are surrounded?* And he said, *There's a group of students who've locked arms around the statue. They're in the middle there.* And I said, *We've got to get them out.*

KENDALL KING, AT THE STATUE: I have no clue what's set off anything, but I remember immediately just like a lot of jostling, a lot of brawling, like a lot of fist fighting.

CHRIS SUAREZ, REPORTER, CHARLOTTESVILLE *DAILY PROGRESS*: I was at the top of the Rotunda looking down when I saw, suddenly, flames being flung at people. They were screaming. Obviously something very bad was happening.

CHRIS SUAREZ TWEET, 10:15 P.M.: White lives matter chant drowning out black lives matter chant. Fighting breaking out now.[10]

DEVIN WILLIS: Tiki torches, still on fire, were being thrown in our direction. They're also being wielded as weapons. They're being swung at the crowd. You're just trying to make yourself as small as possible so you get hit by as few things as possible.[11]

BRIAN MORAN, SECRETARY, VIRGINIA PUBLIC SAFETY AND HOMELAND SECURITY: It broke out into absolute chaos there for, I don't know, it seemed like a long time, but it probably was a few minutes.

DEVIN WILLIS: So at about that moment is when Dean Groves appears. Dean Groves was the dean of students at UVa at the time. He was somebody, I think, whose job it was to know everybody.

ALLEN GROVES: I remembered Devin. We had met his first year. I had asked a student, a fourth-year who was in charge of this group called Black Male Initiative, which was a conversation group, and I said, *Would you mind if I attended one of these? And I promise, I won't say anything, but I'd love to...it would help me grow as a person to hear this perspective.* And he said, *Absolutely, Dean Groves.* So I came and kind of sat off to the side and Devin was a brand new first-year. You could tell he was so gifted and so bright and so thoughtful in the points that he made that evening. And so he and I ended up having a couple of lunches and stayed in touch with each other. And so, yes, I recognized him that night. He was the one person, the one student I recognized.

It didn't surprise me he was there because he was a person of strong values and strong beliefs and he wanted to take a stand against this. But Devin is not a large guy. And I had seen the guys that were surrounding him and I was very worried about violence.

So I just pushed through the crowd and Walt, to his credit, was right behind me. And I don't remember a lot of calculated analysis. I just felt like, *I'm the dean, these are my students. And I've got to protect them.*

I leaned in to Devin and I said, *It's Dean Groves. It's Dean Groves.* I'd taken my hat off so they could see this [white] hair, which is kind of part of my brand, and so I said, *It's Dean Groves. This is terribly unsafe. I've got to get you out of here.*

And I still remember, I never saw it coming: One of the torches comes flying in and hits me. It was thrown as a spear and it hit me kind of in the chest and arm. And I cut my arm and I remember yelling an expletive and kicking the little canister away, the flaming canister away on the ground.

And then just all hell broke loose. They started beating the students and the community members that are around the statue with their torches. There was Mace everywhere. And so I was grabbing students and pulling them out of the way and coming back in and trying to get them out of the mob. I got Maced in the face. I remember doubling over and trying to catch my breath and clear my face.

LARRY SABATO, UVA PROFESSOR: He was right in the middle of it and really tried to get those people away from the students. They were vicious to him and everyone else. I don't know if they knew he was dean of students or not, I'm not sure it mattered one way or the other.

I felt kinda guilty for standing on the steps.

WALT HEINECKE: Within seconds after that, I noticed that one of those leaders of the neo-Confederates was punching one of the lead student organizers in the face. And then seconds after that, the neo-Nazis and the neo-Confederates started Macing us or pepper spraying us. I got hit in the lip and on the leg, I was wearing shorts. And it just turned into a melee.

DAVID FOKY, NEWS DIRECTOR, NBC29: It was like when you see the movies of foot soldiers clashing with hand-to-hand combat.

EMILY GORCENSKI: A fight broke out to my right. They recognized me. They knew who I was, they knew I was trans. They were directing hate at me. They were saying things like, *Oh there's only two genders.* One person was like, *Have you cut off your part, like what kind of sicko are you?* I found out later looking at the Discords, they were stalking me. They were following me that night.

I got punched. I got kicked. I remember getting hit in the head. I thought it was with a torch. I stepped forward at one point and I got shoved back. I thought I was going to die.[12]

DEVIN WILLIS: There's a lot of pepper spray in the air. It's like there's no fresh air left to breathe. All you can do is just try to get lower.[13]

KENDALL KING: I got pepper sprayed in the eye, so I stopped being able to understand what was going on around me, which was also terrifying.

DEVIN WILLIS: I remember that someone from the direction of the mob threw some mysterious fluid. It looked like it came out of somebody's tiki torch canister, and they threw it at the direction of our feet. It seemed like it might be some type of lighter fluid or something like that, and I thought that their strategy was going to be to burn us alive.

It got on and near my shoes, which was really scary. So I tried to break the trail. And so I tried to stand further on the marble of the statue and off of the brick that was now doused. I thought I had made a very terrible mistake and that I might die that night.

NATALIE ROMERO, SECOND-YEAR UVA STUDENT: I felt like a mouse, trapped, like a Salem Witch Trial type, like I'm about to be burned at the stake.[14] It felt like forever.[15]

WHITE NATIONALISTS: White lives matter! White lives matter! White lives matter! White lives matter!

EMILY GORCENSKI'S LIVESTREAM: We are penned in. We are surrounded on all sides by hundreds of Nazis. We have no way out.[16]

EMILY GORCENSKI: The thing that really sticks out in my head is how happy the Nazis were to be doing the violence. They were angry, they were rageful, they were violent. But when they had us surrounded, they were euphoric. There was almost a sexual happiness that they had. There was nothing that they wanted to be doing more than being there, outnumbering a bunch of students, 10 to 1, 20 to 1, and committing massive amounts of violence. If they could have killed us all right then, they would have. If they had guns and if the cops weren't watching, they would have. This was their pogrom; this was their Kristallnacht.

DAVID STRAUGHN, LOCAL ACTIVIST: You couldn't believe how happy they were, shirtless, dancing around. I said, *Oh my God, these are the imps of Satan!* This is what I imagine hell to look like: just crazy fucks dancing around in fire while other people suffer and die.

TIM DODSON, MANAGING EDITOR, *CAVALIER DAILY*: At this point I'm at the part of the Rotunda steps that overlooks the statue. I don't remember seeing any police. Nobody had intervened to break this thing up.

WALT HEINECKE: At 10:04 or something, I called the police, I called 911.

What's the nature of your emergency?

I'm like, *Well, there's 150 neo-Nazis and they're beating people up here and there's no police!*

BRIAN MORAN, SECRETARY, VIRGINIA PUBLIC SAFETY AND HOMELAND SECURITY: Finally, some police arrived.

Both university police and City of Charlottesville police eventually responded.

LARRY SABATO, UVA PROFESSOR: You had a long line of police on the steps of the Rotunda, but they weren't, they weren't interjecting themselves.

ALEXIS GRAVELY, SENIOR ASSOCIATE NEWS EDITOR, *CAVALIER DAILY*: I was on the steps and the police officers were *above* me on the steps. And I'm like, *Why? Why are you up here and not down there?* Like, there's something wrong here. They were just watching. I just remember thinking, like, *They do not seem to be here to stop any of this.*

DAVID FOKY: I have no recollection of police officers, certainly in uniform, being in the middle of that melee trying to stop it.

LARRY SABATO: We were all looking to this line of police, like *What are you going to do?*[17]

At home, Mayor Mike Signer found out what was happening from social media posts.

MIKE SIGNER: I called Pat Hogan, UVa's chief operations officer, and told him what I was watching.[18] He said he was on vacation; it sounded like there were kids in the background. And he said, *I'm not in town right now.* And then—and I'm paraphrasing, but he said, *From what I hear, everything is fine.*

Everything was happening so fast, but it was dumbfounding that he didn't know about it, while it was happening in real time. I was relaying something that I was watching on social media to him. This is real fog of war stuff. It was kind of crazy that I just had to say, *Look at this website,* and then he looked at it and then he said, *I gotta call our chief of police.* And then he was off the line.[19]

REV. SETH WISPELWEY, PASTOR AND COFOUNDER, CONGREGATE C'VILLE, AT ST. PAUL'S: I go back out front within a few minutes and that's when you could see all the fire, all the torches from the steps of the church.

WILLIS JENKINS, UVA PROFESSOR: As the torches came into view at the Rotunda, someone sprinted across the street with an urgent message: Students were holding their ground at the Jefferson statue at the bottom of the Rotunda steps with no one to defend them. She pleaded with us to go assist them.[20]

SMASH CAINE-CONLEY, COFOUNDER, CONGREGATE C'VILLE: I remember saying like, *We're gonna go figure it out right now.* And a few of us went to a room to try to talk about how to respond. I think individually I really shrank away in that moment. I think I allowed other people to make decisions 'cause I was scared and didn't know what to do.

WILLIS JENKINS: The lead organizer instructed us to remain at our posts, for there were hundreds of people in the church and no police in sight; our duty was to protect the assembly. The messenger cursed us in frustration and ran back.[21]

I am haunted by that moment. Of course we should not have relayed to the crowd of untrained people inside the building, many already fearful of the situation outside, an invitation to confront an armed mob, and of course all of us standing guard could not have abandoned our post. But I am a faculty member, and those were our students.[22]

SMASH CAINE-CONLEY: I know why decisions were made to protect people in the church and I don't necessarily disagree with those. I think for me it's more about how I responded individually. I really regretted not directly going to help them. It wasn't random people asking me for help—the folks that were asking for help and some of the students that were at the statue were people I *know*.

I definitely didn't know any of the details of what was happening, I was just being told, *There are Nazis here surrounding the statue. There are people in danger.* And I think that that should have been enough.

I.B.F., LOCAL ACTIVIST: There was a church full of people, if we had just walked across... if we had just gone out the front door and been like, *What are you doing?* Maybe it would have changed things? It almost holds greater trauma because it was just a few folks against hundreds of people with fire, and I was right there and I didn't do anything. I know rationally that there were reasons that everyone made the choices that they did and that it was based on the information we had at the time, and it was the best that we could do. But still I can't help but feel really guilty about it.

REV. SETH WISPELWEY, INSIDE THE CHURCH: [Sekou] made the announcement to the church. *It's come to our attention*... like we're trying not to start a panic. We had them sit down. We really didn't want to create a panic. It was full. We had people of all ages and backgrounds there. And he said, *We've got a situation outside. We're going to keep singing. And this is—it's all right, but we're going to—no one go out the front doors right now.* That was the initial announcement.[23]

DON GATHERS, COFOUNDER, CHARLOTTESVILLE BLACK LIVES MATTER: The service continued, with a heightened awareness of the immediate surroundings. We had people posted at every possible entrance, both inside and out, folks who had literally put their bodies on the line in case it came to that.

No one was coming out. No one was going in.

False rumors spread that the white nationalists were, in fact, marching on the church.

JALANE SCHMIDT, UVA PROFESSOR AND COFOUNDER, CHARLOTTESVILLE BLACK LIVES MATTER: It was like a fog of war kind of thing. There's pandemonium. *The Nazis are marching toward the church.* That's what we heard.

JALANE SCHMIDT TWEET, 10:07 P.M.: Trapped, w 100s, inside St. Paul's church after #defendcville prayer service. Alt-right gathered outside.[24]

REV. TRACI BLACKMON TWEET: They are coming for the church! Police all around. They won't let us go outside. Y'all these KKK are marching with torches!

ROSIA PARKER, LOCAL ACTIVIST: I felt like the four little girls in the Birmingham Church, the girls that got burnt at Martin Luther King's church. You kind of like, this can't be real? It's just like a movie or something playing in your head.

Due to her public activism, Jalane Schmidt had already been tagged as a high-profile target for the white supremacists. She had her own activist security detail that weekend.

JALANE SCHMIDT: We were just like, *Oh hell no, I'm getting outta here.*

I'd been mentioned by name in these forums, these chat rooms and whatnot. So I was warned to really take care and not stay in my house during all this. I didn't stay in my house for eight days.

So we were busting toward a side door to get out.

We went down an alleyway and then hopped into [my security's] car and took back streets out of there.[25]

LISA DRAINE, LOCAL ACTIVIST: [My daughter] Rebecca and I, instead of leaving at that point, we went out the back and came around to the front of

St. Paul's and we're standing on the steps. And from there, we could see this squiggly line of fire. We were like, we should go and see what's happening. So we actually walked down University Avenue until we were directly across from the Rotunda. And then at some moment we heard the chant, *Black lives matter, Black lives matter.*

And I turned to Rebecca and I said, *I bet you Sophie's there.*

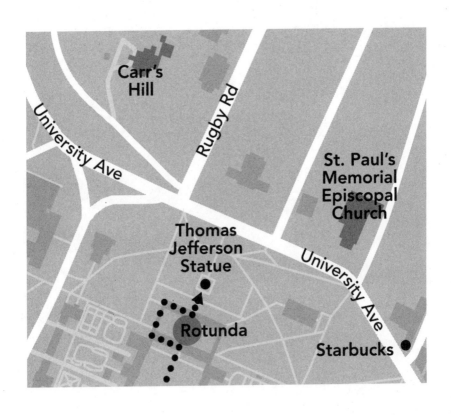

CHAPTER 7

"Does this change what we're going to do tomorrow?"

10:15 P.M.

LISA DRAINE, LOCAL ACTIVIST: So we ran across University Avenue and scampered up through the bushes and we arrived on this scene of total chaos.

DEVIN WILLIS, SECOND-YEAR UVA STUDENT, AT THE JEFFERSON STATUE: It got to a point where I was just so horrified and I was so afraid and I felt like I had a lot to live for. I wanted to leave. I was like, *I'm ready to go.*[1]

NATALIE ROMERO, SECOND-YEAR UVA STUDENT: I was just like, *Which way? How do we get out of here?* You couldn't really see an exit.[2]

DEVIN WILLIS: Eventually we were able to communicate amongst ourselves that we were going to try to escape, but that would require, of course, letting our hands go and collapsing and forming a group so that we could get out. And that was as dangerous as it sounded.

So the plan was that because me and Nat were being targeted and that because we are very obviously people of color—I'm a Black man; she's a Latina woman—that we were in the most danger. And the fight was happening on our side. So our friends formed a circle around us and tried their best to escort us off of the statue, but the minute that we let go of our hands, of course, the white nationalists basically pummeled us. They took advantage of the chaos. And so all the friends were thankfully very quick in collapsing around me and forming a circle around me and Nat. The white nationalists are beating, badly, my friends who are standing between us and them. And so I'm watching—as me and Nat are basically crawling off the statue—I'm watching the people who are standing above me, my friends, take pepper sprays at point-blank range directly into their eyes. I'm watching them take punches and kicks to their backs and the backs of their heads as they're just trying to escort us off the statue.[3]

NATALIE ROMERO: I don't know how they did it.[4]

DEVIN WILLIS: We hobble over to a group of benches and we try to rally ourselves. We try to lick our wounds. People were doing first aid. So I'm watching close friends of mine get milk poured on their eyes. Everyone is coughing, crying, getting themselves together.[5]

I felt like I had just been attacked and driven off of the statue, and that that was, in my 18-year-old imagination, somehow embarrassing.[6]

WHITE NATIONALISTS: Torches out!

ELIZABETH SINES, UVA LAW STUDENT: The torches went out in a wave.

LISA DRAINE: You could see torches going out and people running in all directions, people fighting—like on the ground fighting and then people on the ground. There was some chemical agent in the air. We were like, *Oh my God.*

And we found Sophie and her friends all huddled there and kind of shell-shocked. And it was like, *Oh my God, Sophie, come home with us.* And she was like, *No, no, I need to debrief with my friends and I'll be home later.*

The dinner with friends Sophie had told her mother about was the gathering at Walt Heinecke's house. She had been there with Devin Willis, Kendall King, and the other students.

LISA DRAINE: And, of course, we didn't know what had happened at the time. But if you look at the photos, you'll see a big white banner that says, "VA students against white supremacy." Sophie was one of the people holding that banner.

KENDALL KING, THIRD-YEAR UVA STUDENT: I remember I couldn't find one of my friends and that freaked me out a lot. And I was really scared that they had essentially taken her.

Kendall later tracked down her friend. Other counterprotesters ran over to St. Paul's to get help. At that point, many of them had been Maced and pepper sprayed at point-blank range.

REV. SETH WISPELWEY, PASTOR AND COFOUNDER, CONGREGATE C'VILLE AT ST. PAUL'S: I remember a young Black woman just screaming, *We need help. We need water.* So I'm running back to the kitchen of this church with them like, *Come back, we're filling up these old milk jugs with water.* Then we were looking for milk, which is the better thing.

STAR PETERSON, LOCAL ACTIVIST AND STREET MEDIC, AT THE STATUE: I ended up going to the eye wash station.

KENDALL KING: Street medics came and washed our eyes out.

NATALIE ROMERO: By then I had already been Maced. There was somebody in a wheelchair. It was a student. They were getting their eyes washed out.

ALLEN GROVES, UVA DEAN OF STUDENTS: They had Maced a young woman in a wheelchair! I'm like, *Honest to God...*

NATALIE ROMERO: And then there was a couple of other people on the floor getting their eyes washed out, including me.[7]

STAR PETERSON: Even after you rinse out their eyes, there's not a lot you can do. Right? Except sit there and suffer.

So, there was someone, I had no idea who they were, but I just said, *Hey, do you want to hold my hands?* So, I just sat there, and again, they couldn't even open their eyes, and just held their hands while they went through the worst of the pain.

ALEXIS GRAVELY, SENIOR ASSOCIATE NEWS EDITOR, *CAVALIER DAILY*: The police were there afterwards, but by then it was too late.

ALLEN GROVES: I was trying to talk to the police because they didn't know who the bad guys were and I was trying to yell at them, no, no, no. The people who were still there were students and a couple of townspeople who had been Maced.

WALT HEINECKE, UVA PROFESSOR AND ACTIVIST: The police showed up and were basically saying, *This is an illegal assembly and we're gonna arrest you.* They were gonna arrest the students.

NATALIE ROMERO: There were police that lined up and then started to tell people that they had to leave—including us. They were like, *Everyone has to go.*[8]

WALT HEINECKE: So I told the students, I said, *It's time to go. You guys gotta get outta here.* So, they went off, they all kind of scurried out the back way.

MALCOLM STEWART'S GROUP TEXT, 10:24 P.M.: It's dying down. Interviews are happening. I met Dean Grove's dog. She's a good dog.

ALLEN GROVES: Once people had cleared out, we were there, and Gracie was comforting several people. And we're fortunate that's just her personality.

She was what's called a flat coat retriever, so, imagine a black golden retriever. We had adopted her from the Charlottesville SPCA. We wanted to save an older dog, and so she was eight years old. She had been pretty badly abused. She couldn't be a more chill, easygoing, sweet dog.

I didn't realize I was bleeding until after I pulled my shirt up after it was all done and realized that, yeah, it [the thrown torch] had cut me and there was blood on my shirt and on my arm. Remarkably, not as bad as it could have been—if the flaming gel from the canister and stuff had hit me dead in my chest and that had caught fire, that might have been pretty dicey.

TOM BERRY, DIRECTOR OF EMERGENCY MANAGEMENT, UVA MEDICAL CENTER: We started receiving ambulances and pickup trucks. Some people were throwing their buddy into vehicles and showing up right there at the ER bay. That's when it became real.

TERESA SULLIVAN, UVA PRESIDENT: You know, we had a police officer who went to the hospital that night. He had a knee injury.

As the torch march dispersed and students nursed their wounds, people in the church finally breathed a sigh of relief. It looked like they

weren't being targeted, for now. Organizers at the church officially lifted the lockdown with a closing prayer and a coordinated exit.

CHURCH LEADER, TO THE CROWD: I think it's a good time for a prayer for our enemies. God called us to the hard work of loving our enemies. Lead them and lead us from prejudice to truth. Deliver them and deliver us from hatred, cruelty, and revenge.[9]

DON GATHERS, COFOUNDER, CHARLOTTESVILLE BLACK LIVES MATTER: We then slowly began to allow people to exit the church. No one left on their own.

REV. SETH WISPELWEY: We started evacuating people out the back of the church, through the kitchen, as I recall, and then the side and the back alleys down Chancellor Street. For folks who might not have had someone we insisted on a buddy system, that they meet their new best friend, because we really wanted to make sure people got to their cars safely. But there were so many people, we had people go out in groups.[10]

I.B.F., LOCAL ACTIVIST: We had to evacuate the church. And I remember taking off my hijab, it was white and sea green stripes, and putting on a hat—it was Smash's hat because I didn't have a hat—and then leaving out the back door, and running to the car, and the car driving back to [our activist] headquarters [at an apartment].

REV. SETH WISPELWEY: After the service we were going to use one of their big gathering fellowship rooms to do, as best we could, some of that tactile bodily awareness training for people. We never got to do it.

KATRINA TURNER, LOCAL ACTIVIST: I had called my sons and I told them, *Look, we're locked in the church. They just tried to surround this church with tiki torches. Please come up here and get us. You have to come up here now!* That was just all I had to say. *Please come up here and get us. We need help.* And they came. So both my sons came to the church and started helping people get back to their cars.

REV. SETH WISPELWEY: I don't think the church was fully empty of attendees until maybe 11:30.

DON GATHERS: We had just had a wonderful evening. No one was going to take that from us. That was what their intent was, and we weren't going to allow that to happen.

A valiant goal, but the trauma seeped in. Rev. Wispelwey's seven-year-old daughter, a person of color, was at the service with him.

REV. SETH WISPELWEY: We wanted to be upfront with her and also recognize the tender age.

She was old enough to know what her parents were about and doing, knew it was serious, knew that it was hateful, knew that it was a threat to her, and she freaked out, for lack of a better word. I can only describe it as a panic attack. She was crying uncontrollably.[11]

There was a lot of comforting and she didn't want to leave me because she knew I was part of the response to these people. So just being like, *We're OK. Daddy's gonna be OK and Mommy's gonna look after you.* But like, *These men are dangerous.* These were hard conversations to navigate with a seven-year-old.

After the service, the clergy activists headed to a nearby hotel called The Graduate, where Don Gathers worked his day job.

REV. SETH WISPELWEY: We're waiting for other people to get to the hotel to talk through like, *Does this change what we're going to do tomorrow?* Because by then, word is starting to come, like some bad shit went down at the statue, worse than we already saw.

DON GATHERS: As we got Dr. [Cornel] West down to the hotel, there actually were several of the Nazis gathered outside on the sidewalk. The hotel is right there. So, I mean, it was not a surprise that some of them were actually staying there.

REV. SETH WISPELWEY: And someone looks outside the lobby windows and is like, *That looks like Augustus Invictus.*

Invictus is a well-known white supremacist who was scheduled to speak at Unite the Right the next morning.

REV. SETH WISPELWEY: We're like, *Shit, this is supposed to be the safe space.*

I still have my clergy collar on at this point. A friend of ours, a fellow white man, went out to confirm it was Invictus and document his vehicle. I wanted to make sure he was OK, and hold space by the door, and pulled out my own phone to take pictures, which set Invictus off.

Augustus Invictus starts coming at me. He's, like, backing me up into the lobby. The activists still back in the lobby were not tall, straight, white men like me. They're spooked and crouching behind couches, everything, because these are folks of different marginalized identities and so on. And he's like threatening me and being like, *What church do you go to?* And everything. And I'm just standing there, like, *You'll find out tomorrow.* And he is like, *Well y'all are going down tomorrow.* I stood my ground there in the lobby because I could tell, like, this isn't good. And eventually they back off. They drove off.

But later I got called on this kind of chauvinistic impulse [to confront Invictus]. It was a good learning moment for me too that just because you're doing the "right thing" on paper, I hadn't thought like I'm also bringing risk into this place where these other comrades are.

So eventually, I'd say at least midnight, we went up to the spare room. It's a big room, two queens, and someone had gotten some pizza and we stayed up 'til like 3 a.m. talking through, learning what had happened.

I was listening and everything and we're like, *Do we continue with what we're planning to do?*

SMASH CAINE-CONLEY, COFOUNDER, CONGREGATE C'VILLE: We took in everything that had already happened and tried to process with one another what the rest of the weekend was going to go like. That in and of itself I think was a really hard space to be in because of what had already happened. And then we were trying to figure out how to do the next day.

REV. SETH WISPELWEY: In the end we decided that our presence and the story we hoped to bring should continue.[12]

Across Charlottesville, shell-shocked activists and witnesses headed toward an uneasy sleep.

DIANE D'COSTA, FOURTH-YEAR UVA STUDENT AND LAWN RESIDENT: I didn't want to be anywhere near the Lawn that night. My friend, who lives in

Charlottesville, texted me. And he said, you can stay at my parents' house in Charlottesville, and I gladly took him up on that offer.

He pulled up in the alleyway right next to Pavilion Ten, and I ran out the back of the Pavilion straight to his car. It was like I was fleeing my house and it was wild because I have memories of my family telling me stories of my great-grandmother fleeing Poland. And it felt like fleeing my home from Nazis, but on the Lawn.[13]

Then we drove down and there were still people [including white nationalists] walking, and that was like pretty scary. I just remember crying, thinking that people would see me.

MELISSA WENDER, STREET MEDIC: I don't remember what time I left. I don't remember whether I walked home by myself or with someone else. I don't know what time I got home. Don't know a thing about it.

KENDALL KING, THIRD-YEAR UVA STUDENT: The group of us, which was maybe like 25, 30, found everybody, checked in, walked to the end of the Lawn, sat on the stairs of Cabell Hall and sort of assessed our wounds. And basically we were like, *Is everyone OK? What did we learn about tomorrow? Are we still OK to go out tomorrow? And unanimously: Yes. Yes. Yes.* Everyone was like, *That was horrible. We are traumatized, but we will absolutely be there tomorrow at 6 a.m.* That was a really moving, amazing moment.

NATALIE ROMERO, SECOND-YEAR UVA STUDENT: I didn't know what the effect of the spray was. So I didn't know that you shouldn't shower. I got in the shower to cry. I kind of sat there, and as the water is hitting me, it's just like reliving it all again, because it started to go back into my eye. It spread through my body, my entire body. And, yeah, I sat there in pain from the stinging of it. And I—once I realized I was making it worse, I just kind of sat in the tub trying to make sense of what I had just witnessed.[14]

ALLEN GROVES, UVA DEAN OF STUDENTS, AT HOME: So I get home probably around 1 a.m. I remember going in the shower at my home and turning on the shower and putting my head under it. And my eyes just exploded because the dried Mace on my face was activated by the water. And so the worst impact of the Mace was actually in my shower at home.

KATRINA TURNER, LOCAL ACTIVIST: After church, I just went home, cried a little and went to sleep. That's all I could do. I mean, we knew that we had another day coming. Just had to get my rest, and get ready.

ROSIA PARKER, LOCAL ACTIVIST: And for me, I had to come home and get my community prepared because I live in a low-income neighborhood where the white supremacists have already been. So trying to prepare my community for what was to come: talking to different people and basically trying to be around my children for a time.

I was just praying and going into worship, reading my Bible, doing what I had to do. I knew that I might not make it back home. I was mentally prepared to die that day.

EMILY BLOUT, UVA PROFESSOR AND MAYOR MIKE SIGNER'S WIFE: We were advised by the FBI at that time to not be in our house for the weekend. We were getting a steady stream of white supremacist threats, mostly threats based on my husband's religion, Judaism. I think the ones that were most powerful and scary came through the mail, 'cause they figured out where we lived, and were targeting us in a consistent way. And so we bundled up our little babies, three-year-olds, and we took them to a different location and we stayed in a different place.

MAYOR MIKE SIGNER JOURNAL ENTRY, 1:15 A.M.: There is going to be an unlawful assembly after about 20 minutes tomorrow. And there will be some mayhem. And then there will be a day of *brush fires* around the city, just as Baxter predicted. I do wonder if there will be rioting or some form of it. I'm glad we have our crisis communications guy with us, but this is going to be bad and will be a rough stomach-turning day. These guys tonight were like ISIS, spectacular propaganda and striking where it was least expected and will make the most impact. Spencer is smart that way, this plays right in his strike zone. And the whole weekend is now teed up for maximum impact and maximum fear among the "cucks" as they called them.

TERRY MCAULIFFE, VIRGINIA GOVERNOR: It became clear to me, when Brian [Moran] briefed me and said they literally were throwing the torches at people, that these were jackasses and this was going to be very, very serious. And I said to Brian... *We better be ready 'cause this is gonna be much worse. These people are here to hurt people.*

BRIAN MORAN, SECRETARY, VIRGINIA PUBLIC SAFETY AND HOMELAND SE-CURITY: I got to the room and called the president of the university, Sullivan. And she called me back around midnight and said that somebody had known about this march, but it never got to her. And she said, *I don't know if we're prepared for tomorrow.* Here it is midnight, you know.

TERESA SULLIVAN, UVA PRESIDENT: There was more going on in terms of encoded messages and so on that we just weren't aware of. We just didn't have a sophisticated enough intelligence operation, you know? And in part, I think that's because university police, they're still trained with respect to the Vietnam War–era protests, when the objective is to preserve everybody's rights, but the protest is usually a reasonably peaceful protest, maybe some angry words said, but not much more than that. This was not that. And you know, despite our many days of preparation, we weren't ready for what this was.

I.B.F., LOCAL ACTIVIST: I came back to headquarters and my best friends from the grad programs were there and one of them, she held me and she was like, *Oh my God, you're shaking.* And I didn't, I hadn't realized that.

I think I was more angry because we *knew* that they were going to come. We knew the route they were going to take because they've been tweeting about it and they've been chatting it in Discord. People in front of me had shared it with UVa leadership, with the UVa security to just be like, *just so you know.* And nothing. They faced no resistance, they faced nothing. And so I think I was more pissed that no one had listened.

EMILY GORCENSKI, LOCAL ACTIVIST: What has me jaded about the antifascist community is we talk about *we keep us safe*, but I was fucking there and they weren't.

It was a huge colossal fuck-up. It was a catastrophic mistake. Because you don't leave people undefended. You don't leave people vulnerable, people without protection. The students, the community members, the people of the church. You just don't do that. It was a huge failure.

My wife was watching from home on my livestream, at my house, which had been doxed. My phone died because I was livestreaming the whole thing. Phone died, found a friend, called her, told her I was OK, I'd be on the way home, pack a bag, get something to eat. We're going.

I came home and I was waiting for my other partner to come up from Roanoke, Virginia. And so we put together some bags and I brought Christine, my wife, to one of her friends' places. Yeah, I think before the torch march, I even taught her how to use my nine-millimeter. And basically said, *If anyone that you don't know tries to come through that door, this is what you do.*

I brought her over to her friend's place where I knew that there would be no way of tracing her or finding her. And then my other partner and I went, and we were going to stay home that night, but we couldn't. And so we went to an Airbnb and crashed there, and I packed up my guns and found a safe house. I was just scrolling Twitter, seeing all of the harassment that was being thrown at me.

[The Nazis] walked away and they got away with it. They're coming in here the next day ready to do more. I thought like, *Here we go. Yeah, here we go.*[15]

ALEXIS GRAVELY, SENIOR ASSOCIATE NEWS EDITOR, *CAVALIER DAILY*, ON GROUNDS: As fast as everything happened, it was just gone. I just walked back to the *Cav Daily*'s office in Newcomb, and we started debriefing with Tim and Daniel, and writing, and that was that. I think I left like 2:30.

My grandmother's generation, they lived through cross burnings and church burnings and bombings and things like that. But I felt like that was our generation's first really visual representation of racism.

And so I understand why people would say we never could've believed this would happen because it was so overt versus—the sort of racism that we'd been dealing with up until Trump was systemic and microaggressions and things like that. And so unless you were Black or were a person of color, those were sorts of things that you probably wouldn't be familiar with.

But no I wasn't like, *Oh my God, my dear UVa. Like, the bastion of equality. Like, how could this happen?* Like, no. I'm like, *OK. Yeah, this checks out for a place that was built by slaves.*

Videos of the torch march and the ensuing violence spread rapidly around town. One person watching the videos that night was 32-year-old Heather Heyer. She'd already known the alt-right rally would be happening in downtown Charlottesville the next day, and while she was a vehement supporter of justice, she'd originally decided not to go to counterprotest, fearing violence.

SUSAN BRO, HEATHER HEYER'S MOTHER: She had planned on not going. But when she saw videos from Friday night, she'd said, *I have to go.*

Heather was feisty. Mouthy at times. No nonsense. She was a true Gemini with a heart of gold and yet she could be just as obstinate and stubborn as you'd ever wanna see. But she cared deeply for others and she cared deeply, deeply, deeply for the rights of others. Always did. Always everything had to be explained to her from early childhood in terms of is this fair or not fair. And so I'd have to resort to the, *'Cause I said so and that's the end of it. I don't care if you think it's fair or not.*

She definitely had rough teen years and made life pretty miserable for both of us for a while. But she had moved out finally by age 26, and was then 32 and was getting her life together. She had a career, she was a certified paralegal, she worked at a bankruptcy firm and she helped clients not become clients by offering them some quick suggestions as a way to avoid bankruptcy. She worked very hard to teach her mother to be an antiracist.[16]

I think everybody's aware that Black people don't get a fair shake. I think that we're lying to ourselves if we say otherwise. But it never really brought it home so intensely to me as when her boyfriend was living with us, who was Black, and we would go to dinner, we'd get the dirty looks, we'd get the snide remarks from time to time. I began to realize just how much, day to day, the struggle can be just to be alive and to be Black in America.[17]

She was one of my first teachers.

I think ultimately that's what made her decide that she had to take a stand when she saw them chanting in Charlottesville on the university campus the night before.[18]

She said, *OK, this is beyond what I thought it would be.* She had been going to stay away with her best friend, who was gay—they were staying away for his safety—and she said *I'm gonna do this.*[19]

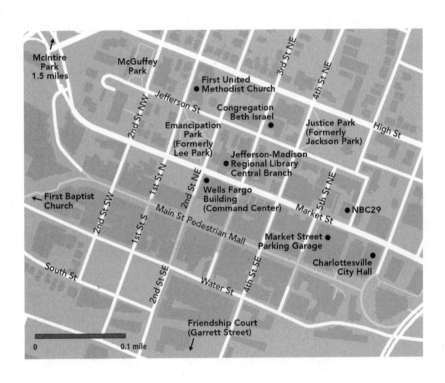

McIntire
Park
1.5 miles

McGuffey
Park

First United
Methodist Church

Congregation
Beth Israel

3rd St NE

4th St NE

High St

Justice Park
(Formerly
Jackson Park)

Jefferson St

2nd St NW

Emancipation
Park
(Formerly
Lee Park)

Jefferson-Madison
Regional Library
Central Branch

1st St N

2nd St NE

5th St NE

First Baptist
Church

Wells Fargo
Building
(Command Center)

Main St Pedestrian Mall

Market St

NBC29

2nd St SW

1st St S

Market Street
Parking Garage

2nd St SE

4th St SE

Charlottesville
City Hall

South St

Water St

Friendship Court
(Garrett Street)

0   0.1 mile

CHAPTER 8

"We need to go confront literal Nazis."

The night of August 11 seemed to bleed into the early morning hours of August 12.

SMASH CAINE-CONLEY, COFOUNDER, CONGREGATE C'VILLE: I got home and tried to sleep for like two hours, which didn't really happen obviously.

TOM BERRY, DIRECTOR OF EMERGENCY MANAGEMENT, UVA MEDICAL CENTER: I didn't feel comfortable going home that night. I kept a cot in my office for whatever—snowstorms, Ebola responses, the floods that occur a lot in the hospital with old pipes that are breaking. So I just went back to my office, set up the cot, got some light sleep.

WEDNESDAY BOWIE, COUNTERPROTESTER: Everybody else was like, *Let's get our rest.* And I was like, *I cannot sleep.* So I stayed up literally all night. I was just anxiety-ridden and reading as much as I could about any articles I could find, anything about what to expect the next day.

DON GATHERS, COFOUNDER, CHARLOTTESVILLE BLACK LIVES MATTER: I'm not certain that I went to sleep. If I did, I'd have to say I was back up by 4:30?

REV. SETH WISPELWEY, PASTOR AND COFOUNDER, CONGREGATE C'VILLE: I got up early, 5:30 a.m., ate a banana with peanut butter, and got in the car.

CHRIS SUAREZ, REPORTER, CHARLOTTESVILLE *DAILY PROGRESS*: I was up pretty quickly, probably 6, 6:30. I really don't even remember making coffee or having breakfast or anything. I just got up, put on clothes, and was out the door. I remember riding my bike up to First Baptist on Main Street.

DON GATHERS: I had organized a 6 o'clock sunrise service at First Baptist Church for that Saturday morning in preparation for what we had to go out and face that afternoon, not knowing what to expect, but knowing that we needed to come together and pray about it as a community.

First Baptist Church was founded during the Civil War, in 1864, as the Charlottesville African Church.

DON GATHERS: I headed to the church to make sure everything was set and ready. And I'll tell you, when I got there, there were already people there— folks who had volunteered to serve as security. There were also plainclothes CPD as well as some in uniform. Eyes and ears all over the church.

REV. SETH WISPELWEY: The band had already gotten set up and everything. People were starting to come. We filled it pretty well. There were a few hundred people.

WES BELLAMY, CHARLOTTESVILLE VICE MAYOR: I drove to First Baptist in silence. No Jeezy, no Chance the Rapper, no R&B, no nothing. Just silence. The sun had yet to come out. Few cars were on the road. It was a surreal moment. Upon arrival, I embraced my brother Deacon Don Gathers, and his energy was one of a warrior prepared for battle.[1]

DON GATHERS: It may well have been one of the most incredible Saturday mornings of my entire life. Just seeing that many people flowing into the building for worship service on a Saturday at six o'clock, 6:30 in the morning, and seeing the sea of people. God, we must've had another 350 to 400 people packed into that church in the morning.

REV. SETH WISPELWEY: It was a waking up. A pump-up-and-go.[2]

SINGER: I need you today!

SPEAKER: Come on, put your hands together!

CROWD: Cheers

SPEAKER: Praise God, praise God, praise God. If you haven't been moved yet this morning, check to make sure you have a pulse.[3]

CROWD: *Laughter*

SMASH CAINE-CONLEY: It was much smaller than the night before. And it was primarily folks who were wanting to engage that day in some way, shape, or form.

It definitely had a different feel too. There was more of an ominous feeling in the air for sure. We were preparing ourselves to leave and to engage something pretty scary.

SPEAKER: It is indeed one of the great honors and moments of my life to be able to stand before you to introduce today's speaker. We have with us today our beloved brother Dr. Cornel West.[4]

The crowd cheered and then stood, one by one, to welcome Dr. West with a standing ovation as he took the stage. Then, just before he even began to speak, another standing ovation.

REV. DR. CORNEL WEST: Are we ready to be a hope this morning in the face of what we understand structures of evil to be? We not here to hate anybody; we here to love. And we're lovin' in such a way that we hate the structures of evil. That's what it's all about. And that's why when they see us with a smile, they gonn' say, "Who are these strange folk of all colors and sexual orientations and religious tradition? Don't they realize that they could get hurt? Don't they realize that some of them might get hit? Some of us might even get shot." That's all right. We are willing to pay the cost of truth, of justice, of beauty.[5]

SMASH CAINE-CONLEY: Cornel West always has really incredible things to say and, I think, a way to get people's spirits in a place where they're ready to engage things that are scary.

REV. DR. CORNEL WEST: This is the time for action. This is not a moment for sunshine soldiers.

When we march this morning, when we hold hands and lock in this morning, when we sing this morning, when we get arrested this morning, when we go to jail this morning, let's try to remember those—the best of those came before—who sacrificed so much for us. Who paid a greater cost than we gonn' pay today.[6]

REV. SETH WISPELWEY: So, I missed some of West's talk actually because I was part of a group kind of having these little huddles in the basement. We're sending kind of "runners" to Market Street to get reports on what the situation was. You know, *Kind of still quiet. Militia's there. They're armed.*

SMASH CAINE-CONLEY: After the service ended, that's when things started to get a little dicey.

DON GATHERS: It was my intention as I was putting this thing together, to cut it off at a point where, OK, those who want to leave and go home safely before the beast is released, so to speak, would have time to do so.

Rev. Sekou stepped forward.

DAVID GARTH, RETIRED PASTOR: He announced that we would divide up in two groups and if we had had nonviolence training and we were willing to be arrested, that we would march to [the site of the rally] Emancipation Park, with the statue of Lee. Those of us who had not had nonviolent resistance training, we would be in a different march downtown, but not at the same location.

MICHAEL CHEUK, SECRETARY, CHARLOTTESVILLE CLERGY COLLECTIVE: I remember Sekou just being really, really frank and clear with the participants there, saying, *OK, it's gonna be dangerous. We could get hurt. We may even get killed. There's no shame if you decide to participate and counterprotest in a different way, but want to be very clear about that.*

SMASH CAINE-CONLEY: We started to get some pushback from some folks. Not any local folks, but some people that had come to be with us. We were kind of being accused of putting people in a dangerous situation.

REV. SETH WISPELWEY: There were accusations being thrown around of being a martyr. And just not knowing the weeks of training that we had.

MICHAEL CHEUK: There was kind of a standoff.

SMASH CAINE-CONLEY: I was just really confounded. I was like, *I can't believe this is happening*, because we were extremely clear with people leading up to this weekend of what we expected. We expected it to be violent, we expected it to be dangerous. And we particularly called for white folks, and I was hoping for white male Christian pastors, to come and put their bodies on the line. So I think getting that pushback from folks about the choices we were making—to be in solidarity with our community and with activists in our community—was really disappointing.

Like, we literally need to leave now to go confront literal Nazis. Now is not the time for me to explain to you why we are doing this and how we've built relationships in our community and how local people of color have asked us to do this work. So that was really challenging.

REV. SETH WISPELWEY: And also, the maxim is, *Listen to local leaders, follow local organizers*. Well, we *were* that. This is our hometown, we were listening to *our* local organizers and activists and our local Black women. Like, me, I'm accountable to Brenda Brown-Grooms and Yolonda Jones and Jalane Schmidt and Lisa Woolfolk and others who we were all consulting this whole time.

Cornel just sat quietly. He was just like, *I follow local leadership.* And he was like, *I'm going with these people. I trust Sekou. We've made our peace with the cross, we know who we're accountable to.*

Most of the out-of-town clergy, many of whom were white, chose not to directly confront the white nationalists. The group that ended up marching to Emancipation Park was much smaller than expected. Even without the strength in numbers they'd anticipated, they continued on.

SMASH CAINE-CONLEY: We went and lined up in front of the church kind of two by two and had a prayer. And we started marching.

=‖=

Across the city, secular activists were also preparing, coming to terms with what the day had in store.

SABR LYON, COUNTERPROTESTER: Waking up that morning, it's the regular anxiety of the day. I was trying to... because my mom came with us, I was trying to give her a realistic expectation. My wife who was then my fiancée, they had both done antiwar rallies and things, and my mom is one of the people who walked out of her high school so they could wear pants when it was wintertime or whatever. So, she had done protests and things, but she had never been to one where it was going to be a war zone.

I knew there was a chance somebody was going to die. I hadn't spoken to my dad for more than six months at that point, but I called him that morning and I said, *In case I die today, I need you to know that I may not be able to be in contact with you, but I love you. I just want to let you know we are going to war. What they're going to say on Fox News that you're going to watch is all going to be lies. Know that when they're telling lies, they're telling lies about me,* and I hung up the phone.

Star Peterson woke up at home with her houseguests she'd met the night before: two medics who had offered to sleep over and keep an eye out for Nazis.

STAR PETERSON, LOCAL ACTIVIST AND STREET MEDIC: I made coffee and cinnamon rolls for them or something. I was so nervous and so ready for it to get over with. I mean, I was very aware that I might die that day.

CONSTANCE PAIGE YOUNG, COUNTERPROTESTER: We all knew what had happened the night before, and so the fear, at least for me, was coming from, *Are there explosive devices out on the street? Am I going to be shot today? Will I be shot at? Will I be physically assaulted?* You kind of go through your head and you ask yourself, *What am I capable of? What am I capable of? How can I protect myself here? I'm unarmed.*

EMILY GORCENSKI, LOCAL ACTIVIST: My wife was like, *You need to promise me after last night that you don't go to the front lines.* And I was like, *I promise you that. I've seen enough action.*

LISA WOOLFORK, UVA PROFESSOR AND MEMBER OF CHARLOTTESVILLE BLACK LIVES MATTER: I remember very early that morning, texting one of my good friends and I said, [*My spouse*] *Ben and I are going to this rally. And if anything should happen to us, I want the boys, our kids, to live with my sister-in-law Molly in New York. And I'm telling you this not because I don't love my sisters, but my sisters live in the South. They live in Texas and they live in Florida. And I believe that the boys will be better served in school by living in Manhattan and going to schools in New York City.*

DAVID STRAUGHN, LOCAL ACTIVIST: We wrote bail support phone numbers on each other's arms and legs with Sharpies. We packed our bags full of water, fruit, and a change of clothes for the impending tear gas. We were ready.[7]

MARCUS MARTIN, COUNTERPROTESTER: My fiancée at the time, Marissa, wanted to go. I couldn't allow her to go alone and her mind was made up. So I was like, *I gotta go.*

We met at the McDonald's downtown. We parked our cars over there and then we started to walk, and that's when a big group [of white nationalists] walked right past us. Like, that's when we first got there. Wow. They walked right past us and that's when Marissa looked at me and grabbed my hand and was like, *I don't want, I don't think we should be, I don't think we should do this.* And then I told her, I was like, *Babe, just hold my hand and don't let it go.*

Many activists came in from out of town.

BILL BURKE, COUNTERPROTESTER: That was my first trip to Charlottesville. I heard about the Unite the Right in Chicago at a socialist conference. It was my birthday weekend, August 13th. So I was like, I'll just go yell at some Klansmen for my birthday.

I had to work Friday and I was planning on leaving really early Saturday morning. So I got up, probably left the house about four, five o'clock in the morning for Charlottesville. It was about a six-hour drive.

CONSTANCE PAIGE YOUNG, COUNTERPROTESTER: I was there once before and I remember I bought a dress from a vintage shop. It's a 1960s-style dress, I think, with a high collar and it's made of raw silk, it's blue, it's very pretty. I went to a couple of wineries out there. Yeah, so that was my only experience with Charlottesville before.

A friend of mine had been arrested in July. Another friend of mine was medic-ing. They told me about it—it sounded horrifying. And it sounded unacceptable. If there's a screaming, abandoned baby, you go and tend to it, you don't ask questions about it. It seemed like this was a situation that should be addressed. So, I didn't contemplate the decision. The decision made itself to just go ahead and go.

WEDNESDAY BOWIE, COUNTERPROTESTER: We got up pretty early. And we went to Bodo's and got bagels. That's a big Charlottesville thing. If you go to Charlottesville, you got to get Bodo's Bagels.

One of the people that came with us was a street medic. And so, my plan for the day was stick with her and just bodyguard her and anybody she needs to take care of.

I went into that situation knowing that it was going to be violent and knowing that it was going to be dangerous and my purpose with it was like, *I'm a large person. I'm six feet tall. I'm no lightweight.* My expectation was, *I'm going to need to physically put myself between people in order to be a protector.*

While activists streamed into Charlottesville from elsewhere, many local Black families chose to leave town entirely.

WES BELLAMY, CHARLOTTESVILLE VICE MAYOR: You see, for a lot of Black people, this issue wasn't necessarily ours to fight.[8]

A large majority of Black people that I spoke with were clear that they weren't going downtown that day. Several encouraged me to not attend. Many people of color believed that it wasn't our fight and that the white supremacists' minds were not going to be changed by Black people confronting them. That instead, they would be more prone to listen to other white people, and as people of color, their time would be better served protecting their own communities, their own peace of mind, and their own bodies.[9]

YOLUNDA HARRELL, CEO, NEW HILL DEVELOPMENT CORP.: There's a very big difference between the Black person and the white person in that situation. For the Black person—like you got several things to think about. I've got a real thought of, *I could lose my life just simply be being Black.* I don't have to say anything. I don't have to do anything. It could just be because someone is so hate-filled. For me, as a Black person, what would I accomplish by being there? Because they're here to demonstrate their hate. Me being there is not gonna change that.

And so the idea that you could actually be out—not even involved in that, in what was going on—and come across a group who is now amped up and feeling like they can do something to you? Now you become a prisoner in your own community.

My husband and I made a decision. We're not even staying in town for that. Like, we're just gonna leave. We're gonna go outta town. Because that just has the potential to just get out of control and we are a little town. What's gonna happen if it gets outta control? And do we wanna find ourselves in a situation where we're fighting for our lives?

DR. ANDREA DOUGLAS, EXECUTIVE DIRECTOR, JEFFERSON SCHOOL AFRICAN AMERICAN HERITAGE CENTER: There are multiple reasons why you would say, yes, there were not many Black people on the streets.

Many people say, *We have bigger problems than this. Those statues don't bother us. We don't occupy those places anyway. So it doesn't matter to us. What matters to us is putting food on the table.* They're working as hard as they can to make ends meet in a service industry. And so that also speaks to the fact that—the African American population in Charlottesville, 39 percent of it is impoverished, right? So 39 percent of 8,000 [Black] people [living in Charlottesville] are impoverished. That's a big number. And of that 39 percent, a good number of those people are young people. So, when you look out and you say, *Where are the Black people?* Well, you know, you're not sending your kids out there. You're not sending your older population out there. And then the numbers become very small, really.

And at the same time, you also have to go defend your home because they were headed towards Garrett Square. And the young men there were like, *You're not passing these gates.*

So that's a real space too, you know: making sure that the alt-right were turned back from these Black spaces was also what some of the Black men, the young men were engaged in.

WES BELLAMY: With this in mind, I would say that less than 20 percent of the people who were counterprotesting were Black.[10]

| **Also gearing up: Charlottesville's reporters.**

HENRY GRAFF, ANCHOR AND REPORTER, NBC29: My mom called me and she was like, *I don't want you to go to work today.* And I'm like, *Well, I have to go to work.*

But did you see what happened on the TV last night?

And I was like, *Yes, I saw. I watched it. I'm very sad.*

And I think it did—yeah, it stacked the deck. If you were holding on hope that it was going to be peaceful, I think by watching the events unfold the night before, that little hope went away.

But we had a meeting, we got our assignments. We were given special [health] insurance cards with IDs because nobody knew what was gonna happen.

TIM DODSON, MANAGING EDITOR, *CAVALIER DAILY*: My car was outta commission for whatever reason. So I was driving my mom's minivan, a Honda Odyssey.

ZACK WAJSGRAS, FREELANCE PHOTOGRAPHER: Being someone who was really obsessed with photojournalism and had encountered a lot of war photography, I had always wondered if I would report on something like that. And what the role of doing that was, with clear danger present.

And just hearing lots of reports of people bringing guns. I was like, *Oh my God, is this something we're going to experience today?* I think literally from the time that we got in the car, my heart basically just started racing from then.

HENRY GRAFF: There were people you knew. Small town, you know, there's Joe Blow from down the street or Carrie you see at the bar sometimes.

It's quiet. I can see police officers, I'm like, *Hey, how are you, be safe today. Please remember me, if you need to pull me out of something, I'm a good guy, please!*

I mean, these are cops you know. I remember walking down Market Street and hugging Tammy Shiflett—she was the officer who parked at 4th Street—being like *I hope you have a safe day.* 'Cause I have interviewed her 100 other times on other random bullshit topics that we cover for the normal news every day. And here I'm like, *I hope you survive.* That kind of stuff where it's like, *God, what are we doing here?*

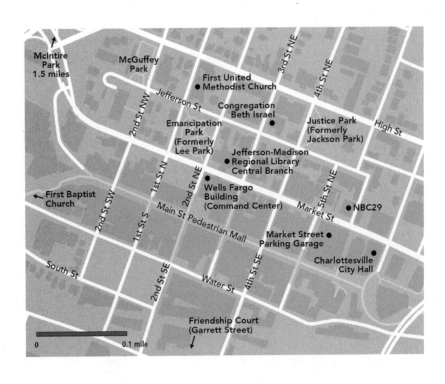

McIntire
Park
1.5 miles

McGuffey
Park

First United
● Methodist Church

3rd St NE

4th St NE

Jefferson St

2nd St NW

Congregation
Beth Israel
●

Justice Park
(Formerly
Jackson Park)

High St

Emancipation
Park
(Formerly
Lee Park)

Jefferson-Madison
● Regional Library
Central Branch

1st St N

2nd St NE

Wells Fargo
● Building
(Command Center)

5th St NE

← First Baptist
Church

2nd St SW

1st St S

Main St Pedestrian Mall

Market St

● NBC29

Market Street ●
Parking Garage

South St

2nd St SE

Water St

4th St SE

Charlottesville
City Hall
●

Friendship Court
(Garrett Street)
↓

0   0.1 mile

CHAPTER 9

"This is fucked up as a football bat."

Meanwhile, the second group of protesters—those who would not engage in direct action—marched downtown.

DAVID GARTH, RETIRED PASTOR: It was a sunny day. We left maybe sometime around between 7 and 8 and started to walk. It was a casual crowd. I noticed that our state senator was there, and I think there were some other people who were my age. I was 74.

KRISTIN SZAKOS, CHARLOTTESVILLE CITY COUNCILOR: I was walking with Don Gathers. It's a pretty short distance. I think we were walking fast. I think everybody was amped up a little bit, but it was quiet, as I remember. We were chanting things and carrying banners and signs, and more of a sense of real determination, girding ourselves for the day.

DON GATHERS, COFOUNDER, CHARLOTTESVILLE BLACK LIVES MATTER: We marched in unison into McGuffey Art Park. There was a separate vigil being held there.

MEDIA ADVISORY FOR MCGUFFEY PARK EVENT: There will be information, teach-ins, and speakers in addition to prayer and meditations, music and art, and an opportunity for respite.

This event was known as the PARJ, the People's Action for Racial Justice, organized by Professor Walt Heinecke. The idea had started a few weeks before, when he had met with Jalane Schmidt and her partner, Mimi Arbeit.

WALT HEINECKE, UVA PROFESSOR AND ACTIVIST: I met with Jalane and Mimi downtown somewhere, and we were just sort of chitchatting about what was going on and how to respond. And they had told me that one of their SURJ members, a young woman who I actually know who was in [one of my] classes, a little bit of a hippieish woman, had gone down and tried to get permits to do some kind of art protest in McGuffey Park. And the city had rejected them. I kind of got the sense that the city kind of just thought she was a lefty kind of crazy person, [and] young. And so they didn't give her a permit. So Jalane and Mimi just said, *Hey, can you help? Can you help us get permits for counterprotests?* And I said, sure.

So the next day I put on a suit and tie—you know, the UVa blue blazer and the khakis—and went down to the Parks Department and filled out a permit for the People's Action on Racial Justice, and they gave me the permit.

And I don't know if they were just being discriminatory against the young woman, or what was going on, but they gave *me* the permits.

Now, part of my motivation for doing that was going back to July 8th—the way that the police treated the progressive protesters. They tend to shut down free speech and assembly pretty quickly on them with no reason. And that whole thing made me think, *Well, if the city's gonna be kind of fascistic about counterprotesters protesting, I want a place for free speech and I want a protected place for free speech and free assembly, so that Antifa and progressive protesters and activists in Charlottesville could come and have a safe space.*

So, I put together a group. I put out a call to the activist networks and I asked for people who wanted to volunteer. And I got a really solid group of diverse folks to sign up. Devin was on that steering committee.

DEVIN WILLIS, SECOND-YEAR UVA STUDENT: I got up early because I promised that I would be at McGuffey Park bright and early so that I could help set up the park.[1] I had already given my word that I would come and help out with like water bottles, set up folding tables, that kind of thing. One, you don't want to, like, quit halfway through the job; and two, I think, based off of how that small, tiny rally went the night before, I was like, OK, these guys are dangerous. They're violent. And what we're doing at the PARJ is more important now than ever. There needs to be a safe space. And yeah, I had responsibilities. I had to go.[2]

When I got to the park that morning, I did my job. I helped with logistical things: unfolding tables, helping point out where porta potties should be, putting down the water bottles.[3]

WALT HEINECKE: We started setting up the medic tents. We set up the rain tents and the PA system. And then security came. We had walkie-talkies and I handed out the walkie-talkies to kind of circulate in the near area and give us intelligence about where these neo-Nazis were marching and where they were coming.

DON GATHERS: There was already a huge vast number of people there waiting. It had been marked a safe space, a safe haven for people who wanted to come and be out with the community. The Care Bears, if you will, and the nursing staff and first aid people were assembled there.

MICHAEL CHEUK, SECRETARY, CHARLOTTESVILLE CLERGY COLLECTIVE: They're called Care Bears. They have little wagons that they actually pull in out in the streets to give people water or Band-Aids or whatever they may need and so forth.

REV. SETH WISPELWEY, PASTOR AND COFOUNDER, CONGREGATE C'VILLE: It's humid as hell. It's August and we're robed up. Like we would have passed out if someone hadn't been shoving water bottles in our hands.

BRENNAN GILMORE, COUNTERPROTESTER AND FORMER US FOREIGN SERVICE OFFICER: People were writing lawyers' numbers on their arms, doing this traditional protection stuff before a big rally, and then handing out leaflets with legal advice.

WEDNESDAY BOWIE, COUNTERPROTESTER: I remember we followed a trail of glitter down the sidewalk to get to the park. And that was nice. It was like, *Oh, I wonder who did this?* It was a nice distraction.

DON GATHERS: Various speakers took the mic. We had clergy from everywhere.

DAVID GARTH, RETIRED PASTOR: There was a band there and people were playing. There was music, recorded music, and there were some stands or tables had been set up and there were balloons and it was basically a kind of a fair. A festival sort of mood intended, I guess, for people who might have gone to the Lee statue but wanted someplace else where the danger would not be evident at all.

KRISTIN SZAKOS, CHARLOTTESVILLE CITY COUNCILOR, AT PARJ: I was going through the motions in a way on the ground as myself, worrying about the bigger picture that I couldn't see. And I was getting texts every now and then from the city manager, the police chief. It was surreal to be on these two planes: both being part of the establishment that was supposed to protect the city and then myself, as a human being. One reason that I chose not to go to the rally itself, the big one, was that I knew because of my work on the statues since what, 2012, that some of the [alt-right] folks organizing this rally knew who I was and that I would trigger it. I would trigger violence and I didn't want that to happen.

It wasn't that I was afraid. I just didn't want to provoke them personally. I had been under a lot of personal scrutiny and ire for almost a year before that from the right, from white supremacists. My home phone number was put on Aryan Nation websites, so people were calling me all the time. And people were telling me what time I went to bed last night, calling to just show me that they were watching my house and threatening horrible things to me and my kids. So, I had been living with that going into that summer.

I just felt if I had been an anonymous person, I probably would've been there, but I felt like it would just make it worse if I went. It would be about me, and that seemed to distract from what people were trying to achieve there.

ACTIVISTS AT PARJ, SINGING:
Over my head I see peace in the air.
Over my head I see peace in the air.
Over my head I see peace in the air;
There must be a God somewhere![4]

KRISTIN SZAKOS: I spent quite a lot of the time on the corners of the park that face downtown—because we started about, oh, maybe 8:30—to see these roving bands of white nationalists coming toward the park. Just trying to, I think, freak us out or something, or I don't know what their intent was. But the first ones looked like they were trying to look like Vikings, and they had these big flags and these Norse avenger fantasy characters. And they were shouting something indecipherable and they were marching toward the park.

DAVID GARTH: I could see alt-right folks coming and going to the Lee statue park. And they had helmets and they were carrying sticks and weapons of some kind. I was genuinely afraid. And for me, that just confirmed that I was in the right place. To go to a safe space.

KRISTIN SZAKOS: And some of the folks who were doing security at the park—just citizen security, not police—were starting to engage with them, shouting at them and throwing things at them. And I remember I went and talked to them and asked if they could try to move that away from McGuffey, because I felt like that was really drawing them in, and they did. They were great.

But I was also texting the police department and saying, *These guys are coming to McGuffey Park right now. The rally's supposed to start at noon, but it's 8:30 and they're already out here. Can you get some folks around this park?* Because they weren't. There was one down on Market Street, one police officer alone or maybe two. And there were a couple more over on High Street, but I had not seen a police presence around the park and I thought it might be a good idea.

They didn't come. I don't know why. The two policemen who ended up on Market Street did come, but there was never any kind of protective cordon or anything at McGuffey Park. So, we really relied on prayer and hope and these few citizen security people who were watching the edges.

CONSTANCE PAIGE YOUNG, COUNTERPROTESTER: I just had this feeling something was going to happen. I had on long sleeves...I was trying to protect my body. And I did see people there who were not ready, who looked very, very green. This was not green stuff. There's nothing about this that would scream fun protests down at the National Mall in DC, where the cops are used to protesters. I think I even saw a couple of minors, and I'm thinking to myself, *Why are you here?*

You can't reconcile flip-flops and Klansmen. There's nothing that's about safety there. There ain't no safety there.

HEAPHY REPORT: Some who marched to McGuffey walked over to the First United Methodist Church [FUMC], where prayer services happened inside while medical tents and counterprotester support organized in the back parking lot.

MICHAEL CHEUK, SECRETARY, CHARLOTTESVILLE CLERGY COLLECTIVE: There were people out in the parking lot. They had set up kind of a security station there.

REV. BRENDA BROWN-GROOMS, PASTOR, NEW BEGINNINGS CHRISTIAN COMMUNITY: I'm a stroke survivor, so I wasn't gonna do well in the street. So I was among those who were deployed to First United Methodist Church. The praying vigil were there. There was also the welcoming station and where people could come in for medical aid.

HEAPHY REPORT: Deborah Porras, a minister who traveled to Charlottesville to support counter-protest efforts, told us that FUMC had installed metal detectors and required white males to have a "sponsor" to enter the building.

REV. PHIL WOODSON, ASSOCIATE PASTOR, FIRST UNITED METHODIST CHURCH: No weapons of any sort would be allowed inside the church. Everyone who sought access to our church's safe space would be subjected to having our volunteers review their identification and submit to being scanned by a metal detector. Unless there was an emergency as determined by the members of the leadership team, armed police officers would also have to adhere to our zero-tolerance rule for weapons in the church. But in the event of an emergency, anyone and everyone who needed sanctuary would be provided with it. This included fire department, emergency response personnel, and armed officers if they were stationed around our churches. If somebody started shooting shit up or blowing shit up, the church was going to open its doors to everybody. That's what we agreed upon.

That morning I spoke with each of those groups—firemen, police officers—early in the morning, and then in no uncertain terms made clear that if a bomb went off or a gunman went rogue, that they were absolutely allowed to come inside for safety.

Using the church's facilities to pee and needing sanctuary are two distinctly different needs. And so there were many times throughout the day when First UMC volunteers had to prioritize the physical and mental care that people were receiving inside and unfortunately had to turn a number of simple "bathrooms seekers" away. If those cops wanted to hand me their guns while they walked inside to pee, we would've had a different conversation.

The rules inside said, *No one calls the cops. If you're inside this church, you do not call the police. That's up to those of us on the outside. Or those of us in leadership positions. Notify one of us that had our pictures up there on the board. These are the people you talk to before you call 911.*

Just two blocks away, Jewish worshippers congregated for Saturday services in Charlottesville's only synagogue.

ALAN ZIMMERMAN, PRESIDENT, CONGREGATION BETH ISRAEL: So my very first memory of when I got downtown was—and this is just a very Charlottesville thing—was, *Hmm, that was easy finding a parking spot.*

And I went to the synagogue. The guard was there. We had maybe, I don't know, 30 people. Yeah, pretty normal size of people that come to services, although the mixture was a little bit different. A lot of the elderly people that regularly came were not there, but then there was some people that I normally don't see at services that came and they were like, *I wanted to be here because I don't want to be chased away from services.*

RABBI TOM GUTHERZ, CONGREGATION BETH ISRAEL: After what happened on Friday night I think we all kind of thought, *All bets are off on this one.* Whatever we were thinking was going to happen—we just really didn't know. Kind of had a very strong feeling about that. We just did not know.

| City officials were also preparing for the day.

ANDREW BAXTER, CHARLOTTESVILLE FIRE CHIEF: So I get up Saturday. I check Twitter and probably NBC29 and CBS19. And I went to Ridge Street to the firehouse, to check with the off-going shift commander. We've essentially got 80 percent of the fire department working that day, plus all these mutual aid resources coming in.

City officials monitored events from two main command centers: Unified Command, located in the Wells Fargo building overlooking Emancipation Park and staffed by top decisionmakers, and the Emergency Operations Center, 2.5 miles away at Zehmer Hall on UVa's Grounds.

Baxter had been planning on spending the day at Unified Command (also called the command post or command center), but says city leaders told him he was not on the list.

ANDREW BAXTER: They said, *We don't need you in the command post.* I think part of that was some hubris on their part. And I think part of it was at that point, [City Manager] Maurice [Jones] and [Chief of Police] Al [Thomas] had started to see me as a nag. And they didn't want me in the room. Hubris is a really... I'm careful using that word, but I think it fits.

INTERNATIONAL ASSOCIATION OF CHIEFS OF POLICE AFTER-ACTION RE-
VIEW: ...not all key personnel were operating from the site
designated by the city as Unified Command at the Wells Fargo
Building overlooking the demonstration site. Several satellite
posts, including the Fire Branch, were working in support of
the event but apart from the Unified Command.[5]

| Also denied entry to the city's command post: Mayor Mike Signer.

MIKE SIGNER, CHARLOTTESVILLE MAYOR: I had asked Maurice Jones if I could go be at the command center, which is at the Wells Fargo building. And he said, *There isn't space for you here.* I had not been—this is really important—I had not been given anything to do.

City Manager Maurice Jones was within his authority to deny Mayor Signer access to the command center due to Charlottesville's system of government, in which the mayor holds a largely ceremonial role. Instead, Mayor Signer considered attending the actual protest.

MIKE SIGNER: I talked to my wife, Emily, about it, and she said, *I won't, I won't allow you. I don't want you to be out there unless you have somebody from the police with you.* And that seemed prudent based on the conversations we had with the FBI and the ADL.

And Al Thomas, earlier that week, had denied me that request. He said, *I'm sorry, we just don't have anybody.* And I was like, *OK, well.*

So, I just went over to City Hall to my office there. I had to walk through the Downtown Mall to get there. And it gives me chills to think about it because I walked through the Downtown Mall. There were hundreds of officers everywhere.

I probably got over to City Hall at like eight o'clock, maybe. It was so weird because it was . . . There was nobody there. I mean, the entire staff was cleared out.

He sat in his office with two outside crisis communications professionals he had hired for the weekend, whom he says were also not invited into the command center.

MIKE SIGNER: It's just us three, like tapping away. Me getting a zillion emails and texts. It's eerily quiet.

Fire Chief Baxter headed instead to the Emergency Operations Center (EOC). When he arrived with his friend and colleague Dan Eggleston, fire chief for Albemarle County (the county surrounding Charlottesville), he was shocked by the limited number of people there—and their relatively low seniority.

ANDREW BAXTER: There's a vice president from the university, a lieutenant from CPD, a sergeant from VSP [Virginia State Police], Deputy County Executive Doug Walker, and a number of other people. Dan and I are both looking at each other like, *This is fucked up as a football bat.* But our responsibility's to make this as good as it can be.

So we had to create, essentially from scratch, a regional emergency operations center with the people that were in that room. And we did. We did an hourly briefing. We tried desperately to get information from the command post, but here's how bad that was: We have a CPD lieutenant sitting in the regional emergency operations center, and the only way she's getting information about what's happening on the ground is by listening to her radio, to one channel on the radio. And we're monitoring Facebook Live and Periscope. And our job is to have situational awareness of everything that's happening, so we can pre-position resources and anticipate what the incident commander on the ground is going to need. Zero communications. It was horrible, absolutely horrible.

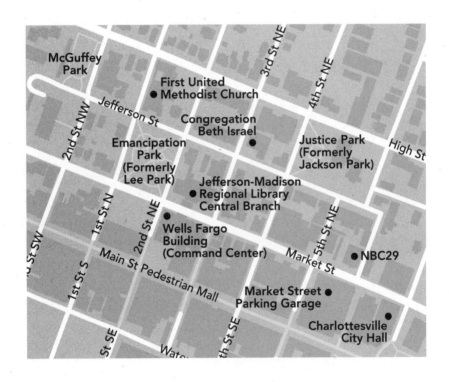

CHAPTER 10

"I remember thinking, Somebody is going to die today."

ABOUT 8 A.M.

SMASH CAINE-CONLEY, COFOUNDER, CONGREGATE C'VILLE, MARCHING TO EMANCIPATION PARK: That morning it didn't feel extraordinarily hot yet. It was overcast a bit. I think it was pretty, in my mind. But it was eerily quiet. I had never seen Charlottesville so quiet before. There was hardly anyone around on the streets anywhere.

CHRIS SUAREZ, REPORTER, CHARLOTTESVILLE *DAILY PROGRESS*: I was just riding along and watching the clergy start marching to Emancipation Park. They weren't chanting or anything. It was just kind of a very solemn thing.

REV. SETH WISPELWEY, PASTOR AND COFOUNDER, CONGREGATE C'VILLE: You could almost smell and feel dread.

Once we turned onto Market Street, we pulled out into a single-file line in front of the sidewalk facing the park.

WEDNESDAY BOWIE, COUNTERPROTESTER: It was early. There weren't any Nazis around yet.

CHRIS SUAREZ: By the time we got close to the Lee statue, that's when I saw all the militia guys. I could pick up on the fact that this isn't law enforcement.

REV. SETH WISPELWEY: It looked like you were going into a militarized zone. Big, burly militia members, big guns, camo.

WASHINGTON POST: The Southern Poverty Law Center, a nonprofit watchdog group that monitors extremist organizations, classifies 276 militias in the country as "antigovernment groups," meaning they generally "define themselves as opposed to the 'New World Order,' engage in groundless conspiracy theorizing, or advocate or adhere to extreme antigovernment doctrines."

REV. SETH WISPELWEY: I remember explicitly, the guy right in front of me. He had a patch that had the Stars and Bars on it. These guys were not neutral peacekeepers, of course.

Other militia members, however, did not wear Nazi or white nationalist insignia. Law enforcement from different agencies, including the National Guard, were also posted in and around Emancipation Park. In many cases, the two groups were virtually indistinguishable.

RABBI THOMAS GUTHERZ, CONGREGATION BETH ISRAEL: Nobody quite knew who was who.[1]

TOM PERRIELLO, COUNTERPROTESTER AND FORMER US CONGRESSMAN: You could not tell who was National Guard and who was white supremacist. They were in full camo. They had earpieces in. They were moving in formations. They had open long guns. They were, in every meaningful way, exactly how National Guard would be out in the streets. And they saw themselves that way.

STAR PETERSON, LOCAL ACTIVIST AND STREET MEDIC: I just remember being like, *Who are those people? I'd really like to know which side they're on because they make me very nervous.* They're in full-on fucking military gear.

HEAPHY REPORT: They carried long guns and wore body armor.

SMASH CAINE-CONLEY: I know that they think they were there to keep the peace, but it's really disconcerting walking towards people with semiautomatic guns and army fatigues. If I see a white man with a large gun, I'm not

really gonna be like, *Oh, are you my friend or not?* I'm probably gonna be like,
I don't wanna be near you right now. It's hard to distinguish.

VSP TROOPER, TO A COLLEAGUE: What are they, like military?
They're more armed than we are.

BRENNAN GILMORE, COUNTERPROTESTER AND FORMER US FOREIGN SERVICE
OFFICER: I remember thinking that I've had more clarity in civil unrest in
war-torn countries in sub-Saharan Africa because there's a cleaner delinea-
tion of who the armed combatants are. As soon as I walked to the main area
of the park I saw all the guns, and I couldn't tell who was legitimate security,
state police, National Guard, or who was militia. And I just looked around
and saw weapons everywhere.

JEFF FOGEL, LAWYER AND ACTIVIST: I went over to one of them and I said
hello. He seemed very stern and very serious. He didn't want to answer me.
And I said, *Well, what are you doing here?* Blah, blah, blah. He eventually said,
Well, we're here to protect people's rights.

It certainly wasn't clear to me how he was doing that, standing in the
middle of Market Street with an AK-47.

BRIAN MORAN, SECRETARY, VIRGINIA PUBLIC SAFETY AND HOMELAND SE-
CURITY: I started sending pics to the governor of these folks with their long
arms, long rifles assembling.

TERRY MCAULIFFE, VIRGINIA GOVERNOR: And I was really astounded because these people have better weapons than our people have. And they're
marching in military procession, they are pretending to be real military, with
outfits like they're real military. They have semiautomatics, they've got their
pistols all strapped to their sides, to their calves, to their ankles.

And so I called Brian and said, *This is not something else we needed added in!*
And so I said, *Well, Brian, go talk, find out who the hell they are.* And he's
got the phone open and I can hear 'em.

BRIAN MORAN: One of the militiamen said to me, *You gotta talk to my CO,
sir, you gotta talk to my CO.* It's like, they're obviously an organized militia.
They had a commanding officer.

TERRY MCAULIFFE: Now we've got all these folks that don't answer to any of us with a lot of guns. So that was very disconcerting to me.

BRIAN MORAN: One point I walked over to see if the farmer's market's open. And son of a—it is! The farmer's market, which is, what, three blocks away? Is open! They're going about their business. I think to myself, *Do you have any idea that there are people two blocks away carrying long rifles and there's about to be a thousand white nationalists two blocks away from you and how many counterprotesters?* And they're going about their business at the farmer's market!

So I got a cup of coffee, walked back. I tell the superintendent, I said, *I just got coffee! They have a farmer's market down there, you know?* And then there was a woman jogging with her dog and her baby stroller. It was like business as usual.

BRENNAN GILMORE: I remember thinking, *Somebody is going to die today. This is going to be bloody.*

REV. SETH WISPELWEY, AT EMANCIPATION PARK: And then, we flagged out into a single file line, basically face-to-face with the militia that were on the sidewalks.

HEAPHY REPORT: There was no barrier between them and the armed militia, who stood just a few feet away.

SMASH CAINE-CONLEY: We spread out and linked arms.

WEDNESDAY BOWIE: Cornel West was out there and a bunch of other people in vestments. And they were holding hands and forming a barrier around the park.

REV. SETH WISPELWEY: There's a weird mix of being so real and yet... What, we're in our full clergy drag in the city that I grew up in? That I went to this library on these same streets where I was 5 and 6 and 7 that I now bring my daughter to at age 5, 6, and 7? It doesn't compute.

And yet that was the clearest call I'd ever experienced that summer. I don't know. It's hard to explain the mix of peace and trepidation—that's why you train that way. It's tactile. It's the training paying off. All I have to do is pass the whisper down the line. *OK, now walk. OK, now we're standing out here, now we're spreading out here. OK, we're gonna kneel.* That was what we worked on.

SMASH CAINE-CONLEY: We didn't carry any sort of weapons, but we also wanted to be really clear that nonviolence isn't just about whether or not you carry a weapon: that nonviolence is about the systems that do harm particular folks in our society.

So we lined up in front of the park and began to sing.

SINGING: Ain't gonna let nobody
Turn me 'round
Turn me 'round
Ain't gonna let nobody
Turn me 'round
I'm gonna keep on walkin'
Keep on talkin'
Marchin' into freedom land.[2]

SMASH CAINE-CONLEY: Some of the militia joined in our hymn singing, which I have to admit was pretty disconcerting to me.

SINGING: This little light of mine,
I'm gonna let it shine.

HENRY GRAFF, ANCHOR AND REPORTER, NBC29: This little light of mine! I started bawling that morning. They were singing and urging for peace.

STAR PETERSON, LOCAL ACTIVIST AND STREET MEDIC: Clergy were singing so I was like, *Well, medic duty.* So I handed out cough drops and they were like, *Thank you,* and I was like, *I know protest. This is what people need. We need cough drops. Hope nobody needs anything more than cough drops today.*

WEDNESDAY BOWIE: The whole street was filled with people from our side.

STAR PETERSON: They already had the cops around the wall of the park. We noticed they were facing out. They faced who they think the threat is. They're facing us.

LISA DRAINE, LOCAL ACTIVIST: Sophie and Rebecca left earlier and met up with students, so I was not with them at the time. I headed on up to

McGuffey and I was trying to hook up with a couple of my friends from Congregate and couldn't find them, it was pretty crowded. So I was like, *I'm just here by myself. I don't really wanna be by myself. I'd rather actually be with my girls.* I was texting Rebecca and said like, *What are you guys doing?* So I walked over [to where they were gathering with their friends] and I show up and the girls were like, *Moooommm!!! What are YOU doing here? Why are you here?*

And I said, *Well I was by myself and I didn't wanna be by myself.* But you know, I could tell they were kind of embarrassed.

So anyway, people, they were getting ready, gathering noisemakers and planning what they were gonna chant and that sort of thing. One of the people that were leading them said, *Everyone needs to make sure you have a buddy.* And of course I turned to my girls and they're like, *No, the two of us are buddies. You're gonna have to find someone else.* So I'm looking around and somebody said, *Who doesn't have a buddy?* And it was like me and a few others. And I ended up being buddies with Devin Willis! We had never met each other. He knew I was Sophie's mom and he was like, *Sure, why not?* So the two of us were together as the whole group walked down Market Street.

SMASH CAINE-CONLEY: It wasn't too long after we got to the park that the white supremacist groups started to march in.

DAVID FOKY, NEWS DIRECTOR, NBC29: These alt-right guys, these Nazi sympathizer guys, that mishmash of people started coming towards the park. They were coming from all points. They were walking down the street, coming in groups in a defensive mode where they march together in tight groups with shields and helmets.

WEDNESDAY BOWIE: It was really very surreal. They would have banners and stuff, and they'd just march down the street.

SMASH CAINE-CONLEY: The streets were getting really full. These white supremacist groups would march past us, oftentimes bumping into us or trying to insult us whatever way they could.

REV. SETH WISPELWEY: They were yelling homophobic, misogynistic slurs. *Is this every lesbian clergy in America?* And *Jesus hates you, God hates you.* They would start chanting, *Fuck you, faggots,* and *White lives matter* and this kind of stuff.

COUNTERPROTESTERS: We're here, we're gay, we fight the KKK! We're here, we're gay, we fight the KKK![3]

REV. PHIL WOODSON, ASSOCIATE PASTOR, FIRST UNITED METHODIST CHURCH: A lot of the people who turned up to resist these Nazis were members of the LGBTQ community. White supremacy takes out everything that is not of itself. And so any person of color was in danger, anything that was not white male cis-hetero Christian was in danger.

COUNTERPROTESTERS: Fuck you fascists, fuck you fascists![4]

REV. SETH WISPELWEY: You have people always that are like, *Oh, it's racist and Islamophobic.* When you get really face-to-face with it, a lot of our experiences, it's really homophobic and really antisemitic.

SMASH CAINE-CONLEY: This very loud crowd was forming of antifascist activists, activists of every stripe, like any type of activist that resists white supremacist violence—everyone was there. So we knew the time was now to do an action.

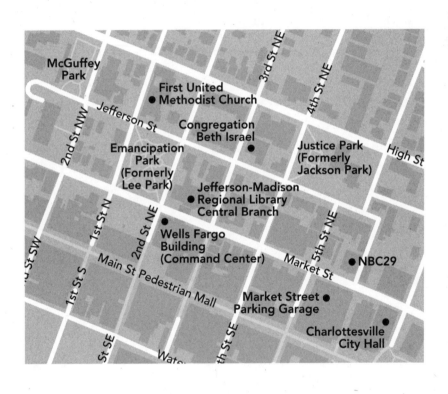

CHAPTER 11

"It seemed like war in downtown Charlottesville."

SMASH CAINE-CONLEY, COFOUNDER, CONGREGATE C'VILLE: We decided that we were going to form a blockade on the stairs that go up to the park.

CHARLOTTESVILLE POLICE DEPARTMENT SERGEANT: That's OK—they keep people out of that area, I'm fine with that.

SMASH CAINE-CONLEY: We were intending to block the stairs even if a group tried to get through. A group did indeed start marching toward us, and Seth and I were on the end of the line that was facing the park.

HEAPHY REPORT: [The white nationalists] marched up the stairs, shields first, and pushed through the line of clergy.

SMASH CAINE-CONLEY: They started marching toward our group, started pushing the front of our blockade with their shields and batons and trying to ram through us.

REV. SETH WISPELWEY, PASTOR AND COFOUNDER, CONGREGATE C'VILLE: I heard yelling—I don't really want to say it, but I heard yelling, *Kill the faggot priests.* I also heard, *Move the fuck aside, clergy*, while they were pushing through.

And then the next thing I knew I was pushed, along with colleagues, into the bushes.

When I stood up and got my bearing again, a large man was just kind of standing over me and yelling, *Fuck you, faggot* over and over in my face.

SMASH CAINE-CONLEY: Somebody in our front line broke the line and let them through! I honestly couldn't believe it. I was so stunned.

REV. SETH WISPELWEY: Part of the reason it caught us by surprise is there's 30 state police officers *right* there.

INTERNATIONAL ASSOCIATION OF CHIEFS OF POLICE AFTER-ACTION RE-VIEW: The Virginia State Police (VSP) dedicated approximately 600 sworn members to the event, the largest deployment in decades.[1]

REV. SETH WISPELWEY: And I'm standing next to Dr. West and he's like, *Oh my God, no one's getting arrested today.*[2]

SMASH CAINE-CONLEY: I was so pissed off. I didn't wanna lose my cool and start cursing at my own folks while the white supremacists were there. So I waited 'til the white supremacists went through. The folks with us started trying to sing "This Little Light of Mine," which was just really embarrassing to me. We've just been run over by group of white supremacists! They're insulting us, calling us names, and you're singing a child's hymn? I was like, this is unreal to me.

After they kind of streamed through, I turned around and I yelled like, *Why the fuck did that happen? How did we let them through? Why did we let them through?*

And I pretty much said, *If you're not here to keep the discipline, then get off the line. Like if we're gonna be here, we're going to do what we said we came to do.*

I think I was enraged for a few reasons. I think I was still feeling my regret from the night before and not showing up the way that I wanted to show up. And we've been training for months and here we're doing our direct action and it failed and, in my mind, it failed miserably.

REV. SETH WISPELWEY: And so I and some of the other leaders of Congregate decided it was still worth making a presence, recognizing that this was an intense situation, but put us as the leaders out in front and lower on the steps.[3]

And then, some of the protesters we had also talked with, they're like, *Well, if you're down with that, we'll stand here with you and hold.* And we're like, *All right, just so we're clear, we're going to hold space, but we're committed to not hitting back if hit.* And they're like, *We're down with that. We'll protect you.* So, that's what I mean when I say Antifa saved our lives.

DAVID STRAUGHN, LOCAL ACTIVIST: If it wasn't for Congregate and if it wasn't for Antifa, much more people would have died that day. Antifa does not get the credit that they deserve for preserving life and for steadfast alliance in the face of just straight-up evil.

SMASH CAINE-CONLEY: After I had my little tirade yelling session at folks, I think people were ready to not let another group through.

HEAPHY REPORT: The clergy reformed their line.

REV. SETH WISPELWEY: And then that's when we saw another large group coming up the street.[4] A huge group of men were walking with shields, flags, different insignias.[5]

DEVIN WILLIS, SECOND-YEAR UVA STUDENT: You couldn't even see into the park because all along the perimeter of the park, these guys are just hanging out on the edges and heckling all the passersby and all the counterprotesters. They seemed more interested in what was happening in the street than what was happening inside their rally.

REV. SETH WISPELWEY: There's this concept of holy foolery. Part of the idea is we're all in our clergy drag. The robes and the stoles and the what-have-you, which is already meant to be this striking *otherness*. It's part of the theater of it, to take attention away.

If there was one do-over, I wish we had waded into the middle of that, right there, that intersection and just started doing the Funky Chicken, in terms of thinking about what could you take the tension away with.

DEVIN WILLIS: The vast majority of [the white nationalists] had some combination of white top, white dress shirt with khaki or navy bottoms, whatever, kind of like a school uniform. But then you also saw a lot of people in riot gear, tactical armor, these militia fake-fatigue kind of getups. You had people wearing helmets, carrying massive Nazi flags, or Third Reich flags, whatever you want to call them. There was a lot more paraphernalia.

It looked like a costume party or something. It was weird.[6]

NATALIE ROMERO, SECOND-YEAR UVA STUDENT: There were multiple people with Hitler on T-shirts, swastikas, lots of that. Lots of that.

MELISSA WENDER, STREET MEDIC: There is an industry in Hitler T-shirts. The fact that someone needed to make them and design them and print them and advertise them—and people ordered them and there was more than one and it wasn't hand drawn.

BRIAN MORAN, SECRETARY, VIRGINIA PUBLIC SAFETY AND HOMELAND SECURITY: They were almost like clans of white nationalists, with different banners, different insignia on their banners.

TOM PERRIELLO, COUNTERPROTESTER AND FORMER US CONGRESSMAN: Now keep in mind, there were like six or seven different tribes. They were wearing literally different outfits. You had the preppy boys all in the khakis and the white shirts and the MAGA hats. You had the people in full-on militia gear. You had the people dressed in sort of medieval cosplay.

HEAPHY REPORT: As the groups marched to the southwest entrance of Emancipation Park, the counterprotesters swelled around that area. Market Street was quickly filling up.

LISA DRAINE, LOCAL ACTIVIST: We were right in the middle of where you saw the whole thing kind of devolving. They started fighting each other, throwing things—like you could see bottles, like just flying through the air. It became just this chaotic scene and all, but I was trying to just concentrate on Devin. I was like, *I'm sticking with Devin, I've got his back* and it was that thought of, *I'm a white woman, I can protect this young Black student, I've got you Devin.*

CONSTANCE PAIGE YOUNG, COUNTERPROTESTER: At one point I was standing shoulder-to-shoulder in a sea of Black people. Dozens of Black people. These fascists are walking by and they're screaming at us, into a sea of dozens of Black people, that Jewish privilege exists. And I'm just like, *Why are y'all telling us this?*

This one guy is uncomfortably close to me. And when I think back about it, it's sort of like—this short white man is screaming at this taller Black woman. He's not screaming racist slurs about Black people to me. He's talking about Jewish people to me. And all of this is just ridiculous. It's just absurd and violent.

And I remember just thinking like, *What the hell? What the hell, why are you doing this?* I spent a lot of time trying to really understand these people. Ain't nothing to understand. It's just hateful.

So this was the first time that I really experienced the sheer hatred for Jewish people. And my boyfriend at the time—my ex-boyfriend is a Jewish guy, and I was dating him when all this happened. And so we had some conversations about this afterwards, and I started getting a better understanding. It felt like, as a Black woman, they would just want me dead. They don't want me around. But the feeling that I got that they had about Jewish people was that they were pissed. They were angry, like they had something to prove there. So it was a different kind of hate. And it was the first time that I was learning this. Actually feeling it.

TWEET FROM CHRIS SUAREZ, REPORTER, CHARLOTTESVILLE *DAILY PROGRESS*, 9:46 A.M.: Another column of #unitetheright protesters have arrived.

ZACK WAJSGRAS, FREELANCE PHOTOGRAPHER: A big group of counterprotesters locked arms and formed this huge wall. I turned around and saw [protesters and counterprotesters] walking at each other, and it wasn't a full-on run, but they just collided at one point. People were throwing hands and things were just swinging around and it was very chaotic very quickly after that.

I took a step back and this woman, right in front of me, charged right into the center of the white supremacists. And I got some of the very first, very crisp pictures of the day of them basically grabbing her by her ponytail, slamming her onto the ground, getting right up towards her face and just punching her. These two or three guys just whaled on this woman for a second. And she just got up and kept fighting.

MARCUS MARTIN, COUNTERPROTESTER: I was with [my fiancée] Marissa, Courtney Commander, and Heather Heyer. And then at the same time, I was on probation. I mean, you expected clashes, you expected fights. So every time we got near a neo-Nazi or something like that, we got away from him. Because if I get into a fight, I'm with nothing but women. That's putting them in a bad spot. I couldn't put 'em in danger, or put myself in the line of it and get myself in trouble. So we got away from it.

NATALIE ROMERO, SECOND-YEAR UVA STUDENT: There's a set of steps. And so a lot of [the alt-right] were up there throwing things into the crowd, throwing liquids, canisters, yelling, spitting on people—doing all kinds of stuff. And they had their shields, their signs, their flags, their poles, et cetera.[7] I saw someone, for example, with a hammer—just, walking around with a hammer on their shoulders.[8]

At this intersection, there was a white police car right there blocking the street. There was a group of women alongside the cop car, not covering the whole street, just alongside the police officer's car. When I saw the group of women—there was white women, some older, younger—and I decided to join them at the very end of the line. It was a small line.

When the protesters saw us they're like, *These bitches*, et cetera. They were saying just really rude, ugly things about women.

And they're like, *We don't care*, like, *Run through them.* Like, *It doesn't matter.* Like, *These bitches are in the way.* Other things like that.

Honestly, I'm in this line thinking, *I'm OK. We're a small group of women. They're not going to do anything. Why would they be violent to a group of women that are literally doing nothing?* And especially because I'm in a group of white women. And I'm thinking, I'm a light-skinned Latina. I'm like, *Maybe they won't notice.*

I just didn't—I didn't see a reason why me being in that line would trigger them. But no, they came directly at me and spit on my face and called me really mean things and asked me what the hell I was doing there. And I should go back to where I came from. I'm from this country. I was born here, you know.

And then they pushed me and they threw me against the cop car and they walked past me. They had no reason. No reason at all to even interact with a line of women, because there was plenty of space all around us. There was sidewalk. There was everything. You had so much space to go around. But no, no. I'm spit on. I got spit on by people who hate me and think that I should not be alive and that I threaten their existence.

I'm just trying to go to school, man. I'm just trying to get out of poverty. They were so happy that they ran through women like that for no fucking reason—I'm so sorry for my language, but—and they went around us. I was just in shock.[9]

DON GATHERS, COFOUNDER, CHARLOTTESVILLE BLACK LIVES MATTER: It seemed like every five, six, seven, eight feet, fights were breaking out. It was like a battle scene from a war. Chaotic. It was just unrelenting chaos.

At any moment, at any second, you were aware that gunshots could erupt. At any moment, you didn't know if a grenade was going to be thrown out at your feet, because they had them. You literally didn't know what to expect. But you knew to expect the worst.

CHRIS SUAREZ, REPORTER, CHARLOTTESVILLE *DAILY PROGRESS*: It just was really chaotic. I saw someone throwing the C'ville newspaper stand. I remember seeing guys burning Confederate flags. I remember hearing people talk about like, *Fire the first shot of the race war,* like hearing that phrase.

DEVIN WILLIS, SECOND-YEAR UVA STUDENT: At that point, one of those militia brigade things pulls up. I just remember seeing a bunch of older, bearded men. And I don't remember much about the color of their uniforms, but they were marching in this quasi-military formation, and they're marching directly for our chain, because why go around us, right? And then they charge into the middle of it and we stand pretty strong, but they are grown men and eventually knock everybody down. So I get knocked to the ground. After that, I'm a nonviolent person, so I fled.[10]

SABR LYON, COUNTERPROTESTER: The stuff that people don't talk about that day are the inch-deep neck wounds from sharpened flagpoles and the guy that had the fricking Taser that almost got my friend. One of the people with a neck wound that I saw refused treatment because they didn't want their name to be [recorded]...just wild shit.

BRENNAN GILMORE, COUNTERPROTESTER AND FORMER US FOREIGN SER-
VICE OFFICER: My worst-case scenario that flashed before my eyes was:
Somebody opens fire, and then it just triggers a free-for-all and people start
drawing weapons and no one knows who they're shooting at, no one knows
who's "legitimate" or not.

WHITE NATIONALIST: I'll shoot you. If you want to play that way,
I'll play.[11]

TOM PERRIELLO, COUNTERPROTESTER AND FORMER US CONGRESSMAN: I did
interview a bunch of these [white nationalists]. They were there to start a
war. They were not subtle about it. They were like, *Yeah, we are ready to die.*
Several of 'em said, *We're ready to kill.*

They were looking for a fight. For very legitimate reasons, people—
including myself—were not gonna concede this space to them.

I think it easily could have been a hundred dead that day.

ANDREW BAXTER, CHARLOTTESVILLE FIRE CHIEF: What I think is just incredible is the fact that nobody got shot. I mean, you had fully armed militias
wandering around the city from different political persuasions with AR-15s,
and SKSs, the civilian version of the AK-47, and everything else under the
sun. And there was only one round of fire, and it didn't hit anybody.

This hasn't been said publicly because I'm sure people are afraid to
say it. But some of the restraint that particularly CPD showed—it is not
unreasonable to say that had they engaged, that there would've been a
blood bath.

I know, from talking to individual officers that were there that day, that
they were afraid that if they engaged—I'm not talking about what they were
ordered to do or not ordered to do, but from a moral perspective and an
ethical perspective, they were confronted with a choice. *If I engage with this
guy, and he pulls out his club, I'm pulling out my Taser. And if he pulls out a Taser,
I'm pulling out my sidearm. And if he pulls out a pistol, I'm pulling out my rifle....*
I mean, that's going to happen, right? And the fact that they didn't begin
that forced continuum process probably saved lives. Again, it's a what-if, but
I'm still amazed to this day that nobody got shot.

You're a police officer, you've had the minimum training at the Virginia Training Center in the Shenandoah Valley. You've been on the job what, 18 months? Two years? And you're in a command-and-control system that from day one was broken, and you still make good decisions? That's amazing.

HENRY GRAFF, ANCHOR AND REPORTER, NBC29: I had a conversation with a cop the next day and he was like, *Yeah, Henry, I mean we probably would have shot a lot of people, so there's this balance of when the cops get involved.*

Most local activists didn't see it that way.

DON GATHERS, COFOUNDER, CHARLOTTESVILLE BLACK LIVES MATTER: I just remember, I continuously was muttering, *My God, my God.* And then I became aware of the positioning and the posture of the police. And the fact that they were standing idly by, arms folded, watching all this happen right in front of them. And was taking no action whatsoever. I was thinking, *This is what anarchy looks like. This is the wild, wild West.* It was hard for me to fathom: seeing them doing absolutely nothing. As all this was happening right in front of them.

SABR LYON, COUNTERPROTESTER: There were [police] snipers on the roof all day. Snipers, watching them fuck with us.

ZACK WAJSGRAS, FREELANCE PHOTOGRAPHER: I had the thought of just, *How is this? How were the police on July 8th ready to shut down everything at the first sign of frustration from counterprotesters? And now there's armed people in this park straight up attacking people. People getting mashed up right in front of each other.*

During this street fighting, with no separation between the protesters and counterprotesters, the police stood behind layers of barricades.

HEAPHY REPORT: Charlottesville resident Tanesha Hudson approached police officers standing at the barricade in Zone 2, just above where the clergy and militia were facing each other...she wanted to know why there were no law enforcement officers on the outside of the barricades. Gibson replied, "We got everyone we can out here to keep people safe....They've gone through weeks and weeks of planning to do the best they

can. There's no one in the middle this second. When things
happen, we'll respond."

Hudson was taken aback. "When they happen?" she asked in dis-
belief. "You're supposed to prevent it from happening."

ZACK WAJSGRAS: And the police are just behind three layers deep in fences,
just watching it happen. And people—including journalists on that little
pod on the side, right between the park and the library—were yelling at the
police and being like, *What are y'all doing? When are you going to stop this?*

HEAPHY REPORT: Lieutenant Hatter...ordered his men to back
up from the barricades as tensions rose. In a conversation
recorded by his body camera, Sergeant Larry Jones explained
to officers that extra space would create a "reaction gap" in
case someone came over the barricade.

As Sergeant Jones stood behind the barricades...he remarked
to other officers that the groups should "save their energy,"
as it was not yet 10:00 a.m.

JEFF FOGEL, LAWYER AND ACTIVIST: Some of us started screaming at them,
like, *Do something. You can't just stand there and watch, you gotta do something!*

I remember seeing a bottle come flying, looked like it was gonna hit one
of the troopers and I'm thinking to myself, *Oh great.* Now *they'll react.* It
didn't hit the trooper. And they didn't react.

A. C. THOMPSON, JOURNALIST: At 10:15 a melee erupted. A group of white
supremacists, some with their hands taped up like boxers, punched, kicked,
and choked people who tried to block their path, leaving them bloodied on
the pavement.[12]

DEVIN WILLIS, SECOND-YEAR UVA STUDENT: They're picking fights with
anybody who they can get to. And they are throwing water bottles that are
filled with urine.[13]

MELISSA WENDER, STREET MEDIC: Some people were throwing urine. There
were urine bombs.

DAVID STRAUGHN, LOCAL ACTIVIST: People were asking me like, *Yo, I heard
Antifa was acting the fool and throwing all this shit at people.* It's like, actually that

was the complete opposite. White nationalists threw bags of feces and urine and bottles at *them*. It's really shameful how Antifa was turned into this great big boogeyman through all of this.

HENRY GRAFF, ANCHOR AND REPORTER, NBC29: My boss [David Foky] came down in the middle of it all, because it was getting very unruly and very dangerous, to protect us. He's a 6'5" guy, he's a big dude, a linebacker build.

DAVID FOKY, NEWS DIRECTOR, NBC29: My thinking was that if I was gonna have crews out in the field in the middle of all this, I needed to be out there as well to try and keep an eye on the situation, to try and make sure that they were OK. This wasn't something to try and manage sitting back in an office.

HENRY GRAFF: So he was covering me and shielding me and I was shielding the photographer, who I had a hand on his backpack because stuff was being hurled. I mean, eggs, everything you can think of. They were throwing bottles of piss. What else were they throwing? It was concrete which they would put in a can, is what state police told me at the time. I don't know who started it. It was concrete and you would put it in a Coke can and that was being hurled back and forth too, so hard projectiles coming at ya.

I've never been involved in war. Don't ever wanna be. I hope that's not a representation of what it was, but it seemed like war in downtown Charlottesville.

JEFF FOGEL: I mean, [the white nationalists] just had lost control of their emotions. They'd lost control of some of their physical capacities. That there were people like this in the country, and obviously there were more than just the people that showed up that day, was a very frightening notion.

BRENNAN GILMORE, COUNTERPROTESTER AND FORMER US FOREIGN SERVICE OFFICER: I had been working in conflict areas for about 10 years at that point, in Tanzania, on the Congo conflict. I have been detained by child soldiers at gunpoint before, and had been in areas where there's border shelling. And I would trade anything for not being in mob violence.

DAVID FOKY: If you had said to me, *You're gonna have dozens of people fighting each other with sticks and poles and bottles of water being thrown, and the cops would watch it and do nothing?* Inconceivable, beforehand. Inconceivable in the moment!

I can remember looking at a Charlottesville police officer who was standing there watching all this. And I remember looking at him and going, *What are you guys doing?* And he looked back at me and he just sort of shrugged like they were just as astounded that they were sitting there watching it as we were, and seeing their inaction.

HENRY GRAFF: David and I, we went up to cops and were like, *What are you all doing? These people are beating the crap out of each other!* And they're just looking at you and they can't respond to you for one, because they know I'm the news guy but, two, they're just waiting for orders.

LEGAL OBSERVER TO POLICE, CAPTURED ON BODY CAMERA FOOTAGE: You tear-gassed us last time, what are you doing?[14]

I.B.F., LOCAL ACTIVIST: It almost felt like they were being really vindictive. That was the feeling at that time like, *Oh, you didn't want us to be involved. You thought we were too involved? Now let us just step back and let whatever the hell happen. We're not going to get involved.*

WEDNESDAY BOWIE, COUNTERPROTESTER: It did not feel like just general ill-preparedness, because they had been pretty prepared and very present during the KKK rally [in July]. There was an air of like, *Fuck you guys. You're on your own.*

TOM PERRIELLO, COUNTERPROTESTER AND FORMER US CONGRESSMAN: Look, there's a hockey fight approach sometimes, which is like, you wait for the fight to happen and then you let them let off steam, and then you pull them apart. They weren't doing any of that. I mean, *I* broke up five fights that day. I was using restraining force many times. I am not a particularly big guy. It was mainly just people like me and Brennan Gilmore and others who were just stepping in and having to break up fights and stuff.

REV. SETH WISPELWEY, PASTOR AND COFOUNDER, CONGREGATE C'VILLE: I remember seeing and recognizing—because I mean, I had supported his first run for Congress—Tom Perriello's out there trying to break up fights.

He has a polo shirt on, he's like, *Hey, Hey.* His polo shirt is getting ripped. That stands out to me.

HENRY GRAFF: I remember looking at my boss one time and I was like, *David, how much longer can we do this? I mean, how much longer can this keep happening before...*

Somebody's gotta step in and do something at some point. You know? Like this is getting out of hand. This is getting dangerous. People are bleeding everywhere right now. There's pepper spray everywhere. I'm tired of being Maced, pepper-sprayed.

It's just like, *What are we doing here?*

CHAPTER 12

"It turned into an all-out battle."

CONGREGATION BETH ISRAEL

9 A.M.

ALAN ZIMMERMAN, PRESIDENT, CONGREGATION BETH ISRAEL: You could just hear the commotion a block away, and there were all kinds of just people milling about on the street in front of CBI. Some of them were Antifa people wearing homemade protective gear. Some of them—there were quite a bunch of yuppy-looking guys, who I later learned were neo-Nazis.

So services started and I was pretty nervous and I was standing out in front of the temple with the guard. Forty congregants were inside.

ANIKO BODROGHKOZY, UVA PROFESSOR AND CONGREGATION BETH ISRAEL MEMBER: We had a rather lightly attended regular service. The stained-glass windows of our 1882-built sanctuary obscured any view of the outside.

For me, going to services seemed the absolutely right thing to do on that day. I'd never felt more Jewish. I had planned to join the antiracist/ antifascist counter-demonstrations following services. Even though I'd done nonviolent direct action training the day before and had participated in other sessions that emphasized the threats we would be facing just being downtown, I can't say I felt frightened or imperiled. I don't think I could quite comprehend what was going to happen that day and what a target our synagogue could be.

ALAN ZIMMERMAN: At one point, there were three guys in camouflage gear carrying long rifles standing in front of the synagogue that were making me very nervous. Had they tried to enter, I don't know what I could have done to stop them, but I couldn't take my eyes off them, either. Perhaps the presence of our armed guard deterred them. Perhaps their presence was just a coincidence, and I'm paranoid. I don't know.

Several times, parades of Nazis passed our building, shouting, *There's the synagogue!* followed by chants of *Sieg Heil* and other antisemitic language. Some carried flags with swastikas and other Nazi symbols.

A guy in a white polo shirt walked by the synagogue a few times, arousing suspicion. Was he casing the building, or trying to build up courage to commit a crime? We didn't know. Later, I noticed that the man accused in the automobile terror attack wore the same polo shirt as the man who kept walking by our synagogue; apparently it's the uniform of a white supremacist group. Even now, that gives me a chill.[1]

MIKE SIGNER, CHARLOTTESVILLE MAYOR: People felt like they were being terrorized there, in front of the synagogue.

WEDNESDAY BOWIE, COUNTERPROTESTER: I saw one, exactly one, cop at the synagogue, which...hah...why would you want more than one police officer on scene at a synagogue that has services on the day of a white supremacist rally?

ALAN ZIMMERMAN: A frail, elderly woman approached me Saturday morning as I stood on the steps in front of our sanctuary, crying, to tell me that while she was Roman Catholic, she wanted to stay and watch over the synagogue with us. At one point, she asked, *Why do they hate you?* I had no answer to the question we've been asking ourselves for thousands of years. At least a dozen complete strangers stopped by as we stood in front of the synagogue Saturday to ask if we wanted them to stand with us.[2]

Then I started getting texts. My wife, Nancy, was home and she was texting me going, *Are you okay? Are you all right? It's on the news. It's on CNN. There's fighting going on.* Other people from outside Charlottesville were texting me, going, *What's going on there? Are you all right?*

I went back into the synagogue to make closing announcements at services. I remember it was getting really hot outside. The synagogue was nice and cool. It seemed much more peaceful in there.

ANIKO BODROGHKOZY: Following services, we moved to the modern part of the building for blessings and a bit of challah. The assembly room on the second floor, O'Mansky Hall, has large ceiling-to-floor windows overlooking the street in front of our building's front entrance. I wandered over to look down at the street.

I saw a large contingent of neo-Nazis with poles and flags marching past. One happened to look up. The first thought that went through my mind: *I hope he thinks this is a church.* Our Gothic-revival building has spires topped with fleur-de-lis decoration. From the ground they sort of look like crosses.

RABBI TOM GUTHERZ, CONGREGATION BETH ISRAEL: I did say to people, *Look, you might not want to go out the front door. You might want to go out the back.* Later on, this got construed as Jews sneaking out of their synagogue. We were not sneaking out of our synagogue. It was more of a case of... It's an unstable situation out there. Many people left the synagogue by the front door. I mean, not everybody left by the side door. And the side door was not a back door, it opens onto 3rd Street. It just seemed less conspicuous, and it was uncertain what was going on out in the street.

ANIKO BODROGHKOZY: Rabbi Tom instructed us to exit the building by the back doors and go in groups. I left with my buddy Cora, but we weren't going home. These two middle-aged Jewish ladies were heading out to stand up against the neo-Nazis outside. I kept my Star of David pendant on for the rest of that awful day.

EMILY BLOUT, UVA PROFESSOR AND MAYOR MIKE SIGNER'S WIFE, AT THE EMERGENCY OPERATIONS CENTER AT UVA: I remember being kind of glued to my phone [later in the day] and then getting a text—*We are looking at social media and there's talk about surrounding the synagogue*—that was just horrifying and giving that information to a local police officer. The police officer said, *Where is a synagogue?*

She was surprised that even the synagogue existed and had no idea where it was. And the synagogue was on one of the side roads adjacent to Emancipation Park right there. And that a police officer in the small little city did not know where the synagogue is was just extraordinary, extraordinary by the fact of the ignorance and is really, really concerning. How can they protect us if they don't even know where the synagogue is?

MICHAEL CHEUK, SECRETARY, CHARLOTTESVILLE CLERGY COLLECTIVE: A little bit later I happened to run into Rabbi Tom, who is the lead rabbi at the synagogue, and he said something to the effect of, *Yes. Yes. There is an absolute threat that the synagogue might be damaged or vandalized, burned, whatever. However, we made sure that our people are safe. That's not like slinking away because some members are actually on the streets with the counterprotesters too. So we are not victims.*

TOM BERRY, DIRECTOR OF EMERGENCY MANAGEMENT, UVA MEDICAL CENTER: We were constantly going through a process of getting updates from the ER, from the ICUs, from the operating rooms because it's not like we closed the hospital. I remember that there were stories of patients arriving who were in labor.

JANE MUIR, EMERGENCY ROOM NURSE, UVA MEDICAL CENTER: I remember I didn't have to go to work until 11, which was nice.

I lived very close, but there were so many barricades to get to the hospital that I remember thinking, *Thank God I can walk to work because I have no idea how I would've gotten to work with all of the redirection.*

I had just graduated. I remember being nervous. I mean, every day you were kind of terrified. What kind of mess, what very scary situation am I gonna be dealing with?

But the hospital had also prepared us very well in terms of email correspondence, saying, *Here's what you can expect and here's our plan.* So that kind of alleviated some of my anxiety.

I just remember like every surgeon in this health system was in our emergency room. But at that point it was quiet. There was a lot of people rolling their ankles on the way, walking downtown, people who got in an altercation with somebody, earlier stages of what was unraveling that day. And they were all being cared for in our express care area. So I was bopping around, jumping in and taking care of people who rolled their ankles, and getting them discharged quickly. 'Cause we were told, *You need to get people out immediately. We are discharging everyone from the hospital. You need to get everybody out of this hospital because you need to make beds available.* I remember patients were distressed because we were being very intense with like, *You need to get out, you need to leave, you need to go home.*

Some of the patients were white nationalists.

JANE MUIR: We were trying to be strategic with where we placed certain people. You can't stick someone who is being really rowdy in a hallway next to someone, you know... like this isn't gonna end well for physical and political reasons. So there was some of that happening.

And I remember having conversations with them about where they came from. And I just remember being amazed at all over the country where these people came from.

ANTI-DEFAMATION LEAGUE: Unite the Right drew white supremacists from at least 35 states.[3]

JANE MUIR: I think every clinician has moments where their ethics are challenged as a provider, as a clinician. You're reminded that your job is really to do what's right for them, and that is helping them heal and helping them get the care that they are [entitled] to. And I think that was one of the first instances where I was fighting some of the anger I had about what was happening in our town, what was happening to groups that have been marginalized. And you have that loyalty to your home, to your community. And that was the first kind of taste of that for me, that challenge against my role as a clinician.

JODY REYES, INCIDENT COMMANDER, UVA MEDICAL CENTER: That's where your Hippocratic oath to do no harm, you have to rise above that. And you have to realize that, *I'm not here to make a judgment on it and I'm not here to take sides. I am here to do a job and that is to provide care to anybody who needs it.*

And we talked about that a lot, because I started off the morning when we kicked off and I said, *This is a raw subject for a lot of people and you all likely have visceral feelings about what's happening today, but I implore you, you have to put those aside. We will care for whatever comes in our door and we will care for them as if it was our family member. We'll sort out all the rest later.*

MAYOR MIKE SIGNER, IN HIS CITY HALL OFFICE: City Manager Maurice Jones is sending out these occasional updates to [City] Council on what's happening. Keep in mind, at that point, I can't see from my window what is happening four blocks down, because my office didn't overlook the street. And so I'm kind of absorbing everything through text and through everything I'm watching online. But it was just really disjointed reality. And then he's sending these texts every 20 minutes to Council.

It was clear that there were riots breaking out in the street. I had no idea until later how bad the policing was because I couldn't observe it and there wasn't coverage in the moment. The crisis communications people I was with said, *You need to be over there* [in the command center] *because the whole country is watching this and the city.*

Mayor Signer texted City Manager Maurice Jones to ask again if he could come to the command center.

MIKE SIGNER: And then I said, *I need to be over there.* And then he said, *You can't be over there. There's not room. You can sit in the conference room.* And then I just said, *I'm going to go over there.*

And I marched over there with the two people from Powell Tate [the crisis communications firm] because I thought it was a crisis and that you needed the government. I sent Maurice these very explicit texts where I'm like, *We need to be unified. We need to be on the same page.* And he said, *There's no disunity. There's no problem.*

And then we had this really awkward confrontation at the Wells Fargo building. I walked in past these Virginia State Police. And then I couldn't get in. [Maurice] denied me entry.

EMILY BLOUT, UVA PROFESSOR AND MAYOR MIKE SIGNER'S WIFE: [Mike] and I tried to get in. It was on the eighth floor of this office building and I was just outraged that they would not let us. The city manager said, *You cannot come in.*

MIKE SIGNER: And it was then we had this altercation. I mean, it was very brief. And then I just left and I went over to the other center, the Emergency Operations Center [EOC], which is where the fire chief was, which is where the university president was and some of these other functionaries. Then that was where I was the rest of the afternoon.

ANDREW BAXTER, CHARLOTTESVILLE FIRE CHIEF, AT THE EOC: I can laugh about it now, but at some point, we've got the vice president of the University of Virginia and the president of the University of Virginia walking into that EOC looking at me and [county fire] Chief Dan Eggleston, and saying, *Can you give us an update?* And I'm like, *Hah, absolutely. But don't you think it's odd that the fire chief from the City of Charlottesville is the person who's giving you the update?* I think it's odd! It was messed up.

HENRY GRAFF, ANCHOR AND REPORTER, NBC29, AT EMANCIPATION PARK: It was just a melee for a while. People were beating the crap out of each other in front of you.

DON GATHERS, COFOUNDER, CHARLOTTESVILLE BLACK LIVES MATTER: Everyone had to do any- and everything that they possibly could to defend themselves. We were on our own. There wasn't anything that the city was going to do or going to be able to do to protect us at that point.

EMILY GORCENSKI, LOCAL ACTIVIST: I was like, *OK, this is a fucking shit show.*

ZACK WAJSGRAS, FREELANCE PHOTOGRAPHER: There became this no-man's-land, basically, in the crossroads of the streets near the library. And the white supremacists were on the corner of the park and everybody else was around the side and people were throwing things at each other and then they would get closer at different points and clash.

I found myself up in the bushes on the edge of the actual park in between the fence line where all the rally people were and where all the counterprotesters were. And then people started throwing things. And that was when I got hit with a water bottle filled with someone's urine on my arm. And it just splashed all over me and it smelled disgusting and it was just...But I just didn't really stop and think about it because it was just like, *Well, OK, this is the type of environment we're in right now.*

Zack Wajsgras had only just graduated from college that May. Two days before the rally, he had interviewed for a staff photographer position at the *Daily Progress.*

ZACK WAJSGRAS: And so, that was another huge reason why I decided to come to the rally too. At one point, I was watching these other photographers. I happened to notice this really famous *National Geographic* photographer was there, and I honestly was trying to look to whoever seemed to be the calmest in the situation. He kept running in and he would jump in and then jump out. And I was trying to keep moving like that. And so, I would jump in when they got really close to each other to try to get where the actual point of clash was. And so, I think at one point I just got a little bit too close and someone's metal pipe just bonked me on the top of the head. And I remember just being really stunned by it.

This woman, right in front of me, I saw pass by me. And a man just popped her right in the face. And she just immediately fell down and was just yelling by how much pain she was in.

It turned into an all-out battle multiple times.

TOM PERRIELLO, COUNTERPROTESTER AND FORMER US CONGRESSMAN: I mean, to me, the shocking thing was not that it started that way, but that this went on for like three hours and the police still hadn't moved in.

CIVILIAN SHOUTING AT POLICE BEHIND THE BARRICADE, CAPTURED ON BODY CAMERA FOOTAGE: This is shameful! I am a teacher, I am a community member, take care of your people! What the fuck are you doing?[4]

WEDNESDAY BOWIE, COUNTERPROTESTER: Basically, the cops were hiding behind the Nazis.

HEAPHY REPORT: Chief Thomas's response to the increasing violence on Market Street was disappointingly passive.

Captain Lewis and Chief Thomas's personal assistant Emily Lantz both told us that upon the first signs of open violence on Market Street, Chief Thomas said "let them fight, it will make it easier to declare an unlawful assembly." Thomas did not recall making that statement, though he did confirm that he waited to "see how things played out" before declaring the unlawful assembly.

Regardless of what he said, Chief Thomas's slow-footed response to violence put the safety of all at risk and created indelible images of this chaotic event.

BRIAN MORAN, SECRETARY, VIRGINIA PUBLIC SAFETY AND HOMELAND SECURITY, AT THE COMMAND CENTER: I'm watching this out the sixth-floor window, command center's down the other end of the hall. I'm watching this thing, going back and forth, walking back and forth saying, saying what's going on and what, what, what are we gonna do? And this thing is escalating.

HEAPHY REPORT: At 10:59 a.m., Captain Shifflett relayed to the Command Center that 2nd and Market Street were once again "getting ready to erupt any second now." A moment later, he reported another fight of "about forty people going at it, they're using sticks." He again radioed, "Weapons are being used on Market and 2nd Street." He added, "Recommend unlawful assembly."

BRIAN MORAN: The last thing people need is some politician in the room making decisions, but I'm watching it live. And I'm on the phone with the governor. And I started seeing what appeared to be Molotov cocktails tossed in the air.

TERRY MCAULIFFE, VIRGINIA GOVERNOR: He really, at this point, is feeling that the fighting is getting out of control. That literally someone is gonna pull out a gun. Someone's gonna get killed. It got to a tipping point.

BRIAN MORAN: And I said, *Governor, this has to stop. You gotta call the state of emergency. This is it. This is, this is way out of control.*

And he said, *Call it, do what you need to do. Call the state emergency.*

CHAPTER 13

"Call the state of emergency."

BRIAN MORAN, SECRETARY, VIRGINIA PUBLIC SAFETY AND HOMELAND SE-CURITY: I ran down the other end of the hall, grabbed the superintendent. I said, the governor's called the state of emergency. It's gotta stop. And then we got the police out there [into the streets]. The directions to the police was call the state of emergency.

HENRY GRAFF, ANCHOR AND REPORTER, NBC29: They're on the bullhorn saying it's an unlawful assembly.

DEVIN WILLIS, SECOND-YEAR UVA STUDENT: The police began using megaphones to tell everyone that it was time to leave.[1] When I heard that, I complied. I was ready to go. So I found my friends, and we started heading along Market Street to leave the city.[2]

HENRY GRAFF: As the news trickles out through the crowd everybody's hearing it, understanding it, digesting it.

ALEXIS GRAVELY, SENIOR ASSOCIATE NEWS EDITOR, CAVALIER DAILY: We could hear it on the loudspeakers, but people weren't really dispersing.

HEAPHY REPORT: At almost the exact moment the unlawful assembly order went out, a smoke grenade was deployed by someone at the southeast corner of the Park. The crowd scattered. Overhead,

the VSP helicopter footage showed the smoke tail of the grenade trailing back and forth as demonstrators and counterprotesters picked it up and threw it back at each other. Out of
the pure happenstance of that smoke grenade, much of the crowd
dissipated—for a moment.

ALEXIS GRAVELY: That was the moment where I was like, *Oh my God, I'm
going to get seriously injured here because the crowd just moved.* And I was like, *Am
I going to get trampled by this crowd moving back?*

NICOLE HEMMER, JOURNALIST: Police eventually did move, starting at the
back of the park. They pushed the white nationalists out into the streets,
right into the crowd of antiracist protesters.[3]

DAVID FOKY, NEWS DIRECTOR, NBC29: And now you're like, wait a minute.
You're gonna push this crowd out of Emancipation Park, out into all the
people that they've been fighting with? You have 'em sort of contained in
that park. And now you're telling them they've gotta leave the park?

HEAPHY REPORT: ...the [Virginia State Police] mobile field
force units pushed the Unite the Right protesters right back
onto Market Street, where a larger group of counterprotesters
were waiting for them.

DON GATHERS, COFOUNDER, CHARLOTTESVILLE BLACK LIVES MATTER: You
gotta know what's going to happen when you do that. And we're not split-
ting atoms here or doing stem cell research. You gotta already know what's
going to happen.

BRENNAN GILMORE, COUNTERPROTESTER AND FORMER US FOREIGN SERVICE
OFFICER: It was like kicking this hive of bees.

HEAPHY REPORT: Lieutenant Hatter described the dispersal of
Emancipation Park on August 12 as the "most messed up thing
I ever saw." Hatter noted that the alt-right demonstrators
were screaming at the VSP and CPD officers as the [VSP] mobile field force pushed from the rear of Emancipation Park,
commenting that "you are pushing us right into the crowd."

Hatter agreed with this assessment, noting that the effort was "causing confrontations and pushing [the alt-right] right into their enemies."

BRIAN MORAN: Now you have these thousand white nationalists and counterprotesters roaming the streets. How do you patrol that? How do you enforce safety?

CHRIS SUAREZ, REPORTER, CHARLOTTESVILLE *DAILY PROGRESS*: [The white nationalists] were being all funneled through the corner of the park and it did—I kind of hate to repeat the characterization that the white nationalists used—but they kind of put them through a gauntlet. That is true.

DON GATHERS: Now you got a plethora of nasty fights breaking out. There are those sticks, flagpoles and bats, and anything that you can imagine.

STAR PETERSON, LOCAL ACTIVIST AND STREET MEDIC: A person went up to an officer and said, *The Nazi pulled a gun on me.* And the officer said, *I don't do guns.* I don't know if they were a fucking school cop or some shit or a fucking parking ticket cop. I don't remember who it was, but I just remember someone being told by a cop, *I don't do guns.* Like working at Subway and saying, *I don't do sandwiches.*

I remember looking over one of the barricades down past the library and I saw this white, masc-presenting cop with this red face. And he's just grinning at us. He's just watching people get hurt and fight and doing nothing but grinning. That's the big thing that stuck out to me from that.

HEAPHY REPORT: Lieutenant Jim Mooney related to us how frustrated he and other CPD officers were, having been removed from their zones almost an hour earlier. "We were sitting there with our thumbs up our asses," he told us.

Lieutenant Hatter lamented the fact that there were "people getting hurt, and I'm standing around behind a steel fence." Rather than breaking up fights, he was "guarding an empty parking lot." Hatter commented that CPD should have been in the street, rather than standing around twiddling their thumbs in a secure area of Emancipation Park.

[CPD] Detective Mark Frazier was more critical. He told us that CPD "failed this community" on August 12.

ZACK WAJSGRAS, FREELANCE PHOTOGRAPHER: The line of state troopers marched in or national guardsman or whatever, and dropped a bunch of colored tear gas and things like that. And just told everybody to disperse and leave the park immediately.

DON GATHERS: Tear gas is going off. And let me tell you, that's some nasty stuff. That stays with you for a while. Literally every part of your body burns. And if it hits your eyes and you touch your eyes trying to clear it, that just makes it worse. It cuts off your breath—your pores literally feel like they're on fire. The recommendation is to get milk for your eyes and face. Water over the rest of your body. It is the most unnerving thing which you can imagine happening to you because you literally feel like you're on fire from the inside out. You're choking, you're gasping for air. It's as though, if you can imagine, your body is on fire underwater. You're burning and you're trying to breathe at the same time and none of it is working.

BRENNAN GILMORE: The heat of the day rises, people are more violent when things get hot.

EMILY BLOUT, UVA PROFESSOR AND MAYOR MIKE SIGNER'S WIFE: It's terribly, sweltering hot in Charlottesville in August. It was oppressive heat, oppressive heat.

TOM PERRIELLO, COUNTERPROTESTER AND FORMER US CONGRESSMAN: It was like a hundred degrees out.

ZACK WAJSGRAS: It was blisteringly hot.

BRENNAN GILMORE: It was a hot day.

JODY REYES, INCIDENT COMMANDER, UVA MEDICAL CENTER: It was hot, but it was a beautiful day.

CHRIS SUAREZ: It was very hot, and it was a very clear day too. There weren't any clouds or anything. You can just kind of imagine that mid-August hot day, right around noon.

REV. SETH WISPELWEY, PASTOR AND COFOUNDER, CONGREGATE C'VILLE: The hot sun baking down.

KRISTIN SZAKOS, CHARLOTTESVILLE CITY COUNCILOR: I grew up in Mississippi. I wouldn't notice.

CHRIS SUAREZ TWEET, 12:05 P.M.: Police have taken over Emancipation Park. Seems like reports of a declared unlawful assembly are accurate.[4]

CHRIS SUAREZ: It was just so chaotic. I had no idea what was going to happen next, 'cause it was like—this was still before the thing was supposed to start at noon. So I was like, *Well, I guess it's over?* Like, *What's going to happen next?*

TERRY MCAULIFFE, VIRGINIA GOVERNOR: We cleared the park and then, I'll never forget it, feeling actually, OK, great! This is done. And this melee did not happen.

Of course, a melee did happen. But the governor says he didn't know, based on what he saw on TV.

I.B.F., LOCAL ACTIVIST: It feels like from national news, the rally is over. And I was very resentful because I was like, *That wasn't like—you think it's done? Like the threat is gone? It's not. I don't.*

MARCUS MARTIN, COUNTERPROTESTER: You couldn't just leave. You couldn't just walk away from it. I may not live down here, but I know people that's a part of this community. I work down here. This is how I provide for myself. So it's like, *I'm part of the community too.* So it's like, *You can't allow that to happen. You can't allow people to come up there and just be bullies.* It was like, *Are y'all serious? Like y'all really feel like this? Over a fucking statue?* It's just like, *You're not even* part of here.

LISA DRAINE, LOCAL ACTIVIST: I lost sight of the girls, 'cause I was keeping my eye on Devin. And I get this call from Rebecca, who's like, *Where are you?* And I'm like, *I'm still at, I'm here on Market Street. Where are* you? And they're like, *Oh no, you gotta get out of there. You're gonna get arrested, Mom!*

ELIZABETH SHILLUE, QUAKER ACTIVIST: We were able to get into First United Methodist Church and immediately went out to the back of the church so we could look out. It was incredible. It had turned into a war zone.

REV. PHIL WOODSON, ASSOCIATE PASTOR, FIRST UNITED METHODIST CHURCH: We had rabbis and other people out on the front porch, praying and singing. We had systems and ways to announce lockdowns in the church. And so we pull all people who were outside, we're saying, *The church is locking down. There's a chance. Get inside.* We pull people in, close the doors, we lock it.

REV. BRENDA BROWN-GROOMS, PASTOR, NEW BEGINNINGS CHRISTIAN COMMUNITY: Somebody let loose a canister of, what's that stuff...tear gas, mm-hmm. And then we closed the church's door, but the gas got into the church and everybody was gasping.

MICHAEL CHEUK, SECRETARY, CHARLOTTESVILLE CLERGY COLLECTIVE: I was a little afraid because if somebody came in, we had no escape other than if the windows were able to be open, then we could jump out. I knew that I could easily be targeted as one of the groups that is part of the problem, in terms of the "browning" of America. And, and yet, in terms of my personal experience, I haven't felt and experienced the level of trauma that could really trigger me. I grew up in a generation where my main goal was to assimilate. I came to the states when I was seven, so I really don't have a Chinese accent. I was part of that generation that said, *You come to America, we gotta find you an American name.* My full name is Cheuk Koon Hung. My aunt, who sponsored us, she gave me the name Michael because she did not want me to be incessantly teased when I was in the second grade. So my identity, frankly, was just kind of torn in some ways.

So I want to just acknowledge that there's a large part of me that has been kind of Americanized by white America. I didn't fit into that binary of white and Black. And so in so many ways, I have been spared from many of the kind of systemic racism and some of the microaggressions that my Black brothers and sisters experience.

But, however much that I identify internally as kind of more white sometimes, there's no way getting around that, externally, I'm Chinese all the way. And if somebody has something against Asians, then I'm an easy target.

At this point the clergy activists from Congregate left the safe zone where they had regrouped and headed back into the street.

SMASH CAINE-CONLEY, COFOUNDER, CONGREGATE C'VILLE: We had gotten word that these white nationalist groups were causing chaos and destruction as they were leaving the park. So we started marching back toward the park.

REV. SETH WISPELWEY: And then—I'll never forget this, especially after what happened earlier—we just marched down in our robes and everything, and this huge cheer goes up. People clapping, a lot of antifascists.

SMASH CAINE-CONLEY: It was the wildest thing. I think that moment was really incredible to me because I felt like we had failed, right? We had failed several times already. And to know that people were *for* our presence?

No one else was showing up, right? The police weren't showing up. No one else was showing up at that intersection to help protect people as white nationalists were doing violence. So the people were glad to see us.

So once we were there, we tried to help usher the white nationalists along, tried to step in when they were doing bodily harm to people as they were passing and then created a roadblock there so that they could not come back.

I remember watching a police officer watching a fight and just wondering, *What the hell is going on here?* And I also feel a little torn because we also don't want heavy police involvement or violence anywhere we are. So in a way you're like, *Yeah, please stay away.* But then you're pissed off because the only time they stay away is when white supremacists are doing harm to community members.

HEAPHY REPORT: We asked the command staff why no order was given to send a CPD squad in riot gear or another field force out into the streets. . . . They explained their view that, had officers been sent into the crowd, officers would have been put into a deadly force situation. Colonel Flaherty concurred with that assessment. He explained that he feels that only "fools rush in" to a situation in which they are not adequately protected.

MARCUS MARTIN: I recall a moment where everybody was taking a break. We was sitting down outside a parking garage. We was under a tree. So the next thing everybody was like, *Where's Heather, where's Heather?* And we look up and we seen Heather talking to a person with a helmet on, in a uniform. So we thinking Heather knows this person. So when Heather comes back over there, we actually were like, *Yo, you know 'em?* And then Heather was like, *No.* And then it was like, *So why was you talking to 'em?* She was like, *Just trying to understand like, why they're down here.* And then Heather was like, *Yeah, but I pretty much told 'em how fucking dumb they was.*

TWEET FROM ALLISON WRABEL, REPORTER, *DAILY PROGRESS:* More heading down Market Street. Pepper spray is lingering in the air.[5]

Among the white supremacists marching out of Emancipation Park was James Alex Fields, who earlier had been seen wearing a black shield. As they marched out of the park, they chanted "Jews will not replace us" and "You will not replace us."[6]

DAVID STRAUGHN, LOCAL ACTIVIST: We watched all of the white suprem-acists march down Market Street, away to McIntire Park. Many of them looked despondent and rejected, but I imagine that to always be the face of a white supremacist: wrinkled and sneering, always angry and full of rage. Soon after, we watched Richard Spencer run down the street, surrounded by a security circle of Nazis. The onlookers cheered and screamed as he sped by with his group.[7]

CHUCK MODIANO, REPORTER: Someone on the hill was saying, *Black lives splatter! Black lives splatter! Black lives splatter!* And I'm fumbling for my phone, and by the time I hit the record button, it stopped. And I was like, *Oh, I wish I got that. I wish I got that on video.*

DAVID STRAUGHN: Then the police in riot gear returned, preparing to disperse the crowds still remaining in the street.[8]

SMASH CAINE-CONLEY: That's when the police obviously got really milita-rized. It very quickly turned from a melee and chaos to feeling like we were under occupation by militarized police.

It's really just a surreal experience to see these militarized police march-ing in unison in all these lines, but that's all one side of you. And on the other side of you, there's white nationalist groups with their very large guns. And then next to them are a bunch of local activists in like T-shirts and their

Nikes. We stayed there for a while to kind of make sure that it was safe and that no one was gonna be harmed by the police.

Now all these actors are in the same space and it's kind of like a powder keg, right? You don't know who's gonna set it off, but you know it's gonna get set off.

HEAPHY REPORT: Once Emancipation Park was clear, the violent conflicts spread beyond the park. Small groups of people wandered through the streets and engaged in frequent skirmishes unimpeded by police. Violence erupted at the Market Street parking garage, Justice Park, High Street, the Water Street parking area, and on the Downtown Mall. Police attempted to respond to these violent conflicts, but were too far away and too late to intervene. The result was a period of lawlessness and tension that threatened the safety of the entire community.

The most notorious incident from those tense moments involved a homemade flamethrower and a gunshot. As alt-right demonstrators left the park and turned right to move west down Market Street, they passed by counterprotester Corey Long [who is Black]. Video taken by a bystander shows Long igniting the spray from an aerosol canister and pointing the flames at passing demonstrators.

COREY LONG, COUNTERPROTESTER: I went out to voice my opinion. To have my freedom of speech. Just like the racist Nazis who took over my town.[9]

THE ROOT: Long said the only weapon he had was a can of spray paint that a white supremacist threw at him earlier, so he took a lighter to the spray paint and turned it into a flame thrower. And a photographer snapped the photo.

But inside every photograph is an untold story. If you look closely at Long's picture, there's an elderly white man standing in between Long and his friend. The unknown man was part of the counterprotests, too, but was afraid, and Long and his

friends were trying to protect him. Even though, Long says,
those who were paid to protect the residents of Charlottesville were doing just the opposite.[10]

WEDNESDAY BOWIE, COUNTERPROTESTER: I remember seeing Corey with
his flamethrower and just being like, *Holy fucking shit. This is some wild-ass
shit, huh?*

Seeing a guy, shirtless, holding off Nazis from attacking an elderly man
with a flamethrower—that was one of the most surreal things that I saw
all day.

HEAPHY REPORT: Richard Wilson Preston, a Ku Klux Klan leader
from Maryland, saw this as he exited the park. He drew his
handgun and pointed it at Long while screaming at him to stop.
Preston loaded a round into the chamber of his gun then fired
a single shot at the ground next to Long.

COREY LONG: At first it was peaceful protest. Until someone pointed a gun
at my head. Then the same person pointed it at my foot and shot the
ground.[11]

ZACK WAJSGRAS, FREELANCE PHOTOGRAPHER: At one point, we heard the
gunshot go off and just, no one even seemed to pause. It just, like, happened. And a few people looked at each other and then people just kept
running at each other and the moment moved on.

PASSERBY, CAPTURED ON VIDEO: That was a gunshot![12]

HEAPHY REPORT: [Preston] holstered his gun and walked away.
VSP troopers, identified by their neon yellow vests, stood
in a line behind two barricades about twenty feet away. None
appeared to react.

**After this incident, Corey Long walked down Market Street with
his friend DeAndre Harris, a 20-year-old high school special-
education aide.**

ZACH ROBERTS, PHOTOJOURNALIST: I saw a young African American man
[DeAndre Harris] chased by a bunch of white protesters—saw one with a

red Make America Great Again hat on, a bunch of them in full combat gear, like kind of fake combat gear, wearing helmets and waving batons. They basically chased after him.

HEAPHY REPORT: At about 12:07 p.m., the group [of white suprem-acists] stopped in front of the Market Street garage and a fight broke out.

CHUCK MODIANO, REPORTER: It all happens really, really fast. I'm walking up the street and I hear a bunch of commotion and I hear and I see the white supremacists running back towards the garage. So I immediately turn and run that way. And as I'm running, you know, it's chaotic.

HEAPHY REPORT: From our review of the ample open source video footage of this confrontation, it appears that a counterpro-tester attempted to yank a flag away from a Unite the Right demonstrator who resisted and fought back. During that strug-gle, a second counterprotester named DeAndre Harris rushed in and used a club, possibly a Maglite flashlight, to strike the alt-right demonstrator's head or shoulder. Nearby demonstra-tors rushed over to fight back and deployed pepper spray.

DEANDRE HARRIS, COUNTERPROTESTER: I was here as a counterprotester, but just to voice my opinion about the KKK and white supremacy and things like that. I wasn't out here being violent. I wasn't out here to be violent.[13]

COURT DOCUMENTS: Harris intended to simply attend the counter-protest to show solidarity with those advocating for equality and love over racism and hate.[14]

HEAPHY REPORT: The struggle moved into the parking garage. Harris appears to have tripped or been pushed to the ground, which left him defenseless against a mob of angry alt-right demonstrators that descended upon him with flagsticks, shields, and pieces of wood.

WHITE SUPREMACISTS: "Go, go, go, go, go, go!"[15]

With Long nearby, multiple white supremacists converged on Harris, attacking him with a large wooden plank, a tire thumper, a flagpole, and bare fists.[16]

ZACH ROBERTS: There was probably six to ten people actively trying to attack DeAndre. And he ended up being almost thrown into a parking garage arm and it broke. And then one of the Unite the Right people grab that parking arm and started beating him with it.

DEANDRE HARRIS: I kept falling. I didn't even realize I was being hit at the time. I was just trying to get up and run, but then I fell, then I got up again, then I fell. When your adrenaline is running so high, you don't feel none of it until after the fact.[17]

TWEET FROM CHUCK MODIANO, REPORTER: Fight broke out. Nazis beat black kid w/sticks at end.

COREY LONG: The white supremacists told us to "die, n****r" in the garage.[18]
   The fact was that [photographers] just stood around recording everything. The fact that they didn't help us. . . . It was outrageous.[19]

Only one journalist did: Chuck Modiano kicked one of the men who was on Harris.

CHUCK MODIANO TO WHITE SUPREMACISTS, RECORDED ON VIDEO: "Yo! Yo! Get the fuck out of here! Yo, get the fuck out of here!"

CHUCK MODIANO: I tried to do something. I very feebly tried to kick a guy. I thought I kicked him harder than I did, looking at the video. I'm upset I didn't do more, if being quite honest with you.

ZACH ROBERTS: Chuck's a great guy. He was much, much closer than I was. And basically from that moment, they all kinda scattered.

WHITE SUPREMACIST, RECORDED ON VIDEO: "Yo! Let him up, let him up!"

Long helped Harris get into a stairwell to hide.

COREY LONG: The Nazis tried to force their way into the stairway that we were hiding in.[20]

DEANDRE HARRIS: I got hit in the head and I had to get staples in my head to seal it back up. I broke my wrist right here. I busted my lip. I chipped my tooth. I'm on my knees just getting beat with poles and signs and being kicked and hit. It's crazy.[21]

COURT DOCUMENTS: Harris suffered several physical injuries as a result of the assault, including a spinal injury, broken wrist, chipped tooth, concussion, head wound requiring 10 stitches and other internal injuries.[22]

There was only one law enforcement officer in the garage, who eventually tried to render aid and called an ambulance: Sheriff James Brown, who is Black.

HEAPHY REPORT: Charlottesville Sheriff James Brown was standing outside the CPD headquarters, which is located next to the Market Street garage.

Someone stopped him and said that a Unite the Right member had drawn a firearm, but then Brown heard the sound of heavy sticks hitting the pavement. Sheriff Brown turned and saw Harris being beaten, attempt to get up, and then stumble to the stairwell. Brown went to assist Harris. As he walked towards him, he picked up a 36-inch baton that had been carried by a Unite the Right demonstrator.

Sheriff Brown reached Harris and attempted to render aid in the stairwell. Harris's head had been split open and he was bleeding. He described the scene as "surreal." When Brown looked around, he realized he was the only law enforcement officer in the garage.

At 12:08 p.m., a radio call went out. . . . A few minutes later, the CPD SWAT unit arrived in their Bearcat armored vehicle. Street medics and police officers moved Harris across the street to the alcove in front of NBC29's studio.

WRAL-TV REPORT: Harris said he's alive thanks to a stranger he only knows as Karen.[23]

DEANDRE HARRIS: She talked to me and kept me calm and really kept me awake. I was fading and she woke me up.

HEAPHY REPORT: By 12:28 p.m., paramedics arrived and transported Harris to the triage center at COB McIntire.

ZACH ROBERTS, PHOTOJOURNALIST: I walked down to the street, I saw what I believe is a state trooper, and I was just like, *I just witnessed this* [*assault*]. And I was showing him the photos on the back of my camera and he just shrugged his shoulders and walked away. That was the moment where I'm just like... Here's evidence of a brutal beating by multiple people who are still in the vicinity most likely, 'cause it was like five—maybe not even five minutes afterwards—and the police officer had no interest whatsoever at even looking at the photos!

DEANDRE HARRIS: I was losing so much blood, the people at the hospital told me I was lucky.[24]

TERRY MCAULIFFE, VIRGINIA GOVERNOR: At this point, to be honest with you, it's over. It's done before it started. It had fist fights, but no damage done, no property—nothing set on fire, not a window had broken. Subsequently we did hear a couple of people were hurt. Remember that young Black kid in the parking garage but we, you know, we didn't know that at this point. It's over.

REV. PHIL WOODSON, ASSOCIATE PASTOR, FIRST UNITED METHODIST CHURCH: The police pushed them into the community. And so what we had for hours after that were bands of Nazis roaming through downtown with a lot of north downtown cut off from their access, but a lot of southern downtown, like Friendship Court, where we have a lot of subsidized housing and where a lot of other Black and brown people live and well into Belmont area, it pushed them towards these low-income, predominantly Black neighborhoods and pushed them in that direction.

And so even just the setup of the police was guarding this north down-town, white, single-family housing neighborhood. And so they come this far but no further, but pushed them into the walking mall where people were, and then down towards Friendship Court apartments, and other areas that are predominantly Black and low-income housing in the city.

DAVID STRAUGHN, LOCAL ACTIVIST: This was an attempt to cause harassment and violence at multiple locations. Not just one place in the Downtown Mall. That's another thing where people get it twisted. They thought [the alt-right groups] were all coming to meet together. Oh no. They were com-ing to catch bodies. They were coming to get one. They were like, *Yo, they beatin' Black ass in Charlottesville in August. You wanna roll? Hell fucking yeah!*

That was the point. It wasn't for free speech. It wasn't to meet under-neath the flag and celebrate constitutional rights. No, it was about possibly murdering and beating the shit outta Black people and having the autonomy to do it.

SMASH CAINE-CONLEY, COFOUNDER, CONGREGATE C'VILLE: Then we re-ally just started marching around, particularly downtown as we heard that something was happening in a particular place. We would get some com-munication that there was a white nationalist group in this spot and they were causing some sort of harm or disruption. And we would march in that direction and then we would hear that there would be somebody some-where else. So we would march in that direction, and really just try to put our bodies into places where there could be violence and try to support people with our words or our actions.

DAVID FOKY, NEWS DIRECTOR, NBC29: By and large, it was—we thought it was winding down and we could start putting our stuff together for the six o'clock news.

And then one o'clock came.

CHAPTER 14

"It was like the resistance camp at the end of the world."

HEAPHY REPORT: Many of [the counterprotesters] regrouped at Mc-Guffey Park, where they waited to determine where they should go next.

REV. SETH WISPELWEY, PASTOR AND COFOUNDER, CONGREGATE C'VILLE: Everyone's like, *OK, the streets feel safe enough.* We're all pulling back.

ELIZABETH SINES, UVA LAW STUDENT: When I look back on what happened, this is what I will choose to hold onto; it was the first time I felt at peace. There were no Nazi groups or white supremacists on site—just counterprotesters. It was like the resistance camp at the end of the world.[1]

There was a soft breeze. Balloon bouquets were everywhere, someone had made a papier-mâché statue of Sally Hemings. There was diversity in age, race, gender, and ability.[2]

SMASH CAINE-CONLEY, COFOUNDER, CONGREGATE C'VILLE: There were protest puppets and there was music and there was free food. It was a space of community, a celebration. That was really beautiful to be in and it was a stark contrast to what we had been doing the rest of the day.

NATALIE ROMERO, SECOND-YEAR UVA STUDENT: We were at the park with swing sets, eating oranges and kind of sitting, hanging out, drinking waters. People were just sitting in circles in groups, getting to know each other.[3]

WEDNESDAY BOWIE, COUNTERPROTESTER: I remember I went and got on the swings, because I hadn't been on swings in a really long time, and realizing that the day was ending and that we'd probably be heading home and being surprised that I was still in one piece.

DAVID STRAUGHN, LOCAL ACTIVIST: I remember positioning my bookbag as a pillow, finding a shady spot below a large tree, and lying underneath it. I basked in the glory of the moment.[4] Shit's over.

I thought the day was won. We all did.[5]

CHELSEA ALVARADO, COUNTERPROTESTER: People were just talking, eating food, because there was snacks and stuff.[6]

REV. SETH WISPELWEY: Someone shoved a peanut butter sandwich in my face. I remember having half.

SMASH CAINE-CONLEY: We had been marching throughout the city all day and standing and hadn't slept for awhile. And it was hot. It was August and we're wearing clergy robes.

STAR PETERSON, LOCAL ACTIVIST AND STREET MEDIC: Somebody was there making vegan burritos. I remember telling my friend like, *Oh gosh, they have vegan food*, and being all excited.

SMASH CAINE-CONLEY: I ate a burrito and that was fantastic.

ELIZABETH SINES: A DJ was playing reggae.[7]

Lisa Draine found her daughters in the crowd and they relaxed a bit together.

LISA DRAINE, LOCAL ACTIVIST: We're sort of like, *Wow, I guess it's over.* So eventually I was like, *I'm just hot and tired.* And then I was like, *I think I'm just gonna go on home.* So I left the girls with their friends.

SMASH CAINE-CONLEY: At some point, the clergy left there and went back to [regroup].

EMILY GORCENSKI, LOCAL ACTIVIST: That's when the call for support came.

NATALIE ROMERO: Someone started to let people know that the white nationalists were near Friendship Court, harassing people in that direction.[8]

WEDNESDAY BOWIE: That didn't really mean anything to me, but it was explained that it's a low-income, predominantly Black neighborhood and that it would be really bad if Nazis started shit there.

Friendship Court, often called "Garrett" after its Garrett Street address, is a Section 8 housing development that is home mostly to people of color. It's across the Downtown Mall from McGuffey Park.

STAR PETERSON: They were like, *We're going to send scouts out.* So I was like, *Well, let's fucking go now.* I used to be a fast walker. So I ended up being at the front of that crowd.

DON GATHERS, COFOUNDER, CHARLOTTESVILLE BLACK LIVES MATTER: Through our intel and then from things that they had left behind, we found that they had maps with targeted areas that they planned on going into to wreak havoc. And there were places on some of those maps that, please forgive me, but this is what they called them: they were n*****hoods and we found out that they were planning to head over to Garrett.

NATALIE ROMERO: We were walking towards Friendship Court.[9]

BILL BURKE, COUNTERPROTESTER: We get down there and there were no Nazis around. But there were people who lived there in the place. So some of our people went over and talked with them.

STAR PETERSON: I remember a lot of people coming out of their homes and looking at us. We're told, *Hey. The threat's gone right now.*

BILL BURKE: They decided that a huge group of us being there would probably draw the Nazis [back] to them. So we decided we'd leave a couple of people in the area so that they could run back up the hill and get us if they needed to or whatever.

STAR PETERSON: I remember coming around the corner near where the parking garage is. We could see the Downtown Mall. I remember seeing another group of people. It was clear that they were on our side. And I just remember it being really joyous and lots of celebrating. And the thing was, the Unite the Right rally was shut down. They didn't get to have any of their hate speech. So I just remember it being really joyful. One group was coming down this way and we came up and then merged with them and then all walked together.

The group swelled to a couple hundred counterprotesters.

KATRINA TURNER, LOCAL ACTIVIST: Once we merged together, we just started celebrating and singing and chanting "Black Lives Matter," and just celebrating at that point, because [the white nationalists] had left Friendship Court and everything.

NATALIE ROMERO: It was two groups of people coming together. People were just kind of happy to see each other. Kind of like, *How are you all? Great to see you all.*

Natalie Romero was marching with a group of friends, including Kendall King and Lisa Draine's daughters, Sophie and Rebecca.

KENDALL KING, THIRD-YEAR UVA STUDENT: I just was like, *Oh my God, this is the best moment of the day.*

ZACK WAJSGRAS, FREELANCE PHOTOGRAPHER: At one point, there was a group of people who were dressed as clowns. I have a picture of five people dressed as clowns, just standing on the corner while I was walking past them.

BILL BURKE: It was the most pure, ecstatic joy.

Counterprotester Marcus Martin joined the crowd with his fiancée, Marissa Blair, and friends Heather Heyer and Courtney Commander.

MARCUS MARTIN, COUNTERPROTESTER: We found that big crowd of happy people: cheers, clowns, people singing kumbaya and shit.

ELIZABETH SINES: It felt like we had won: We had taken back our town and protected our people.[10]

EMILY GORCENSKI: Everyone was celebrating, but my thought is like, *We're on a street that's not closed to traffic. The cops are still out. There's National Guard out, got a helicopter flying over us. And we are in a kettle zone. We're not in a good spot.* So we need to get back to the streets that we're allowed to be on and get back to the parks where we're supposed to be. So I'm like, *OK, let's start walking back up to the park.*

ROSIA PARKER, LOCAL ACTIVIST: So that's when we turned around to come back up to the Downtown Mall.

This one particular officer came from just out of nowhere. It's almost like he was an angel. He looked at me and Katrina and he was like, *Don't go down 4th Street, because I'm warning y'all, everywhere that y'all go, it's going to be considered an unlawful entry. Black Lives Matter, y'all are a danger right now, do not go down 4th Street.* So me and Katrina and her son, we looked at each other. We started talking among ourselves and we was like, *We've got to lead these people and make sure we don't go down 4th Street.*

KATRINA TURNER: We got to a spot and didn't know which way to go. And somebody hollered, *Which way do we go?*

ROSIA PARKER: And we was like, *Don't go down 4th Street. Anywhere but 4th Street.*

KATRINA TURNER: And this is what we were trying to tell one of the members of Black Lives Matter: that we were told, *Don't go down 4th street.* But he was the one in charge of the bullhorn and all that. We know he says, *Go ahead, go left.*

ROSIA PARKER: And that was 4th Street.

NATALIE ROMERO: Someone said: *Turn left.* I don't know who. We started making a left.

BILL BURKE: There's a saying in the leftist world, when you don't know, *Always go left.* So we started chanting, *Always go left,* and that's when we decided to turn left and go over Water Street there.

ELIZABETH SINES: 4th Street is pretty narrow, I would say much narrower than an ordinary street. And it's buildings on both sides, so it adds to the feeling of it being pretty narrow.[11]

It was packed. There were a lot of us all in a line, like a big group. So it was a tight squeeze. We had to converge and kind of like—I don't know how to describe it best—take a big group and put it into something smaller.[12]

ZACK WAJSGRAS: Everybody was packed into there and still cheering and stuff. I was going around the edges, but then I just wedged myself right into the center of the crowd in the intersection. Just smack in the middle.

KATRINA TURNER: My son Timmy and another Black Lives Matter member were right there with Heather, walking with Heather.

SUSAN BRO, HEATHER HEYER'S MOTHER: My daughter Heather was wearing black because she was tending bar that afternoon. She worked two, sometimes three jobs, just to live on her own. And she hated to walk in the heat and here it is an August day and she's dressed in black with her full-length hair in a long thick braid because that keeps it under control. But just the fact that my daughter was out there walking tells me how passionate she was about that.[13]

HEAPHY REPORT: The group of several hundred counterprotesters paused for a moment as they decided where to go. Some within the crowd started to move north up 4th Street SE, back towards Justice Park. They maneuvered around two cars that appeared to be stuck at the intersection after having driven south on 4th Street.

Stuck in one of those cars were sisters Tadrint and Micah Washington, 27 and 23 years old. They had heard about the rally but had no plans to get anywhere near it.

TADRINT WASHINGTON: I was coming from a friend's house in Friendship Court. There were a lot of detours that way, which brought me down to Water Street. All the people was right there. We was at a stop sign behind a van. And we got stuck because of the crowd.

ELIZABETH SINES: That was when the car came.[14]

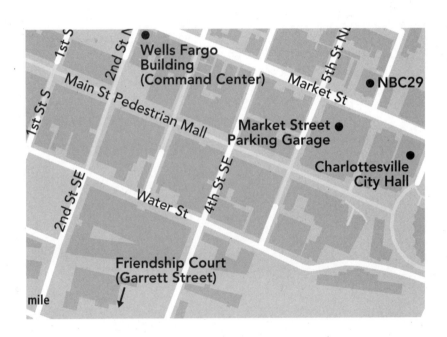

CHAPTER 15

"I heard a car revving."

RYAN KELLY, PHOTOJOURNALIST: I saw the car backing up the hill. I thought nothing of the car. I assumed it was turning around the block to get out of the way and get on wherever he was trying to go. So I started taking some pictures.[1]

MARCUS MARTIN, COUNTERPROTESTER: I was just walking behind Marissa, and I was looking at my phone about to go on live, like let everybody know that *Hey everything's fine. Everything's fine.*

And then I heard the tires screech.

ELIZABETH SINES, UVA LAW STUDENT: You heard it before you saw it.[2]

S.L., COUNTERPROTESTER: I heard a car revving.[3]

BRENNAN GILMORE, COUNTERPROTESTER AND FORMER US FOREIGN SERVICE OFFICER: I heard from behind me, a squeal and acceleration.[4]

WEDNESDAY BOWIE, COUNTERPROTESTER: I was in a space between one parked car and a black pickup truck that was parked, and that was about a car-length's worth. I remember seeing something in the corner of my eye.

BRENNAN GILMORE: When it hit the mall, because there's a big dip there, it slowed for a second. And I remember having this split-second thought, *Oh, he's just . . . This guy's trying to scare this crowd. That's really fucked up.* It was an instant, but then it's no sooner that I had that immediate thought that he then really accelerated and slammed into the crowd.

CONSTANCE PAIGE YOUNG, COUNTERPROTESTER: The only thing that I could think of was, *We're all getting struck. We're about to get struck.* I didn't think, *Jump. Run.* There was nothing there. It was just, *We're about to get struck.*

I remember being consciously aware that this was happening. This was going to happen.

ELIZABETH SINES: In my mind, I can still see it in slow motion. You just see a car fly down the road and hit this large group and crash into a car that had been at the base.[5]

STAR PETERSON, LOCAL ACTIVIST AND STREET MEDIC: I never saw the car coming. So never, ever had a chance to get out of the way.

ELIZABETH SINES: It sounded like if you would take a metal baseball bat and slide it across a wooden fence. Something I'll never forget.[6]

MARCUS MARTIN: I looked up and just see people in the air. So I did what any person would do, I got my loved one out the way. I pushed Marissa out of the way.[7] And then I got hit.

ZACK WAJSGRAS, FREELANCE PHOTOGRAPHER: Just the sound of bodies hitting metal and then very shortly after just piercing screams.

EMILY GORCENSKI, LOCAL ACTIVIST: Thump, thump, thump, thump.

KATRINA TURNER, LOCAL ACTIVIST: Wop, wop, wop, wop.

STAR PETERSON: I just heard three bumps. Two of them were his left tires going over my leg.[8]

DAVID STRAUGHN, LOCAL ACTIVIST: I just see people flying up into the air. People in the air. People on the ground.[9]

KATRINA TURNER: All's we saw was bodies fly. All I saw was people in black. And I didn't know who it was, I didn't know if it could have been my son.

ELIZABETH SINES: I jumped over someone who had been hit who was unconscious on the road.[10]

ROSIA PARKER, LOCAL ACTIVIST: It's a movie. It's a movie, and I'm standing. Right there. And I'm watching how many times when Heather got hit. I'm watching it, looking directly at her, counting how many times that she twirled around in the air and when she hit and rolled off the car, and I'm like, *Oh shit.*

STAR PETERSON: I didn't know Heather Heyer, but I saw this white femme-presenting person flying through the air facing me. Everything slowed down and I remember thinking, *That's what someone's eyes look like when they're dead.*

ROSIA PARKER: Our Care Bears pushed us out the way, so we hit the brick wall.

SABR LYON, COUNTERPROTESTER: There's no time for thought and in the moment I pushed my then-fiancée so hard, I left a hand print on her back. I pushed her hard enough to push my mom out of the street.

TADRINT WASHINGTON, SURVIVOR: Before I know it, my head was in the steering wheel. I remember hitting my head, seeing a lady come over on my windshield.

L.Q., COUNTERPROTESTOR: I did not feel the impact, and I did not feel my legs break as he drove into me. And I was still confused as I flew upside down through the air. Then as he plowed into Tay Washington's car, I heard the cars crashing around me right before I landed on her hood. If she had not been there, I believe I would be dead.[11]

TADRINT WASHINGTON: I'm still in shock. I'm still like, *Am I seeing this or am I not?* Really, to be honest with you, I thought somebody bombed us. My vision wasn't really there because I hit my head so hard.

ZACK WAJSGRAS: Right after it happened, it was just black. My senses were not receiving information.

NATALIE ROMERO, SECOND-YEAR UVA STUDENT: I get hit and the next thing I know is just darkness.

I could hear my heart beating. You know in movies, those war scenes where they were just hit or something, and it's just flashing? I couldn't see too much, but I felt dripping on my face.[12]

KENDALL KING, THIRD-YEAR UVA STUDENT: It smelled terrible, like burning rubber. It was very quiet for one second while everyone figured out what the fuck happened. Then it was absolute, total chaos.

CONSTANCE PAIGE YOUNG: I just remember it felt like there were a thousand pounds tied on my lower body. And I was just grabbing at anybody. Grabbing at anybody to try to...and I remember I had tunnel vision. So, I couldn't see on the sides. I could only see literally what was directly in front of me. And it was almost like I had this vision as if it were in a movie. Nothing, nothing existed. This was just the only thing that my brain was thinking was, *You get the hell out of here. You got to run.*

S.L., COUNTERPROTESTER: The very edge of my thigh made impact with the car and it knocked my feet out from under me, so I landed on my face a few yards from where I had been standing.[13] I knew my face was wet with blood. I was in shock, and I did not know what happened to me. There was a moment I thought I could be dying.

BILL BURKE, COUNTERPROTESTER: Next thing I know I was on the side of the road and there was a girl telling me that my head's bleeding, that I had a cut or a hole in my head, and I was looking at her and the words weren't making any sense. And she took my hand and put it up where my head was bleeding and I tried to stand up and I felt the most excruciating pain I've ever felt before. I mean, instantly took me to my knees and I closed my eyes and I was like, *Oh, man, this is it.*

RYAN KELLY, PHOTOJOURNALIST: I knew immediately that something horrible had happened and I knew it had happened intentionally.[14]

ZACK WAJSGRAS: I was frozen and I took a step back. So, I just was like, *OK, I didn't get hit.*

LISA WOOLFORK, UVA PROFESSOR AND MEMBER OF CHARLOTTESVILLE BLACK LIVES MATTER: I looked up and I saw a shoe, just a shoe floating in the air. And I looked at it and I was like, *What is happening? Is someone throwing shoes? Are people throwing projectiles? What is this?* [Someone] had been hit by the car with such force that his shoe had flown off his body and into the sky about 10 feet.

ELIZABETH SINES, UVA LAW STUDENT: I don't know exactly how we made it over to the side of the road, but we jumped to the right side of the road.[15]

STAR PETERSON, LOCAL ACTIVIST AND STREET MEDIC: The next thing I remember is just being in the street and being like, OK. *I need to get out of the street in case there's more cars coming.* So I tried to move and it was too soon to even feel pain yet. I just registered my right leg doesn't work. So I yelled. Somebody pulled me out of the street and onto the sidewalk.

S.L.: John pulled me up off the street and we ran. Our only choice was pushing up against a brick wall on 4th, John shielding me with his body.[16]

BRENNAN GILMORE, COUNTERPROTESTER AND FORMER US FOREIGN SERVICE OFFICER: I could have reached out and touched his car. I was right next to it. The window was darkly tinted, and I could just see that it was a man with close-cut hair. Couldn't tell much more than that.

The driver was James Alex Fields, the white supremacist seen earlier in Emancipation Park carrying a black shield and chanting "Jews will not replace us" after the unlawful assembly was declared.

WEDNESDAY BOWIE, COUNTERPROTESTER: I just was running towards the car because I could see that there were people on the ground and that people were hurt. I wasn't processing anything. I didn't have any thoughts of like, *This is on purpose.* I just knew that we needed to get to people. And I had a medic. But I got two feet away from the bumper, a foot and a half, two feet away from the bumper, and I saw the reverse lights come on.

S.L.: At that moment Fields slammed his car into reverse.[17]

WEDNESDAY BOWIE: I very clearly remember having the thought, *I'm going to get hit by a car. And I hope this doesn't suck.*

And actually, getting hit by the car did not suck because he was not going very fast when he caught me on his bumper, so that was fine. It was just getting picked up. But I got stuck on his trunk. I was bent in half. I was basically lying on his back windshield with my legs down, and I was like, *Don't go under the wheels. Don't go under the wheels.*

He ended up smashing me into the black truck, into the driver's side door of the black truck, ass first, basically. And because of that, I didn't get run over. But I broke my pelvis.

I'm not sure if it was when I impacted with the truck and my face hit his back windshield or if it was when I impacted with the ground, but at some point, I broke my orbital socket. I think that was the blow that caused me to lose consciousness. I was unconscious when I hit the ground.

SABR LYON, COUNTERPROTESTER: There's this person down with an obvious head wound. My mom goes to grab them out of the road and I see the car starting to back up and I screamed bloody murder. She almost got run over a second time.

ELIZABETH SINES: He started backing over the people that he had hit.[18] That's when the panic really set in for me. It became obvious that he was trying to kill as many people as he could.[19] We started screaming.[20]

DAVID STRAUGHN: That's when everyone starts to scream. I try to scream, but there's no sound that comes outta my mouth.

The car appeared suddenly, right in front of me. A gray Dodge Charger with the windshield smashed, and the bumper torn away from its right side. A man in front of me began whaling on the car with a large stick, bashing out the back window.[21]

S.L.: Despite the confusion, it was clear to both John and I that we were under attack. We felt completely vulnerable and desperately hoped Fields would not veer into us or emerge with a weapon.[22]

TWEETS FROM EMILY GORCENSKI, LOCAL ACTIVIST: After the car hit, I ran through the crowd because I was concerned he might pop out and start shooting. I pulled my weapon—no round was chambered—just in case that happened.[23]

EMILY GORCENSKI: I had done a lot of work mentally to prepare myself for what my limit of violence was and what I would do in those situations. And this was one of those situations where it's like, if there's a possibility of lethal force, I'm going to be willing to defend. So basically, at that point, it was like, *If this guy gets out and tries to shoot somebody, I'm going to try to shoot him.*

BRENNAN GILMORE: So I ran up the street and was shouting, *Go, go get out of this canyon that we're stuck in!*[24]

ELIZABETH SINES: Someone yelled, *Go to the alleys, go to the alleys!*[25]

NATALIE ROMERO, SECOND-YEAR UVA STUDENT: Somebody—I heard someone pull me. I felt someone pull me.[26]

BRENNAN GILMORE: We ducked around the corner.[27]

ELIZABETH SINES: People flocked to the alleys and began climbing ladders and staircases to get to higher ground.[28]

NATALIE ROMERO: I believe that if I hadn't been pulled, he would have run over my legs.[29]

BILL BURKE, COUNTERPROTESTER: I tried to get up and...I was an EMT beforehand. So my first instinct was to kick in and help somebody. And I tried to sit up and I don't even think I made it to my knees, I just went back down and passed out again.

MARCUS MARTIN, COUNTERPROTESTER: I stood up and I stepped on my right leg first and then when I went to go step with my left, like everything just pushed up in my leg and I collapsed and that's when the pain started. My ankle was broken and my tibia was actually really bad: The injury came from my knee, the crack spiraled all the way down my bone.

The medics just start running up to you. And I didn't know where Marissa was. And so when the medic was running up, *Are you OK?* I was just, *Go find her. She's wearing white shirt, blue shorts.* I would say about five, six times they ran up to me, asked me what's wrong. And I told 'em, I gave 'em all the same answer: *Find her.*

And then I heard her voice. Then I laid eyes on her and then that's when I could worry about myself.

KATRINA TURNER, LOCAL ACTIVIST: So after I was pushed out the way of the car, like Rosia said, we got separated. So Rosia was gone. I couldn't find Rosia. I couldn't find my son. And I just get hollering, *Rosia! Timmy? Rosia! Timmy!* I just kept hollering for 'em.

But one of the [activist] security came and said, *We will find Rosia. We will find Timmy, but you have to get to safety right now.* So he took me into an alley and there were other people that had ran into this alley. So he told me, he said, *You'll be safe right here. I'm going to find your son. We're going to get you to him.*

RYAN KELLY, PHOTOJOURNALIST: I actually chased the car, thinking he would get pulled over or get in a wreck or arrested. I thought I would capture that. But none of that happened.[30]

DAVID STRAUGHN, LOCAL ACTIVIST: I chase after the car 'cause I just don't know what to do. It was long out of sight. I ran in futility. I had to do something. I had to do more.[31]

RYAN KELLY: By the time I got up to the cross street, he was long gone. I asked a couple of people who saw what happened, they said he got further than I could have made it.[32]

NATALIE ROMERO: Chaos. Blood. People didn't know what to do. It was terrifying. It was straight out of like—you've seen domestic terrorism before in the news or random places that weren't in my life. That's what that was. That's what it looked like.[33]

TADRINT WASHINGTON, SURVIVOR: I closed my eyes to try to get my vision back because my head was hurting so bad. I just remember kept saying, *What happened, what happened?* And as I'm trying to get my vision back just something struck me: *your little sister. You can't panic.*

MICAH WASHINGTON, SURVIVOR: As soon as I hit the dashboard—for some reason, I always snap into protective mode when crazy things happen. I know she's the older sister, but I'm the one that snaps in protective mode and immediately, I was worried about her. She kept asking, *What happened, what happened?* I'm telling her, *I'm not sure what happened, but we're OK. You're OK. We're OK.*

And at this point I'm not sure what's going on with her because she's laid straight back into her seat, arms by her side and her eyes are closed. She's slightly shaking all over. So at this point I'm really, really scared, but I'm still trying to comfort her saying, *We're OK, it's going to be OK. It's going to be OK.*

TADRINT WASHINGTON: I'm also an EMT. I'd just graduated. We are somehow taught to be prepared for some of these things, but you can't really prepare for these things. So I was trying to remain calm for her, but I don't know how well I did that.

And I just remember when I got myself back together, I started to wiggle my fingers because I wanted to see if my blood was circulating. My finger's moving. I tried to wiggle my toes to make sure my spinal cord wasn't messed up in any way. I still couldn't really see—I had spots in my eyes. So I'm just trying to make sure I'm not bleeding. My extremities are moving.

NATALIE ROMERO, SECOND-YEAR UVA STUDENT: The flashes, the noise. A lot of people are trying to talk to me. A lot of people are trying to keep me awake. I was holding a pole because I—I just wanted to lay down, but I knew if I laid down I would fall asleep. And if I fell asleep, I might not wake up. In trainings we were taught that all the time: *Keep consciousness. Keep your consciousness, because you could die.* So that's what I thought was about to happen. I thought that I was about to die. I was like, *These are my last seconds of breath. I need to call my mom right now.*[34]

CHAPTER 16

"I always wondered: *Was she afraid? Did she see him coming?*"

1:41 P.M.

REV. SETH WISPELWEY, PASTOR AND COFOUNDER, CONGREGATE C'VILLE: At that point I was about a block and a half up Water Street. A restaurant owner who liked what Congregate was about at the time was running Escafe. He was a big fan of what we were doing. And so that had been set aside as a safe space for us, for anyone who wanted to just check in and get a bite maybe.

Escafe was the city's only downtown establishment known for a roaring dance floor. As the only gay bar in downtown Charlottesville, it also served as a safe space not only for queer people in town but also for people of color and others who felt they didn't fit in with the majority.

REV. SETH WISPELWEY: I stood out on the outdoor patio for a smoke, just to catch a breath. We're like, *What's going on? We're going to take stock.* I sat down two, three minutes, halfway done with the smoke and was alone on the patio, and this woman runs up red-faced, hyperventilating, distraught.

At first she's like, *Please help, please come.*

And I was like, *What's going on? Take a seat.*

She's like, *No, no, no, no, no, you need to help.* And I stand up. *You guys have to come down. A car hit a bunch of people. There are bodies everywhere. People are hurt.*

I stick my head in like, *Clergy, we need to go. Hey, Congregate, Clergy, where's Smash?* I said that something's happened—a bunch of people are hurt.

SMASH CAINE-CONLEY, COFOUNDER, CONGREGATE C'VILLE: So I was talking to this reporter. I had my clergy robe open. I'm trying to air out and it's like halfway on.

REV. SETH WISPELWEY: And because we were disciplined, I remember asking Smash for permission, *Is it OK with you if I, and some others, run down?*

SMASH CAINE-CONLEY: I told Seth, I was like, *Go, run, I'm right behind you.*

REV. SETH WISPELWEY: We just started sprinting down Water Street.

DON GATHERS, COFOUNDER, CHARLOTTESVILLE BLACK LIVES MATTER: Seth and I were running together, not imagining what it could have been because we had just left from that area. I just knew I had to get there.

SMASH CAINE-CONLEY: I told the reporter, *I'm really sorry, I have to go.*

I just remember running as much as I could, 'cause I was exhausted. My body honestly felt like it wasn't really working. I don't really have my clergy robe on, it's like flapping through the wind.

REV. SETH WISPELWEY: I remember I can hear the fire engine right on my heels the whole time, getting louder and louder, screaming, and I slowed down just as I came up on 4th Street.

DON GATHERS: And we get there. And when I tell you that it literally looked as though a bomb had been dropped in the middle of that intersection… there were bodies scattered literally everywhere. Blood, bruises, broken bones. It's…. there is just no describing the carnage that existed there.

REV. SETH WISPELWEY: There was blood everywhere. There was a young Black woman just writhing on the ground at the corner of the intersection. There's medics everywhere. There's glass, there's blood.

DON GATHERS: We got there before emergency services did. We got there before the police did.

REV. SETH WISPELWEY: There were people performing CPR on a woman. And right next to them, I just kind of yelled in their ears, *What do you need? How can we help?* And they said, *We need space. We need space. Please help clear the street.*

So we turned around, and at that point more of my Congregate colleagues were catching up, and so we helped clear the road.[1]

SMASH CAINE-CONLEY: We were trying to get people onto those sidewalks because ambulances were on their way and the streets were just filled with people. A really striking moment to me is me and a few other clergy folks are trying to get people onto the sidewalks, and these two guys were just standing there talking to each other, having a normal conversation.

I don't know what they were talking about, but they weren't moving. I screamed at them. I was like, *Get on the sidewalk!* We're trying to move them and people are on the ground dying and they're just having a normal conversation. They eventually got on the sidewalk and looked at me like, *Calm down.* And I—I still remember that. Like, *I can't believe that in that moment you told me to calm down.*

STAR PETERSON, LOCAL ACTIVIST AND STREET MEDIC: When I switch into emergency mode, I'm in "we're taking care of this" mode. Sometimes I get bossy. As I'm laying on the ground, I just started ordering around whoever was near me and I was like, *OK. There's a phone in the front pouch. Open the front pouch and go to such and such and tell them that we need an ambulance here.* Because I knew that we needed to alert the core medics so everybody could find out, and obviously we needed EMS. But I wasn't at all, I don't think, aware of—I don't know, the amount of damage or whatever, or that my leg had been crushed. All I knew was my leg didn't work when I tried to get out of the street.

At some point, medics jumped in, got my head in a safe place, had me on my back. And a friend from earlier that day was there just standing over me, looking really concerned. And I was like, *I need to see someone's face. I need you to stay there so I can see your face.*

TADRINT WASHINGTON, SURVIVOR: We were still in the car. I remember my sister just asking me, *Are you OK, we going to be fine?* And what she's seeing and what I'm seeing it's not the same thing because I'm on this side of the car. And basically when I pull myself back together, she was just like, *Tay, they trying to resuscitate some woman over here.*

MICAH WASHINGTON, SURVIVOR: I'm looking outside. It was almost surreal. I would've never expected to see someone coming down my sister's windshield, to look back in the rear and see EMTs fighting as hard as they can to revive someone. I mean, as hard as they can. I could see the intensity, the passion that they had behind trying to bring this woman back.

TADRINT WASHINGTON: I didn't see the woman on the other side, which we later learned was Heather—I didn't see her but Micah did. And she's like, *They're having trouble,* because I guess she can see them really trying to save her. And she's like, *How bad are you hurt? Can you go try to help them?* And me being the person that I am, I was willing...I wanted to go help this lady but my legs was so messed up because I guess I hit the dashboard or whatever, that I couldn't really move.

ROSIA PARKER, LOCAL ACTIVIST: I'm trying to help the lady in the silver car, which her legs went up under the steering wheel. So I went from being a victim to survivor now.

So her legs, I'm trying to get her out of this car and her legs are pinned up under the steering wheel. We're trying to help them get out the car and we can't get them out of the car. There is no police, no nothing out there. So everybody's hollering.

So by this time, I see my daughter out there. And so my daughter looks and she was like, *Oh my God, Heather!* 'Cause my daughter knew Heather. So we start hollering for medics. They tried to do CPR.

BILL BURKE, COUNTERPROTESTER: I was going in and out of consciousness. And one time when I woke up, they were doing CPR on Heather Heyer. I was right on top of her. My head was right on top of her chest. And they were doing CPR on her, and I was trying to count how many repetitions they were doing on her to try to stay awake. And I remember counting 29, and that was the last number and I was out again.

HEAPHY REPORT: Ms. Heyer succumbed to her injuries at the scene. Chief Baxter told us that she had already died when CFD

[Charlottesville Fire Department] arrived, but given the raw
emotions of the crowd fire fighters continued to perform CPR
on her.

ANDREW BAXTER, CHARLOTTESVILLE FIRE CHIEF: People that are in cardiac
arrest when we arrive on the scene, who've died from blunt trauma, don't
survive. Heather Heyer's already passed away. In a mass casually incident, the
correct thing to do is to write this patient off. That's what triage is: We're
going to try and save some other people's lives.

But the first-to officer makes a decision. He read the tenor of the
crowd. He said, *We're working this*, meaning we're going to do CPR and
whatnot.

I talked to him at length afterwards and I think it really was a conscious
decision on his part. And the ability to make that decision and do that,
where you've got these street medic folks and law enforcement folks trying
to help from various agencies, and the chaos of that scene, that's like PhD
level responder stuff right there. Just amazing.

SUSAN BRO, HEATHER HEYER'S MOTHER: I always wondered: *Was she afraid?
Did she see him coming?* She was deaf in one ear, so...

KENDALL KING, THIRD-YEAR UVA STUDENT: My buddy and I knew, *OK, we
have friends who are ahead of us*. We found Sophie, and Sophie's sister Rebecca
was like, *I've got her. You get Natalie*. So we picked Natalie up, just 'cause it
was like total fucking chaos. At this point I was extremely distraught. I was
not well. And my buddy, thank God, had a much more level head and was
basically just like, *Kendall, call an ambulance and tell them, tell them to meet us
at the Market Street parking garage*, 'cause we had to get out of there. I mean,
Heather Heyer was going through CPR right next to us and we were just
like, *This is so horrible*. Like we can't have this person who's bleeding a lot and
very delirious also be swarmed and stormed by all of these fucking reporters,
who just have these big-ass cameras in our face. I was like, this is absolutely
absurd. You're in the way of us trying to get out. And I got so angry at the
reporters. 'Cause I was like, *This is my friend and she is really badly hurt and she
looks horrible. Like she looks like she's gonna die. And if you take another picture of
her, I'm gonna kill you.*

But basically as fast as we could—'cause there were so many reporters trying to take pictures of us and literally in our way—my buddy picked up Nat, I called the ambulance.

NATALIE ROMERO, SECOND-YEAR UVA STUDENT: They were like, *We need to take you to the ambulance.* But the ambulance wouldn't be able to make its way towards me. Because there was people on the ground and stuff. And I couldn't walk. So I had both arms on people's shoulders and they took me.

We were walking past people. I could see the ambulance. Once they grabbed me and sat me down, I lost consciousness then.[2]

DON GATHERS, COFOUNDER, CHARLOTTESVILLE BLACK LIVES MATTER: The adrenaline is still pumping through you. You're aware of your surroundings, but it's like you're outside of yourself, looking back at yourself. As weird as that might sound.

It was then that I saw that...I stood right there on the corner where the paramedics were working on Heather. Working as feverishly and as delicately as they can. Or as they could. And I know it sounds over-the-top, but I literally saw the life leave her body. There just wasn't anything that they could do...

I think it was at that point, it was at that moment that I think all the fight left my body. I just didn't have anything left.

WEDNESDAY BOWIE, COUNTERPROTESTER: I was basically in the middle of the street when I landed and I was unconscious, and some people dragged me back so that I was out of the street a little bit. And when they sat me up is when my memory from the day kicks back in.

Because I remember I said, *My legs won't move. Something's broken. My hip's broken.* And I remember seeing the face of one of my friends that I had driven with. One of my friends had also run at the car with me. And so, I was very concerned that they had also been hit by the car. I was screaming for them. And then my other friend was freaking out and she's calling my husband at the time. Thank God she had his number because my phone got smashed.

Oh, also my can of Mace that was in my backpack exploded. I also got Maced while I was getting hit by a car.

REV. SETH WISPELWEY, PASTOR AND COFOUNDER, CONGREGATE C'VILLE: All of a sudden I hear, *Father, this woman needs help.* And he's looking at me and I guess mistakes me for a Catholic priest. And he just pushes this young woman into my arms, who's kind of falling down sobbing and everything. She had just seen Heather Heyer die and everything. I just hold her for a bit.

ELIZABETH SINES, UVA LAW STUDENT: Not long after, a truck pulled up and no one knew if this was another vehicle—if that was part of an organized attack. All we could do was run. It was awful. People were lying in the streets. People were bleeding. People were having panic attacks.[3]

ROSIA PARKER, LOCAL ACTIVIST: It's like a movie, that this shit really—excuse my French but like—this shit really fucking happened. And you're standing there. You don't know if you're pissing, shitting or . . . like you're in complete . . .

KATRINA TURNER, LOCAL ACTIVIST: Shock.

ROSIA PARKER: Yeah, and you might not even call it shock. It was just so much.

ELIZABETH SINES: You saw people trying to shield people receiving medical treatment with their banners.[4]

TWEET FROM ALLISON WRABEL, REPORTER, *DAILY PROGRESS*, 1:46 P.M.:
Injured people are limping down Water Street.[5]

ROSIA PARKER: We knew we weren't supposed to go up that street. And to go up that street anyway and everything that took place on that street? It's almost like for me—I feel responsible. I still hold myself accountable for the actions.

BRENNAN GILMORE, COUNTERPROTESTER AND FORMER US FOREIGN SERVICE OFFICER: At that point I thought there were probably a dozen people dead. It had just been bodies, bodies, bodies. And the speed at which—the violence of the incident—I thought there were probably a lot of dead people there.

There's no other explanation for what I just witnessed than an intentional attack on these people. During the summer, as I had dug more into this movement, I had started seeing these memes about Black Lives Splatter, and how to trick out your car to better run over protesters. And this was something that was on social media. Even people I knew, conservative class-mates from high school and folks that I did fishing tournaments with and stuff, were posting these jokes on Facebook based just about running over protestors.

So, I remember at some point right in the aftermath, thinking, *One of these guys has seen these memes and decided to be the one to do it.*

CHAPTER 17

"Where were the cops? How did this happen?"

EMERGENCY OPERATIONS CENTER
UNIVERSITY OF VIRGINIA
1:41 P.M.

MIKE SIGNER, CHARLOTTESVILLE MAYOR: There was a big conference room where they had these tables arranged, sort of like a U. And there were probably 20 people seated with laptops around them, and they had a big monitor, a screen where live feeds were being projected.

ALLEN GROVES, UVA DEAN OF STUDENTS: We were essentially using other people's Facebook and Twitter feeds of what was happening to watch this. We see Heather Heyer and everyone hit by the car.

MIKE SIGNER: I had been working in this separate room across the hall from there. I literally heard somebody scream. And then I came in and somebody said, *There's been a car attack.*

EMILY BLOUT, UVA PROFESSOR AND MAYOR MIKE SIGNER'S WIFE: A man on the phone in this operation center screaming out, *Mass casualty event. We have a mass casualty event.* And everyone just absolutely froze. Everyone there froze. And it was everything that we were worried about.

MIKE SIGNER: And then I sat down and I watched the video wherever it was being played. And it was so horrifying.

My very first instinct was that it had to have been an accident. Somebody like an elderly person, who had fallen asleep or had had a spasm, or...

I looked at the video a few more times. And then it was so clear that it was intentional.

BRIAN MORAN, SECRETARY, VIRGINIA PUBLIC SAFETY AND HOMELAND SECURITY: Then I called the governor.

TERRY MCAULIFFE, VIRGINIA GOVERNOR: He said, *Are you sitting down?* And I said, *Yeah I'm sitting down and watching the TV.*

BRIAN MORAN: I said that the unspeakable has happened—that guy's driven into a crowd. There's gonna be...we don't know the extent of it, but you can...the speed that he drove. I mean, it...it's gonna be bad.

TERRY MCAULIFFE: We did know that a lot of people had been hurt.

ANDREW BAXTER, CHARLOTTESVILLE FIRE CHIEF: One of the things we realized very, very quickly: We need to gain control of the emotional state of this room. Someone had slapped some of the video up onto the big screen in the front of the room. And I went to the IT guy and I said, *Turn that off. Because now we're just watching people's trauma, and we need to be in a position to make decisions, and that's not informing our decision making. It's just trauma for us. So we need to*...And we turned the lights down.

Then I got the group together and said, *OK, this is a horrible event. We plan for this. Folks are executing the plan. Let's contact the people that you're responsible for, make sure they have everything they need. If there's critical information you think we need to know at an executive level, please make sure it gets up.* And then the room kind of calmed down.

NBC29 STATION
DOWNTOWN CHARLOTTESVILLE
1:41 P.M.

DAVID FOKY, NEWS DIRECTOR, NBC29: We heard over the scanners that there had been protesters hit by a car, and it was literally a couple of blocks from the station.

HENRY GRAFF, ANCHOR AND REPORTER, NBC29: We hear on the scanner, *Mass casualty incident.* Myself and a photographer went running out the door.

DAVID FOKY: I didn't run—I have bad knees—but I moved as quickly as I could. I was down there fairly quickly 'cause I remember watching CPR being performed on one of the people that had been hit.

HENRY GRAFF: I watched them do CPR on Heather Heyer, who died. I remember calling work and talked to a boss who was like, *You've never sounded so shook before in my life.*

We were so close. We got down there before a lot of police and medics were able to. It was just—I mean it was a lot of bodies everywhere.

I remember interviewing people and I was asking them, *Are you sure this wasn't some scared senior citizen or someone who just got spooked or someone who just didn't know what was going on?*

And people were like, *No, this was very deliberate. The person, they like backed up, they rammed,* and it was like, *God, how could this happen here?*

TIM DODSON, MANAGING EDITOR, *CAVALIER DAILY*: Suddenly, now that a car attack had happened, police seemed interested in trying to control the situation.

ZACK WAJSGRAS, FREELANCE PHOTOGRAPHER: The first thing that arrived, of course, was a giant armor-clad vehicle with a dude with the big gun hanging out the top of it. So, not the most reassuring thing at first.

SMASH CAINE-CONLEY, COFOUNDER, CONGREGATE C'VILLE: All of a sudden, police roll in with a tank and try to get everyone out of the way. It's just heart wrenching and enraging.

EMILY GORCENSKI, LOCAL ACTIVIST: I was trying to get people off the street, trying to clear the way so that the ambulance could come. And so then what did the police do? They bring a fucking Bearcat.

HEAPHY REPORT: The CPD SWAT team drove the armored Bearcat vehicle down 4th Street to secure the roadway north of the injured counterprotesters.

WEDNESDAY BOWIE, COUNTERPROTESTER: It was just a couple of feet away from me. And I remember there was a guy out the top of that vehicle and

he was pointing a freaking gun into the crowd. And I remember just like...
I was just absolutely flipping my total shit at him. I was screaming. And any
cop that came near me, I was just like, *You motherfuckers!* Blocking the closest
access for an ambulance to get to me.

EMILY GORCENSKI: I wanted a fucking ambulance. I wanted them to bring
everything you've got. Because, I knew that they [the police] had ambulances up there. I knew that they had these little John Deere gators, these
four- or six-wheel carts with medical aid. I knew that police should have
first responder training. Fucking get people here that could help save lives!

SMASH CAINE-CONLEY: The presence of a tank and the presence of aggressive
police officers is not what you need when you've just experienced a horrific
crisis. It was really jarring for folks and I think really traumatic for folks, and
just added to the layers of trauma that folks were already experiencing.

I guess it was a crime scene, so they're trying to clear it out and preserve
it perhaps.

SABR LYON, COUNTERPROTESTER: Guns pointed at us, tanks right behind
them. They have a big-ass torpedo-looking motherfucker, pointing at my
mother and my fiancée and this head-wound victim.

And my friend who was with us, he's a Black man and he's got a gun
pointed at him and he's just emphatically trying to talk to this guy, like,
Why are you pointing this gun at us? Why are you pointing it at us? and just the
obvious reasonable emotional response to this.

So I stand in between the gun, looking this officer in the face and I'm
like, *This man behind me is my brother. He is a human being. He is my dear, dear
friend. He is just going to talk to you.* I said, *He is not going to put his hands on
you. He is just going to talk to you. We are upset. That is a reasonable thing to be
in this situation, don't you think?*

And the guy looked a little surprised that I asked his opinion. And I was
like, *Don't you think that being upset right now is reasonable?* I repeated myself.
This part of the day is the most ingrained in my head.

He kind of looked around and was like, *Yeah.*

I was like, *I understand that you have to come in, so that the ambulance can
come in, because you don't know if there are enemy forces here.* I'm talking to him
like we're in a battle, because we are, right? I'm like, *I'm aware you have to*

secure the hospital people, like the true EMS people. I get that, but can you put your
gun back up and let this man talk at you?

And he was like, *OK.*

And I was like, *Fine.*

And I stepped back and I looked at my friend and I was like, *Keep talking*
at him, he's open now. I connected to this man. I think you can too.

And that gave me this idea in this moment. It's just chaos. People are
screaming, there's crying, and again, in this moment my brain goes into this
hyper focus of: What am I able to do now?

Well, the people that are injured are taken care of. So I just start going
down the line of these [police officers]. They're taught to stand apart or
whatever, and you just go from one to the next to the next and I just con-
nect with them.

I understand that this whole "humanize me" thing doesn't change anything, but it plants a seed. There's this little seed: *I'm human like you.* So one
guy I actually got to tear up, which was one of the things I'm proudest of
in my life.

MELISSA WENDER, STREET MEDIC: We hear people shouting, *Medic!* There's
chaos, there's screaming. And we do not know what's happened. We heard
something about a car crash. We come upon this young woman, maybe 20
years old, who something's happened to her leg, she's crying, she's got a
friend with her, and we decide to help her. When we start to take out our
scissors to cut off her leggings, she's like, *Oh no, don't cut off my leggings.* You
know, like she likes those leggings. So we started to try to pull her leggings
up and it obviously hurt her a real lot. And she's like, *Cut them.*

Her friend is with her this whole time. And at some point we turn our
attention to the friend who's in a sort of panicky way. And she's so worried
about her friend and her friend's leg. We're like, *Are you OK? She's like, yeah,*
I hit my head, but I'm fine. And then we look at her and she has blood coming
from her nose.

Which like, OK, you possibly have a head injury. We talk with her about
the unlikely situation that she could have had an internal bleed or something
like that. And she decides to go be checked out by the hospital, which I
think makes sense.

Then we find out that Star, who I had just run with the night before— her leg was seriously, seriously crushed.

WEDNESDAY BOWIE: I waited quite a while for an ambulance because they were getting other people that were closer to the scene first. I don't know if they even knew I was there for a while. But I was actually . . . My femoral artery had been damaged when my pelvis broke, so I was actually bleeding out internally.

I remember, they put me on a stretcher finally, and they rolled me down the street and somebody got a picture of that. And it ended up everywhere, on CNN and stuff. And that's actually how my parents found out I was in Charlottesville. My mom's best friend since kindergarten, her daughter's husband saw that on the news and said, *Amy, call Marjorie.*

TADRINT WASHINGTON, SURVIVOR: And at that point, I think so much time went by I couldn't even tell you exactly the time. But I just know we sitting there a while and I started to get really, really hot. And I'm starting to realize what's going on and I see all these people around me trying to save people. And I still didn't know how we got in the situation, but I just know it's a lot of people everywhere, screaming. It's a lot of people hurt. And I just remember a couple EMTs coming to me and this one Samaritan—I don't know her name, she wasn't from Virginia, but she was an EMT. And she stayed there with me for a while before a Virginia EMT came.

And when they came, they checked me over. I told them I wasn't bleeding or anything. I told them I guess my legs is really screwed. And they helped me out the car into the ambulance.

WEDNESDAY BOWIE: I remember getting put in the ambulance, and they were putting multiple people in at a time. And I remember there was one person in the ambulance who was a man, and I was really worried about him because he kept saying his name.

STAR PETERSON, LOCAL ACTIVIST AND STREET MEDIC: I remember the ambulances being double stacked, which is fucking creepy. Again, I couldn't see much. They put the real neck brace on me. And honestly, the medics saved my ability to walk by having me supported and immobilized there because I found out later I had two broken parts of my back. And about

25 percent of paralysis actually happens after an incident when the broken parts of your spine cut your spinal cord. So very grateful that they had me immobilized until the ambulance got there.

And then they popped me in the ambulance. I can't look anywhere but up, but I remember, I think I asked for something for pain. I remember just spelling out my legal name very—I don't know—robotically maybe, or just clearly.

BILL BURKE, COUNTERPROTESTER: I remember being in the ambulance and there was a young Black kid, a brand new EMT. And the paramedic was telling him what to do and he was hesitant. And he said, *I'm afraid I'm going to hurt him.* And I said, *Bro, everything hurts. Ain't nothing going to hurt me more.* I said, *Just do what you got to do, man. I'm OK.*

HEAPHY REPORT: EMS personnel classified the injuries according to severity and prioritized transport to hospitals accordingly. Seventeen required hospitalization, and all 17 were transported to hospitals...

DAVID FOKY, NEWS DIRECTOR, NBC29: I was seeing a lot of people who had been hurt. I was seeing a lot of angry people. *I'm* angry that this had happened. I was seeing emergency crews responding. And then people wanting to tell us the stories of what they had seen. And, *Where were the cops? Where were the cops? How did this happen?* Just anger and frustration and fear and confusion. All of the things that you can imagine in a situation like that, just on such clear display.

That's when I ran into Don Gathers.

DON GATHERS, COFOUNDER, CHARLOTTESVILLE BLACK LIVES MATTER: I began to walk up Water Street. Just done. Spent. Head bowed, shoulders slumped, tears just streaming out of me. And I remember, very distinctly—and I will never forget this, this stands out in that day as much as anything—someone grabbing me and just holding me and squeezing me. And whispering in my ear, *Don, you can't give up. You can't stop.* And that somebody was my friend David Foky, the news director over at 29.

He just held me and squeezed me and just told me, *You can't give up. You can't.*

DAVID FOKY: I'd known Don for a couple of years and he was so clearly upset that, without asking, I just embraced him. I couldn't think of anything to do that was a better decision in the moment, than to give him a hug and let him know that he wasn't alone in this.

Don is such an important person in this community. That he was talking about he didn't think that he could go on doing this anymore, that would be a tragedy—if he stopped fighting for what he believed in because of this. And we talked about that, just the two of us. There were so many people around, but in that moment, it was just the two of us.

DON GATHERS: And after that, I kind of got myself together. We got reports and calls that some of the Nazis were on the mall and were threatening some of the businesses. So you had to just put your big boy underwear on again and go back to work.

UVA MEDICAL CENTER
1:41 P.M.

JODY REYES, INCIDENT COMMANDER, UVA MEDICAL CENTER, IN THE HOS-PITAL COMMAND CENTER: We were all watching these Periscope things. We watched it in real time. We were only a mile away.

JANE MUIR, EMERGENCY ROOM NURSE, UVA MEDICAL CENTER, IN THE ER: I just remember the charge nurse getting the call, like, *OK, now we're having a mass casualty incident. A car ran through the crowd.* She was so calm and then the rest of us being like, *This is gonna be something . . .*

JODY REYES: If you're panicked, people are going to lose faith. They're gonna lose confidence. So, you gotta watch some idiot drive a car into a crowd of people. I don't have time to sit there and think about how horrible that is. You have to say, *OK. And now what, how are we going to react?* We had no idea how many people were hurt. It could have been 15 people dead as fast as he was going.

JANE MUIR: You don't even know how many people are coming. That's the scariest part. And I was newer. So that was very frightening.

Then people started mobilizing and coming up with, *This room is gonna be for this person, that we name this.* All the people who are traumas have a name designation that's a country. So like Bosnia, or whatever. So, they started writing: like, here's the room and here are gonna be these people coming up with a plan.

TOM BERRY, DIRECTOR OF EMERGENCY MANAGEMENT, UVA MEDICAL CENTER: We went into our mass casualty protocol. The ER—because it's a teaching hospital, it's just not practicing MDs and RNs. There were also a lot of students all the time. And so that's what really made it so crowded within the ER. But all I remember is the images of trauma teams that were preparing to receive patients into the trauma rooms, within the ER operating rooms. I think just the energy is what I remember most.

JANE MUIR: We all had prepared for which rooms we were gonna be in. They were prepared for so many patients, that there were like four of us in a room [including only two nurses].

Muir was used to more medical professionals responding to a trauma case, especially more nurses.

JANE MUIR: And I remember that being kind of scary, like, *Am I gonna be able to do everything with my other nurse?*

And then you don't know what the injuries are gonna be. So you have to basically pull out all the resources that you have. We have a trauma cart—if you've cracked the cart, that [means] it's potentially gonna be something severe, because the trauma cart is to place arterial lines, give rapid blood, put central lines in, basically get some surgical things started.

I remember in the room, the surgeon at the head of the bed saying, *This is like every other patient we've had, this is no different from any other situation we've had, we're gonna do what we always do. They're gonna come in, we're gonna assess their airway. We're gonna be methodical. We're gonna do good communication. It's no different from how we usually work together.* And I remember that being very grounding and important because it was scary.

HEAPHY REPORT: Those taken to UVa were admitted through the main lobby, where the treatment teams were standing by according to plan. The speed of the response is particularly impressive given the large number of people crowded at the scene of the homicide.

JODY REYES: So again, you gotta think about logistics. You gotta think about how things happen. If you need to have 10 ambulances coming in all at the same time, you're not gonna do that through the emergency department opening, right? The doors are not made for that. So we rerouted all the ambulances to come through the front door.

STAR PETERSON, LOCAL ACTIVIST AND STREET MEDIC: The next memory I have is being in the ER.

MARCUS MARTIN, COUNTERPROTESTER: When we got to the hospital, they wouldn't let Marissa come back there with me. I kind of got a attitude about that, *Like, what? Nah, she's coming with me with like, what the fuck y'all talk about.* And then they wouldn't allow her to come. So they put her in a room.

Then Marissa overheard some cops talking and was like, *One girl died.* And then that's when they told Marissa it was Heather. And then, and then Marissa texted me: Heather died.

STAR PETERSON: Some police officer asked for permission to speak with me and I remember the nurse or whoever just being like, *Two minutes*, and they asked me what the car looked like.

I was like, *I don't know. I just remember seeing a truck when I was down on the ground.*

Marcus Martin says another police officer came into his room and asked to take his clothes as evidence.

MARCUS MARTIN: She was being a dickhead. She literally told me to take off my clothes and I'm looking at her like, *Are you serious right now?* Like, *Will you look at my fucking leg like a bent-up paper clip? And you really want me to take my clothes off right now?* I was like, *Ma'am, can you please just get out? Just leave me alone.*

Marcus Martin says the police officer told him she'd just go get a warrant if he refused to hand over his clothes.

MARCUS MARTIN: And then when she said that, I kind of let her have it. Like, *Look lady, you need to get the fuck outta my face. I just literally got hit by a fucking car.*

STAR PETERSON: I remember asking, *Am I going to be able to walk again? Am I going to be paralyzed?* And I had no idea who was dead or alive at that point. So I remember just thinking, *What can I deal with? I can deal with being in a wheelchair for the rest of my life. I can't deal with my friend being dead.* And that was just what was going through my head.

I remember being very eager for them to get me into surgery because I was in so much pain and I knew that at least I could be unconscious during the surgery, and I wouldn't have to be frightened and in pain for a little while.

WEDNESDAY BOWIE, COUNTERPROTESTER: I remember getting to the hospital, and I remember them putting me in a CT scan. And I remember being examined by trauma doctors. And then, I think that was at that point when the blood loss started to get to me because after the doctors first examined me, I didn't remember anything anymore.

NATALIE ROMERO, SECOND-YEAR UVA STUDENT: I regained consciousness in the hospital. At first I couldn't even remember who I was for a second. I'd say, *What happened to me? What happened?* No one really wanted to tell me. When I woke up, I came in and out multiple times, but some of the upperclassmen folks from my scholarship were there.

I asked them and the nurse that was there, like, *What happened to me?* And they said, *Nat, you were hit by a car.* And then I asked them, *Am I going to be able to walk? Do you know if I have a spinal injury? Is that what this is? Am I paralyzed?*

No one answered me. No one answered. Everyone just stared at me. No one could say yes, no, not the nurse, anyone. So I just sat there crying and fell back asleep.[1]

BILL BURKE, COUNTERPROTESTER: They take me to do the x-rays and CT scans and all that kind of stuff. And by then I was really wigging out because I couldn't get hold of my wife. And one of the x-ray techs let me use her cell phone to call my wife. And I told her what happened. She said, *Yeah,*

I seen it on the news. And the next thing I said, *I think the girl died.* And then that's when she said, *Yes, she did.* My wife told me that I was right on top of her, and that they reported that she was dead.

NATALIE ROMERO: It was maybe the fourth time that I woke up that they said that it was going to be difficult, but they think I was going to be able to walk. And then I found out I had MRIs and all this stuff done to me while I was unconscious.

There was a skull fracture and they, while I was unconscious, stitched it up. I had a tooth fractured. That's a dead tooth in me now. It pushed back, and the impact of the tooth and everything cut open my lip. So I had multiple stitches also done while unconscious. It was ginormous. I couldn't drink water. I could barely eat. There was some leg injury, et cetera. So I had a severe concussion, skull fracture, lip laceration, the shattered root of a tooth, amongst other things.[2]

LISA DRAINE, LOCAL ACTIVIST: I got home and I swear not 20 minutes later, I get a call from my friend who says to me, *You gotta get back down here. Sophie's been hit by a car.* And I was like, what? And in my mind, I'm thinking it's been an accident. I knew there were lots of people in the streets. Most of the streets were shut down, but I was like, somebody sideswiped her, or, you know—I just didn't think at that point that anything bad had happened. So my husband Joel and I jump in the car.

And all this time, I'm trying to call Rebecca 'cause I knew they were together. I knew they were buddies. So I'm calling Rebecca, who's not answering. So I still have no idea what's happening. The ambulances can't get through.

Rebecca finally answered.

LISA DRAINE: And all she could tell us was that Sophie's head was bleeding. Three minutes later she calls and says, *We're now in an ambulance, but they've diverted us to Martha Jefferson.* So we drive all across town and pull up at the emergency room of Martha Jefferson, we jump out of the car and there's Rebecca standing outside the emergency room doors. And she just breaks down when she sees us—she obviously had been holding it together, and she still couldn't really tell us, I mean, imagine, at this point we don't really know what has happened, but she couldn't tell us what has happened. She was just crying. And she was saying, *They wouldn't let me go in with Sophie. They're barring the door.*

So there's a security guard at the door to the emergency room. And he says, *We're not letting anyone except for the patients in. We're in a lockdown situation.* And we were like, *Lockdown?* And he said, *It's a mass casualty situation.* And we're like, *what?!* Again, I'm still thinking she was just, you know, hit by chance. And at the same time there are ambulances arriving. So it's clear that she's not the only one that's injured at this point. And maybe about 20 minutes later, a guy comes back and says, *OK, one of you can go in to be with your daughter.* My husband is a physician. So of course we send Joel in.

Hours later, Sophie was discharged and was able to see her mother for the first time since the car attack.

LISA DRAINE: So she comes out, [they] wheel her out, and her leg was broken, but they couldn't tell how badly 'cause it was really swollen. So we get her home, and that sort of just begins the whole unfolding of figuring out what happened.

Another mother in the Charlottesville area got a similar phone call that afternoon: Susan Bro, the mother of Heather Heyer.

WASHINGTON POST: Bro's trailer home in Ruckersville, Va., is tucked away amid farmland...she spent her spare time knitting, crocheting and designing patterns. She called herself a homebody and enjoyed batch cooking and making cheeses.[3]

On August 12, around the time of the crash, Bro was at her friend Cathy Brinkley's house.

SUSAN BRO, HEATHER HEYER'S MOTHER: I was at my best friend's house and I get a phone call.[4]

My son calls and says that he has called Heather's phone, somebody picked it up and said they don't know what happened to his sister. He saw her—he saw the car attack on TV.[5]

I'm a little frantic because I don't even know anything about a car that's hit somebody.[6]

I was 45 minutes away. My friend is driving [us] in. And I kept calling the hospitals, as my friend was driving.[7]

There's only two hospitals in Charlottesville. We're searching frantically for what hospital she's at. Both hospitals I'm calling are saying, *We don't have a patient by that name. We don't have a patient by that name.* Her ID was apparently not on her; her phone was nowhere to be found. Nobody for sure knew who she was as far as I can tell.[8]

So I finally get a hold of her friend Marissa, who I had only met one time. I found out from her, who found out from one of the girls she was with, who actually located her in the hospital by showing her picture around and saying, *OK, we can't find this person. Can you find them?* And then they, of course they wouldn't tell her anything. They just said, we need the next of kin.

Marissa says come to the far side of UVa from the emergency room. That the emergency room is barricaded. And that's all she will tell me.

So I get there, they search my backpack, I tell Cathy to wait outside for my husband 'cause he was actually out of town that day. And they search my backpack and they don't say anything to me and I don't even know if that was law enforcement or who that was exactly. And they tell me, *Stand over here.*

They hand me a number 20 on a piece of paper that I still have on my refrigerator, and nobody says anything to me, looks at me, talks to me.

And suddenly two strangers that I don't know, two women, grab me on either side and walk me up this ramp. This is the same ramp that I would walk down on my dinner break when I was pregnant with Heather, cause I used to be a switchboard operator in that same building.

And I walk into the room and a gentleman identified himself and he just said, *I'm sorry. Your daughter...* I don't remember the words he used now... *was pronounced at such and such time* and the full meaning of that hit me and I sat down and this awful wail came out of me.[9] It was something between a scream and a wail.[10]

CHAPTER 18

"Senseless deaths for a rally that should have never happened."

ABOUT 2 P.M.

HEAPHY REPORT: After the car attack, many counterprotesters were on edge. Anger burned.

SMASH CAINE-CONLEY, COFOUNDER, CONGREGATE C'VILLE: I don't think we had any indication that the attack that just happened wouldn't somehow happen again. We didn't know if that was part of a calculated, broader attack. We had no idea who it was or what group they were a part of or anything like that. I don't think it felt like it was over.

That's why we were still marching around downtown for a little while.

CONSTANCE PAIGE YOUNG, COUNTERPROTESTER: We didn't know—bombs could be somewhere. We didn't know what the hell anything was.

CHRIS SUAREZ, REPORTER, CHARLOTTESVILLE *DAILY PROGRESS*: And then it just got even crazier.

TERRY MCAULIFFE, VIRGINIA GOVERNOR: At that point I determined, I gotta get down there. So my helicopter, the one we use for the governor called Trooper One, that helicopter is in Charlottesville, but it's doing surveillance actually. They're the ones that followed James Fields's car. And so the state police get Fairfax One, the helicopter they use here if there's a car accident they land on the highway, to fly me down.

MIKE SIGNER, CHARLOTTESVILLE MAYOR: We got news that the governor was coming to Charlottesville. That was a surprise. And when the governor comes, that's going to be a big deal.

We have a meeting scheduled at probably five o'clock to talk about the press conference that is going to happen with the governor. Like, *What do we say? How are we going to do this? Who's talking when? What the hell are we saying?*

Chief Al Thomas looked down at his phone and he said, *Oh. A helicopter has just gone down.*

DAVID FOKY, NEWS DIRECTOR, NBC29: One of the first things that pops into your head is, *Well if Governor McAuliffe is flying here in a helicopter and a helicopter just crashed, did the governor of Virginia just go down in a helicopter?*

BRIAN MORAN, SECRETARY, VIRGINIA PUBLIC SAFETY AND HOMELAND SECURITY: *Chopper down. Chopper down.*

There were moments there when we didn't know whose helicopter it was. I'm standing next to the superintendent, I'm in the command room and we're just looking at each other.

KASEY HOTT, ANCHOR, NBC29: They thought for sure at the time that it was the governor's helicopter that had gone down. We knew that he was in the air. We just thought that was his. The implications of that... it was crazy.

People on the governor's staff started calling and calling the governor. His phone went straight to voicemail.

TERRY MCAULIFFE: I'd been burning my phone up and stupidly, I probably should have had a charger. So I get on the helicopter and my phone dies. It is dead literally two minutes after I get on.

No one was able to reach me for 20 minutes, since my phone was dead, and they were in a panic.[1]

They were actually looking to find out where the lieutenant governor was because they thought I'd gone down on the helicopter.

CHRIS SUAREZ: People were speculating or tweeting, *What? Someone shot down a helicopter?* I'm thinking to myself like, *No, come on, like this* can't *be real. This cannot be real. Like this isn't* Grand Theft Auto, *you know, this isn't someone shooting like a rocket launcher at a helicopter that went down.* This is just so nuts. Like this is unreal.

HENRY GRAFF, ANCHOR AND REPORTER, NBC29: You're just like, *Jesus Christ, what else could happen?*

TIM DODSON, MANAGING EDITOR, *CAVALIER DAILY*: There were rumors that were spreading that maybe these far-right militia members had blown up a police helicopter. Some of these guys were well armed. I think a lot of people were thinking that at the time, which maybe that seems absurd but these people had better weapons than some of the police did.

DON GATHERS, COFOUNDER, CHARLOTTESVILLE BLACK LIVES MATTER: I don't know much about aviation, but it was always my understanding that helicopters are basically...They don't just drop out of the sky. It was a clear sky.

MIKE SIGNER: It sort of strained credulity to think that it could have been brought down, but on the other hand, not crazy. I mean, what if you did have some kind of attack on a helicopter, right? I don't know how that could have been done and why you would have a helicopter attacked in the city of Charlottesville or Albemarle County, but it's not crazy. And, I mean, I had some fear in my mind that it could have been intentional or sabotage or something.

ANDREW BAXTER, CHARLOTTESVILLE FIRE CHIEF: So we were sending units. They tried to make a rescue, but it was too late.

KASEY HOTT: We found out later that it was the VSP helicopter that had gone down and not the governor's.

DAVID FOKY: It wasn't his helicopter that crashed. It was the state police helicopter that had been circling Charlottesville that day with two state police officers on board.

Both Virginia State Police officers were killed: Lieutenant H. Jay Cullen and Trooper Berke M. M. Bates.

MIKE SIGNER: There weren't any indications that it was intentional that I was hearing. Nobody had cited anybody, and nobody had claimed any credit. And so it seemed like it was more just tragic.

DAILY PROGRESS: Authorities have said there is no indication that foul play was a factor in the crash.[2]

ANDREW BAXTER AT THE EMERGENCY OPERATIONS CENTER (EOC): There was a sergeant from VSP in the EOC with us. He's an old salty, VSP guy. He's a smoker too, which is odd. You don't see that in VSP anymore really, and it's probably grandfathered in somehow. I doubt they still let you do that. So he would leave the EOC once every 90 minutes or so to go outside and suck down a cigarette in about 13 seconds and come back in. But I saw him walk outside at some point after we learned what had happened, and I went outside to talk to him. And he was dear, dear close friends with Jay Cullen, the lieutenant who was killed.

And I said, *Man, you take the time you need. If you need to . . .* And he's like, *No, I'm OK.* And five minutes later, he came back in and did his job.

BRIAN MORAN: What was already just a devastating mood through the course of the day just got even worse, if that's fathomable.

ALLEN GROVES, UVA DEAN OF STUDENTS, AT THE EOC: Looking at the faces of some of the state police people when their helicopter goes down and they know these guys . . . there was just so much that day that was so powerful and so overwhelming.

BRIAN MORAN: At that point, the governor came.

TERRY MCAULIFFE: There are moments you never forget and that was one of them. I let out a high sigh and slumped down and stared at the table. I was frozen for a moment, having a hard time believing it really could be true. Jay was my regular pilot and led our State Police Aviation Unit, and Berke, a newly minted pilot, had been on my Executive Protection Unit (EPU), which made him like a member of my family. Berke was definitely a character. He was always larger than life. My thoughts were racing. I thought of both Jay and Berke, all the times we'd joked around together, all the talks we'd had, all the kindness they'd shown my family.[3]

BRIAN MORAN: [The governor] had to call [his wife] to tell her who was in the copter, because Berke was an Executive Protection Unit agent, and the family had become very fond of him, very close. So I remember him calling Dorothy about who died, Berke Bates. That was horrible.

TWEET FROM EMILY GORCENSKI, LOCAL ACTIVIST: These were senseless deaths for a rally that should have never happened.[4]

TERRY MCAULIFFE: After Jay and Berke went down, it was just tremendous anger and tremendous sadness.

DON GATHERS, COFOUNDER, CHARLOTTESVILLE BLACK LIVES MATTER: At that point, I think that the day in and of itself was winding down or had already wound down. And folks began to disperse and head home as quickly and as safely as they could.

CHRIS SUAREZ, REPORTER, CHARLOTTESVILLE *DAILY PROGRESS*: It started to rain.

EMILY BLOUT, UVA PROFESSOR AND MAYOR MIKE SIGNER'S WIFE: I remember the pouring rain after the stifling oppressive day, just a deluge.

ELIZABETH SHILLUE, QUAKER ACTIVIST: I remember thinking, *Thank God for the rain*. And hopefully that was going to end everything. Anything else that might happen was going to be over.

MIKE SIGNER, CHARLOTTESVILLE MAYOR: There was a lot of nervousness about what was going to happen at night. Had they left? Had they really disbanded? And so there was this real nervy, eerie, horror movie feeling as the dark started to settle.

REV. SETH WISPELWEY, PASTOR AND COFOUNDER, CONGREGATE C'VILLE: It's getting later, the shadows longer. At some point, we ate a little bit, we regroup, things are getting quieter. We are going to kind of do our own sweep. There's reports of white supremacists on motorcycles. I remember still sweeping around downtown.

DON GATHERS, AT HOME: My phone did not leave my hand that entire day because I knew at any moment we may have to get out and assemble again, not knowing where they were or what they may be doing at that point. But that we might have to rally en masse and get the troops up and ready to go again.

I'm not certain that I slept that night. Because at this point, I'm looking and listening for any bump in the night outside the house. And just prepared to take whatever action is necessary.

WALT HEINECKE, UVA PROFESSOR AND ACTIVIST: As it became evening time, I was left with just a couple of volunteers. And I figured the parks were kind of trashed, so I cleaned up the parks. I went to each park with trash bags and cleaned them up, and turned off the water that we were using, and just kind of got the parks back in shape.

ANDREW BAXTER, CHARLOTTESVILLE FIRE CHIEF: I slept at the firehouse that night. We were unsure of the degree to which we need to, or should, demobilize.

TWEET FROM EMILY GORCENSKI, LOCAL ACTIVIST, 7:52 P.M.: I don't look forward to my nightmares for the next few weeks.[5]

SUSAN BRO, HEATHER HEYER'S MOTHER, BACK AT HOME: It was a long and hellish evening. I couldn't sleep. Every time I closed my eyes, I was back in the ER with them telling me. And then my brain kind of clicks into practical mode. So I did laundry all night.

L.Q., COUNTERPROTESTER: The first night in the hospital I woke up with my heart racing, terrified that the white supremacists would come to kill me. They are terrorists. I was terrified. After some discussion of what to do, the hospital ended up hiring a security guard for me. I am not sure how protected I was, but I felt better.[6]

KENDALL KING, THIRD-YEAR UVA STUDENT: I remember I was like, *I just wanna go see Nat, I just wanna go see Nat, I just wanna go see Nat.* And a lot of our comrades were like, *Hey, just so you know, there's likely also these people* [white nationalists] *in the hospital. Decide how you're gonna act, if you see them.*

Marcus Martin refused to even stay the night in the hospital.

MARCUS MARTIN, COUNTERPROTESTER: Didn't trust anybody. Just wanted to be in the comfort of my home.[7] They took me out the back.

STAR PETERSON, LOCAL ACTIVIST AND STREET MEDIC: I remember being super afraid, and asking them not to put my name on the outside, in the hallway on the outside of my room, just because I was so afraid of Nazis. I remember a friend coming to visit me in the hospital and being like, *Oh yeah, just standing next to somebody with Nazi tattoos in the elevator*, because they weren't just treating us.

SUSAN BRO, HEATHER HEYER'S MOTHER: Those of us who miss her, miss her forever.

Her best friend said, *You know, it's kinda weird. I'll get to be an old man and she'll always have been 32.*[8]

LISA DRAINE, LOCAL ACTIVIST: The next week we were able to get in to see an orthopedist at UVa. They still weren't sure how bad was the break? So they then x-rayed Sophie and said, *There's no question. She's gonna need major reconstructive surgery.* Her tibial plateau was broken—the bone around your knee—all of the ligaments around the knee were torn or ruptured. So the next week, she was in the hospital having surgery on the day that she was supposed to start classes for her fourth year. Instead of being in class, she was in the hospital.

Sophie and Rebecca said then, and they'll say now, *We don't regret it*, and I don't regret it. You would think that we would, you know, and then I know there are people that are like, *Why did you let your daughters . . . ?* And of course, it's not like I could really stop them. They were 21 and 23, but I was very convinced that this is something I needed to do, and I would've been fine if they had opted out, but they really wanted to be there and we don't regret it.

I came to find out that Sophie was right next to Heather and Marcus. And so it's very unsettling. I now know Susan Bro, and she is an incredible woman, but it's very hard for me to be around her because I know that I came like this close to *being* her: losing my daughter. And she could not be more gracious—she always asks how Sophie's doing.

For a long time, I beat myself up about going home and not being there. Like, if I had been there, maybe I would've seen the car, maybe I would've been able to push her out of the way, you never know these things. Yeah. But you know, in the end, my daughter's alive and hers isn't and for no reason, but maybe a few inches.

KRISTIN SZAKOS, CHARLOTTESVILLE CITY COUNCILOR: For the next week, you'd see some kind of paunchy, white guy in a baseball cap. And I love some paunchy, white guys in baseball caps, but you see people who look like they might have been at the rally and you think, *Are they planning something else? Are they going to do something? Are they armed?* I found myself really jumpy for a long time after, wondering if they were going to come back.

SABR LYON, COUNTERPROTESTER: For the next couple weeks anytime I left the house, I would drive the neighborhoods, because around where we lived at the time were a lot of predominantly Black neighborhoods. So there was absolutely more than once that there was just a truck full of white dudes driving around trying to harass people.

So yeah, the vibes in the town afterwards, it's high alert. You're on high alert for forever.

HEAPHY REPORT: The City of Charlottesville protected neither free expression nor public safety on August 12.

BRIAN MORAN, SECRETARY, VIRGINIA PUBLIC SAFETY AND HOMELAND SECU-RITY: I don't think we should blame the law enfor—you know, there was a breakdown in some communications. There was a breakdown in communication. I think our law enforcement is oftentimes held to a standard that we don't hold our leadership to.

Charlottesville did not prepare adequately.

EMILY BLOUT, UVA PROFESSOR AND MAYOR MIKE SIGNER'S WIFE: There was just like one week of unity where people joined together and helped each other and solidarity. After that, it all fell apart. It was like the whole city just fell into itself and it started eating itself alive. It was just so dramatic and so painful because everyone wanted answers. How could such a horrible thing happen? How could the police not intervene and watch people be beat up?

CONSTANCE PAIGE YOUNG, COUNTERPROTESTER: Why didn't y'all stop it? Why didn't you stop it? I mean, because honestly you can't tell me that had there been hundreds of Black people with long guns walking down the street that they would've been able to come back multiple times and rendezvous, terrorize people, fight, scream racial slurs. So I don't want to hear this free speech argument. No, I'm not trying to hear that.

EMILY BLOUT: [Mike] did everything humanly possible and more to try to stop this. Every single step of the way, every single resource he had, every single pathway he could find, or hope to find to stop this or to contain it, was thwarted and undermined by the city government itself. And specifically, the city's lawyers but also Maurice Jones, again, who was *way* over his head and was undermining any attempt that Mike was making to stop this thing.

MIKE SIGNER: In my last [city council] meeting I said...you know, *I want to apologize to Emily Gorcenski, because you did bring that [dossier] to us. And we...* It was like we couldn't legally have stopped the rally. But if there was...I forget exactly what the apology was, but I wanted her to hear that we could have amplified it more.

It was so hard because it didn't meet the legal standard for a credible threat. It didn't. Nothing that was in the dossier met what the FBI standard is, or the Court's.

KRISTIN SZAKOS: After the event, people from Charlottesville got very angry at the city for not protecting them, and I shared that. I was angry too. So, I just took it. Even as they were yelling at us, I couldn't help but love them and feel like we'd let them down. But we also had shared their experience. We felt the same way. At least I did.

DON GATHERS, COFOUNDER, CHARLOTTESVILLE BLACK LIVES MATTER: Where we go from here, I don't know.

It's still laughable when people say, *Well, that's not...that wasn't Char-lottesville.* Yeah, it was and yeah it is! This was a community that is very visibly divided. And I just don't see anything on the horizon, bridging those chasms that exist.

REV. BRENDA BROWN-GROOMS, PASTOR, NEW BEGINNINGS CHRISTIAN COMMUNITY: If I heard it once I heard it a million times: Everybody kept saying, *But this is not who we are. This is not who we are.* Yeah. It's exactly who we are. We don't want to admit it, but it's exactly who we are.

Can we be someone else? Of course, we *can* be, but it takes work. It takes commitment. It takes being willing to be uncomfortable.

CONSTANCE PAIGE YOUNG, COUNTER-PROTESTER: There's life before the car attack and there's life after the car attack.

Some of the people who I've met who were also injured in this car attack, I will love for the rest of my life. And I think I am more brave because they are brave. And I can continue to exist here and do good work because they are able to do it too. I found a community of people who keep trying and of people who have lost so much. I mean, we have lost so much and we keep going.

I want people to know that a whole bunch of brave people showed up, regular people. A lot of regular brave folks showed up to do an extraordinary thing that day, and I think we did make a difference and we paid a big price for it. And that's all.

ROSIA PARKER, LOCAL ACTIVIST: We are still fighting.

As elders of the community, it took us a long time to get respect, because they didn't understand why we were going off in the way we were going. We became the angry Black women. Well, why are we angry Black women? Because this has been going on for generations and generations.

We grandmamas out here in the streets, you know, because we was planning for such a time as this. But our babies don't have an understanding. Our babies are constantly coming from trauma. And until you treat that trauma, it is going to get worse.

ALEXIS GRAVELY, SENIOR ASSOCIATE NEWS EDITOR, *CAVALIER DAILY*: We can't just be complacent. If all these people and all these systems just sort of provide the breeding ground for these ideas and these people and these views, then yeah, it's going to happen. And if we don't change anything, then it's going to happen again. It's not just something that you ignore and it goes away.

ROSIA PARKER: It's a continuous fight. All we see is a constant fight, until— Trina, what's your favorite song? We have one particular song, a slave song, that Katrina holds in her heart. And before we leave out the house, she sings it.

KATRINA TURNER, SINGING:

Oh, freedom, Oh, freedom, Oh freedom over me
And before I'd be a slave
I'd be buried in my grave
And go home to my Lord and be free!

ACKNOWLEDGMENTS

First and foremost, thank you to those whose voices make up these pages. Thank you for trusting me to tell your stories. Thank you for reliving your trauma in order to share the truth. Thank you for the work you have done, and continue to do, to fight fascism. This book is for you and by you.

Thank you to my own Charlottesville community, those who made the city feel like home, and especially my NBC29 family who gave me my first real journalism job and stuck with me as I learned the ropes—and learned how to turn on a broadcast camera.

This book would never have progressed past the idea phase without my inimitable agent, Wendi Gu. Thank you for believing in this book from its inception and continuing to stand by me through the whole process. And to my editor, Catherine Tung, and the whole team at Beacon Press, who saw the importance of this story and helped bring it to life. I'm also so grateful to Noor Alzamami, Arya Royal, and Amalia Schwarzschild for assisting on the oral history and research that forms the backbone of this book.

Thank you also to my colleagues during my time at CNN, who supported this book project from the beginning, especially John Berman, who reviewed an early draft and provided detailed feedback. And special thanks to CNN's Anderson Cooper and Charlie Moore, who trusted me to field-produce their Charlottesville coverage after I had only officially worked for them for a few weeks. And even before that, thank you both for giving me my first journalism internship, my foot in the door at CNN, and the best training as a journalist I could have asked for.

Thank you to my parents, Mike and Karen, and siblings, Jack and Julia, for encouraging me to embark on a book project of this magnitude. Mom and Dad, thank you for editing the very first drafts of this book's proposal, and even more so, for encouraging my journalism and writing careers from as early as I can remember. And thank you to my in-laws, Kendal and Andy, and brother-in-law Gerrit, for being such cheerleaders of my writing career.

Finally, to my spouse, the love of my life, Lex. This book would not exist without you. Thank you for walking alongside me throughout this writing process, cooking me dinner after tough hours-long interviews, and serving as my ultimate sounding board, consultant, editor, and supporter. I love you forever.

NOTES

Chapter 1

1. Mark Kavit, email message to Charlottesville city officials, August 10, 2017, University of Virginia Library of Special Collections, MSS 16386, Unite the Right Rally and Community Response Collection, series 1, subseries 1, Correspondence, etc., box 1, folder 1.

2. Thomas Jefferson, *Notes on the State of Virginia* (Philadelphia, 1785), https://docsouth.unc.edu/southlit/jefferson/jefferson.html.

3. "The Illusion of Progress: Charlottesville's Roots in White Supremacy," Carter G. Woodson Center at the University of Virginia, Citizen Justice Initiative, 2017, https://UValibrary.maps.arcgis.com/apps/Cascade/index.html?appid=3e111d6024 53478cad8452ba551138b6.

4. Wes Bellamy, *Monumental* (Newport News, VA: BlackGold Publishing, 2019), 47.

5. Bellamy, *Monumental*, 102.

6. Screen capture included in email message from local lawyer to friends, May 4, 2017.

7. Screen capture included in email message from local lawyer to friends, May 4, 2017.

8. Email message from local lawyer to friends, May 4, 2017.

Chapter 2

1. Bryan McKenzie, "Police Prep of 2 Fronts," *Daily Progress* (Charlottesville, VA), August 11, 2017.

2. Bellamy, *Monumental*, 102.

3. Emily Gorcenski, "Terry McAuliffe Still Doesn't Understand What Happened in Charlottesville," *Slate*, August 8, 2019.

4. "Solidarity C'ville Documents Threats of Violence Planned for August 12," *Solidarity C'ville*, July 17, 2017, https://solidaritycville.wordpress.com/2017/07/17 /solidarity-cville-documents-threats-of-violence-planned-for-august-12/.

5. Bellamy, *Monumental*, 143.

6. Bellamy, *Monumental*, 150.

Chapter 3

1. Chris Suarez, "Faith Leaders Gather on the Eve of 'Hate-Driven' Unite the Right Rally," *Daily Progress*, August 11, 2017.
2. Joe Heim, "A Stark Contrast Inside and Outside a Charlottesville Church During the Torch March," *Washington Post*, August 19, 2017.
3. Heim, "A Stark Contrast."
4. Nicole Hemmer, host, "The Summer of Hate," *A12: The Story of Charlottesville* (podcast), Miller Center, University of Virginia, https://millercenter.org/A12.
5. Willis Jenkins, "Ethics under Pressure: An Autoethnography of Moral Trauma," in *Charlottesville 2017,* ed. Louis P. Nelson and Claudrena N. Harold (Charlottesville: University of Virginia Press, 2018), 165–66.
6. Heim, "A Stark Contrast."
7. Heim, "A Stark Contrast."
8. "Charlottesville Mass Prayer Service: Dr. Cornel West and Rev. Traci Blackmon Speaking to #CvilleClergyCall," Facebook livestream, August 11, 2017, https://www.facebook.com/SojournersMagazine/videos/10154913829892794.
9. #CvilleClergyCall Mass Prayer Service program, August 11, 2017, University of Virginia Library of Special Collections, MSS 16386, Unite the Right Rally and Community Response Collection, series 1, subseries 1, Correspondence, etc., box 1, folder 4.

Chapter 4

1. Tweet from It's Going Down (@IGD_News), August 11, 2017, https://twitter.com/IGD_News/status/896155204617248768.
2. Tweet from It's Going Down (@IGD_News), August 11, 2017, https://twitter.com/IGD_News/status/896139934116962304.
3. Day 13 official court transcript, *Elizabeth Sines et al., Plaintiffs, v. Jason Kessler et al., Defendants. Sines v. Kessler,* Civil Action No. 3:17-cv-00072, (W.D. Va.), 44.
4. Day 5, *Sines v. Kessler* (hereafter *SvK*), 167.
5. Day 5, *SvK*,167.
6. Day 5, *SvK*, 21.
7. Day 5, *SvK*, 90.

Chapter 5

1. Day 13, *SvK*, 45.
2. Heim, "A Stark Contrast."
3. Hemmer, "The Summer of Hate."
4. Day 8, *SvK*, 118.
5. Day 8, *SvK*, 117–24, 131.
6. Day 5, *SvK*, 22–23.
7. Day 6, *SvK*, 69–70.
8. Day 5, *SvK*, 171.
9. Day 5, *SvK*, 22–23.
10. Day 5, *SvK*, 23.
11. Day 5, *SvK*, 21, 24.
12. Day 5, *SvK*, 172.

13. Day 5, *SvK*, 176.
14. Day 5, *SvK*, 24.

Chapter 6

1. Day 5, *SvK*, 176.
2. Day 5, *SvK*, 172.
3. Day 5, *SvK*, 172.
4. Maggie Mallon, "Elizabeth Sines and Leanne Chia Were in Charlottesville When White Supremacists Descended—This Is What They Saw," *Glamour*, August 18, 2017.
5. Day 5, *SvK*, 25.
6. Day 5, *SvK*, 176.
7. Day 5, *SvK*, 177.
8. Day 5, *SvK*, 28.
9. Day 5, *SvK*, 28–29.
10. Tweet from Chris Suarez (@Suarez_CM), August 11, 2017, https://twitter.com/Suarez_CM/status/896193287257821184?s=20.
11. Day 5, *SvK*, 180.
12. "Documenting Hate," *PBS Frontline*, 2017, https://www.pbs.org/wgbh/frontline/film/documenting-hate-charlottesville/transcript/.
13. Day 5, *SvK*, 181.
14. Day 5, *SvK*, 28.
15. Day 5, *SvK*, 29.
16. "Documenting Hate," *PBS Frontline*.
17. Hemmer, "The Summer of Hate."
18. Michael Signer, *Cry Havoc* (New York: Hachette, 2020), 205.
19. Signer, *Cry Havoc*, 205
20. Jenkins, "Ethics under Pressure," 165–66.
21. Jenkins, "Ethics under Pressure," 165–66.
22. Jenkins, "Ethics under Pressure," 165–66.
23. Day 13, *SvK*, 47.
24. Tweet from Jalane Schmidt (@Jalane_Schmidt), August 11, 2017, https://twitter.com/jalane_schmidt/status/896191494020792320.
25. "UVa Prof on UVa's Historical Ties to KKK & White Nationalist Alums Richard Spencer & Jason Kessler," *Democracy Now*, August 14, 2017, https://www.democracynow.org/2017/8/14/UVa_professor_on_schools_historical_ties (these two sentences only).

Chapter 7

1. Day 5, *SvK*, 183–84.
2. Day 5, *SvK*, 30.
3. Day 5, *SvK*, 185.
4. Day 5, *SvK*, 30.
5. Day 5, *SvK*, 186.
6. Day 6, *SvK*, 79.
7. Day 5, *SvK*, 30.

8. Day 5, *SvK*, 30–31.
9. Heim, "A Stark Contrast."
10. Day 13, *SvK*, 46–47.
11. Day 13, *SvK*, 49.
12. Day 13, *SvK*, 49.
13. Day 8, *SvK*, 125.
14. Day 5, *SvK*, 31.
15. "Documenting Hate," *PBS Frontline*.
16. Humanity Over Hate Forum, The Leadership Conference on Civil and Human Rights, May 19, 2022, https://m.facebook.com/events/982057595675771/.
17. "My Daughter Was Killed at Charlottesville—Susan Bro—What I've Learnt," *Channel 4 News* (UK), August 12, 2018, https://www.youtube.com/watch?v=YI8vBx967GI.
18. Humanity Over Hate Forum.
19. Humanity Over Hate Forum.

Chapter 8

1. Bellamy, *Monumental*, 156.
2. Day 13, *SvK*, 51; personal interview.
3. Congregate C'ville Facebook livestream, August 12, 2017, https://www.facebook.com/congregatecville/videos/461977134182807.
4. Congregate C'ville Facebook livestream, August 12, 2017, https://www.facebook.com/congregatecville/videos/461977134182807.
5. Congregate C'ville Facebook livestream, August 12, 2017, https://www.facebook.com/congregatecville/videos/461983787515475.
6. Congregate C'ville Facebook livestream, August 12, 2017, https://www.facebook.com/congregatecville/videos/461977134182807.
7. David Straughn, "I Witnessed Terrorism in Charlottesville from a Foot Away," *Scalawag,* August 16, 2017.
8. Bellamy, *Monumental*, 162.
9. Bellamy, *Monumental*, 161.
10. Bellamy, *Monumental*, 162.

Chapter 9

1. Day 5, *SvK*, 191–92.
2. Day 5, *SvK*, 191–92.
3. Day 5, *SvK*, 195.
4. Tweet from Allison Wrabel (@craftypanda), August 12, 2017, https://twitter.com/craftypanda/status/896355589772763136.
5. International Association of Chiefs of Police, "Virginia's Response to the Unite the Right Rally: After-Action Review," 15, https://www.pshs.virginia.gov/media/governorvirginiagov/secretary-of-public-safety-and-homeland-security/pdf/iacp-after-action-review.pdf.

Chapter 10

1. CNN, *Anderson Cooper 360*, August 17, 2017, 8 p.m.
2. Tweet from Allison Wrabel (@craftypanda), August 12, 2017, https://twitter.com
/craftypanda/status/896369731506188289.
3. Recorded on personal videos.
4. Recorded on personal videos.

Chapter 11

1. International Association of Chiefs of Police, "Virginia's Response to the Unite the
Right Rally," 11.
2. Hemmer, "The Summer of Hate," 25:48.
3. Day 13, *SvK*, 58.
4. Day 13, *SvK*, 60–61.
5. Day 13, *SvK*, 60–61.
6. Day 5, *SvK*, 199.
7. Day 5, *SvK*, 40.
8. Day 5, *SvK*, 40.
9. Day 5, *SvK*, 40–43.
10. Day 5, *SvK*, 208.
11. "Documenting Hate," *PBS Frontline*.
12. "Documenting Hate," *PBS Frontline*.
13. Day 5, *SvK*, 204.
14. Heaphy report, 144.

Chapter 12

1. Alan Zimmerman, "In Charlottesville, the Local Jewish Community Presses On,"
ReformJudaism.org, https://reformjudaism.org/blog/charlottesville-local-jewish
-community-presses.
2. Zimmerman, "In Charlottesville, the Local Jewish Community Presses On."
3. Anti-Defamation League, "Have Hate, Will Travel: The Demographics of Unite
the Right," October 8, 2017, https://www.adl.org/resources/blog/have-hate-will
-travel-demographics-unite-right.
4. Heaphy report, 144.

Chapter 13

1. Day 5, *SvK*, 211–12.
2. Day 5, *SvK*, 211–12.
3. Hemmer, "The Summer of Hate," 27:55.
4. Tweet from Chris Suarez (@Suarez_CM), August 12, 2017, https://twitter.com
/Suarez_CM/status/896402363568795648?s=20.
5. Tweet from Allison Wrabel (@craftypanda), August 12, 2017, https://twitter.com
/craftypanda/status/896397870320021507.
6. Official court transcript, *United States of America v. James Alex Fields,*
3:18-cr-00011-MFU, (W.D. Va.), sentencing hearing, 22.

7. Straughn, "I Witnessed Terrorism."
8. Straughn, "I Witnessed Terrorism."
9. Yesha Callahan, "Interview: How Corey Long Fought White Supremacy with Fire," *The Root,* August 14, 2017, https://www.theroot.com/interview-how-corey -long-fought-white-supremacy-with-f-1797831277?rev=1502737785317.
10. Callahan, "Interview."
11. Callahan, "Interview."
12. ACLU of Virginia, "Video Shows Man Firing into Crowd in Charlottesville," as posted by *IBTimes UK,* August 27, 2017, https://www.youtube.com/watch?v= C2ro7U_Yoc4, 0:31.
13. "'I was losing so much blood': Counterprotester Beaten with Poles, Signs in Charlottesville," WRAL, August 13, 2017, https://www.wral.com/charlottesville-rally -organizer-condemns-violence-gov-says-incident-made-us-stronger-/16877938/.
14. Complaint, "*DeAndre Harris, Plaintiff, v. Jason Kessler et al., Defendants.*" Harris v. Kessler, Case No. 3:19-cv-00046, (W.D. Va), 15.
15. Tweet from Chuck Modiano (@ChuckModi1), August 12, 2017, https://twitter .com/ChuckModi1/status/896409728959606789.
16. *Harris v. Kessler,* 2–3.
17. Ian Shapira, "The Parking Garage Beating Lasted 10 Seconds. DeAndre Harris Still Lives with the Damage," *Washington Post,* September 16, 2019.
18. Callahan, "Interview."
19. Callahan, "Interview."
20. Callahan, "Interview."
21. WRAL, "'I was losing so much blood.'"
22. *Harris v. Kessler,* 17.
23. WRAL, "'I was losing so much blood.'"
24. WRAL, "'I was losing so much blood.'"

Chapter 14

1. Mallon, "Elizabeth Sines and Leanne Chia Were in Charlottesville When White Supremacists Descended," *Glamour.*
2. Mallon, "Elizabeth Sines and Leanne Chia."
3. Day 5, *SvK,* 48.
4. Straughn, "I Witnessed Terrorism."
5. Straughn, "I Witnessed Terrorism."
6. Day 12, *SvK,* 17.
7. Mallon, "Elizabeth Sines and Leanne Chia."
8. Day 5, *SvK,* 48.
9. Day 5, *SvK,* 48.
10. Mallon, "Elizabeth Sines and Leanne Chia."
11. Day 15, *SvK,* 64.
12. Day 15, *SvK,* 66.
13. Humanity Over Hate Forum.
14. Mallon, "Elizabeth Sines and Leanne Chia."

Chapter 15

1. CNN, *Anderson Cooper 360*, August 17, 2017, 8 p.m.
2. Day 15, *SvK*, 66.
3. Official court transcript, *United States of America v. James Alex Fields*, 3:18-cr-00011-MFU, (W. D. Va.), sentencing hearing, 90–91.
4. Hemmer, "The Summer of Hate," 30:33.
5. Day 15, *SvK*, 66.
6. Day 15, *SvK*, 66.
7. Day 13, *Svk*, 12.
8. Debbie Elliot, "As Trial Begins in Charlottesville Protest Death, Community Reflects," NPR, November 26, 2018, https://www.npr.org/2018/11/26/669377175/as-trial-begins-in-charlottesville-protest-death-community-reflects.
9. Straughn, "I Witnessed Terrorism in Charlottesville from a Foot Away."
10. Day 15, *SvK*, 67.
11. Official court transcript, *United States of America v. James Alex Fields*, 111–12.
12. *Sines v. Kessler.*
13. Official court transcript, *United States of America v. James Alex Fields*, 90–91.
14. CNN, *Anderson Cooper 360*, August 17, 2017, 8 p.m.
15. Mary Wood, "Standing Up for Charlottesville," University of Virginia School of Law, August 16, 2017, https://www.law.virginia.edu/news/201708/standing-charlottesville.
16. Official court transcript, *United States of America v. James Alex Fields*, 90–91.
17. Official court transcript, *United States of America v. James Alex Fields*, 90–91.
18. Mallon, "Elizabeth Sines and Leanne Chia."
19. Wood, "Standing Up for Charlottesville."
20. Mallon, "Elizabeth Sines and Leanne Chia."
21. Straughn, "I Witnessed Terrorism."
22. Official court transcript, *United States of America v. James Alex Fields*, 90–91.
23. Tweet from Emily Gorcenski (@EmilyGorcenski), August 12, 2017, https://twitter.com/EmilyGorcenski/status/896476017753300992?s=20.
24. Hemmer, "The Summer of Hate," 31:37.
25. Wood, "Standing Up for Charlottesville."
26. Day 5, *SvK*, 51.
27. Hemmer, "The Summer of Hate," 31:37.
28. Mallon, "Elizabeth Sines and Leanne Chia."
29. Day 5, *SvK*, 51.
30. Katti Gray, "Ryan Kelly: 'The Day of the March Was Probably the Most Fear I'd Ever Had,'" The Pulitzer Prizes, https://www.pulitzer.org/article/ryan-kelly-day-march-was-probably-most-fear-id-ever-had.
31. Straughn, "I Witnessed Terrorism."
32. CNN, *Anderson Cooper 360*, August 14, 2017, 8 p.m.
33. Day 5, *SvK*, 52.
34. *Sines v. Kessler.*

Chapter 16

1. Hemmer, "The Summer of Hate," 32:32; Day 13, *SvK*, 62.
2. Day 5, *SvK*, 52–55.
3. Mallon, "Elizabeth Sines and Leanne Chia."
4. Day 15, *SvK*, 68.
5. Tweet from Allison Wrabel (@craftpanda), August 12, 2017, https://twitter.com /craftypanda/status/896427648552927234.

Chapter 17

1. Day 5, *SvK*, 56–57.
2. Day 5, *SvK*, 56–57.
3. Ellie Silverman, "From Wary Observer to Justice Warrior: How Heather Heyer's Death Gave Her Mom a Voice," *Washington Post*, February 1, 2018.
4. CNN, *Anderson Cooper 360,* August 14, 2017, 8 p.m.
5. Humanity Over Hate Forum.
6. Humanity Over Hate Forum.
7. CNN, *Anderson Cooper 360,* August 14, 2017, 8 p.m.
8. Humanity Over Hate Forum.
9. Humanity Over Hate Forum.
10. "My Daughter Was Killed at Charlottesville," *Channel 4 News* (UK).

Chapter 18

1. Terry McAuliffe, *Beyond Charlottesville: Taking a Stand Against White Nationalism* (New York: St. Martin's Publishing Group, 2019), 5, 20, 103.
2. Dean Seal, "2 State Troopers Die in Helicopter Wreck," *Daily Progress,* August 12, 2017.
3. McAuliffe, *Beyond Charlottesville,* 5, 20, 103.
4. Tweet from Emily Gorcenski (@EmilyGorcenski), August 12, 2017, https://twitter .com/EmilyGorcenski/status/896495361166123008?s=20.
5. Tweet from Emily Gorcenski (@EmilyGorcenski), August 12, 2017, https://twitter .com/EmilyGorcenski/status/896519668919291904?s=20.
6. Official court transcript, *United States of America v. James Alex Fields,* 112–13.
7. Day 13, *SvK*, 20.
8. "Documenting Hate," *PBS Frontline*.

INDEX

ABOUT THE AUTHOR

NORA NEUS is an Emmy-nominated journalist whose reporting has appeared in CNN, VICE News, the *Washington Post*, and more. Neus field-produced Anderson Cooper's coverage of the 2017 white nationalist riot in Charlottesville, Virginia for CNN. Before joining CNN, she worked as a local news reporter and fill-in anchor for the CNN affiliate in Charlottesville, WVIR NBC29. She is the coauthor of the young-adult graphic memoir *Muhammad Najem, War Reporter: How One Boy Put the Spotlight on Syria*.